ECLIPSE OF FAITH

Eclipse of Faith delivers the honest, inner struggles most of us share about our faith but sometimes are reluctant, or embarrassed, to discuss in polite company.

—Cary Smith, Global Business Executive and CFO, CloudFactory

Steve Whigham offers us here a compelling narrative of a spiritual journey consisting of many convoluted paths all which providentially lead back to the certainty of the One who is the Truth. Indeed, this account recaptures for us the vivid story of many a Christian saint who emerges from the valley of doubt to the summit of divine truth. This work is engaging, thought-provoking, and delightful.

—André Gazal, PhD., Professor of Historical and Systematic Theology, Co-author of *Scripture and Royal Supremacy in Tudor England*

Thorough, well-researched, and refreshingly readable, this book deals with the most important question of our lives: "Why are we here?" in a way that will challenge you—and ultimately change the way you think. This book will have a profound influence on the way you view your life.

—Jonathan Bailie, Co-Founder & C.M.O.,

Lamplight Marketing Group

The walk of faith in Jesus Christ was never promised to be a painless or smooth path. And doubt can often be a formidable companion. But what if you were able to walk along with another who transparently exposed his own eclipse of faith? This book does that in a most remarkable manner. Though it took me through some very dark valleys, this book had a most amazing ending. Insightful and thought provoking, this book left me rejoicing and with a more clear view of the centrality of Jesus Christ.

—Antone Goyak, EdD Chief Academic Officer,

Northland International University

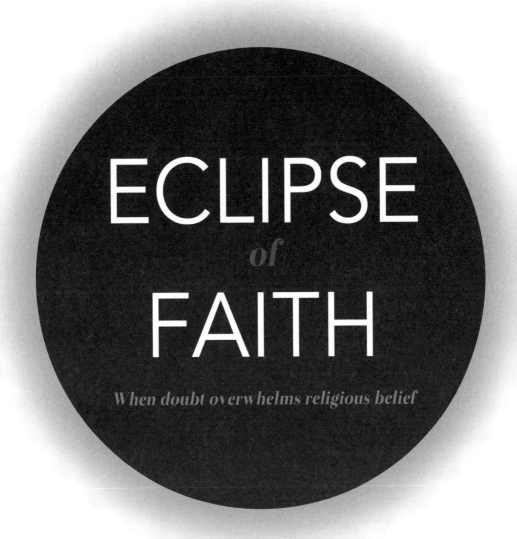

ECLIPSE

of

FAITH

When doubt overwhelms religious belief

STEVE WHIGHAM

AMBASSADOR INTERNATIONAL
GREENVILLE, SOUTH CAROLINA & BELFAST, NORTHERN IRELAND

www.ambassador-international.com

Eclipse of Faith
When doubt overwhelms religious belief

Printed in the United States of America

ISBN: 978-1-62020-218-0
eISBN: 978-1-62020-317-0

Book design and typesetting: Matthew Mulder
E-book conversion: Anna Riebe

AMBASSADOR INTERNATIONAL
Emerald House
427 Wade Hampton Blvd.
Greenville, SC 29609, USA
www.ambassador-international.com

AMBASSADOR BOOKS
The Mount
2 Woodstock Link
Belfast, BT6 8DD, Northern Ireland, UK
www.ambassadormedia.co.uk

The colophon is a trademark of Ambassador

I would like to dedicate this book to my wife, Beth, and to my four children: Bo, Chet, Elissa, and Abby. They put up with so much as I took this journey, and I owe so much to them. The support they showed from start to finish is nothing short of epic. I love all of you!

TABLE OF CONTENTS

FOREWORD

I HAVE JOINED OTHERS IN encouraging Steve to tell this story. Not only has he gone through a very deep and intense struggle with his beliefs, he also has developed a unique ability to articulate and communicate this struggle toward a meaningful resolution.

I am convinced that there is a very large and growing segment of our society that is plagued with doubts and accompanied fears when battling with the questions of truth and the meaning of life. These private and lonely wars within the soul do not always find resolution. Even those who have travelled the path and come to grips with truth find it easy to remain silent about their journey. But there is too much at stake for us to be quiet. We need to open the door for future leaders to question, ask, doubt, explore, and openly wrestle with what they believe. Only then will they truly own their faith.

Steve and I met during the summer of 2008. It began as a business relationship, but we soon became very close friends as we shared the same passion for truth and for preparing college age young people for life. For the next four years we worked together side by side, pouring ourselves into faculty, staff, and students at Northland International University; believing they will change the world they live in.

I have appreciated the fact that Steve has constantly challenged my thought processes by asking provoking questions and encouraging me to think outside the box. That's just the kind of friend he is. He has helped me increase my awareness and sensitivity to how other people think and feel. My mind and soul have been stretched and my life deepened by his influence.

Steve and I have also talked a great deal about being committed to do the right thing, with the right spirit, no matter what the cost. Sometimes the cost is high, but we have been determined to walk that path together. He has been as "iron sharpening iron". The ideas of "Love and Truth" have been transcendent themes that we continue to come back to again and again. For Steve, these are inseparable.

We find a freedom to grow and learn when we can say that "It's ok" to have doubts, fears, and uncertainties. We can work through these together. Steve has stepped up with both boldness and humility to open up honest and transparent discussions that invite us to work through these struggles with him. This book will help you in your pursuit of truth and it will help you help others in theirs.

—Dr. Matthew R. Olson,
Former President, Northland International University

ACKNOWLEDGEMENTS

So many people to thank, so little time . . .

I want to thank all the great thinkers who participated in the Great Conversation before me. Their commitment to seeking truth has been nothing short of inspiring. I realize I merely stand on the shoulders of giants. If it were not for Dr. Peter Kreeft in particular, I'm not sure how I would have managed the process of discovery and analysis; I might have given up. His clear mapping of reason and philosophical inquiry in his books and recorded lectures helped me immensely. Most of my thinking, I am assured, can be sourced within unintentionally purloined ideas that were originated by so many thinkers before me—quite a few ideas of which, I'm sure, I could not even begin to recognize nor trace to the first time they were imagined and communicated. I wish I could tell you that all insights and understandings found in this book are unique creations of my own. They are not. Some of my ideas are so ingrained in so many facets of the Great Conversation that I do not know where my thoughts begin and another's end.

Even so, there are some personal friends I must thank as well. I need to thank my publisher, Sam Lowry, for his interest in this project and his generous sharing of ideas to make every part of this book better. I want to thank my wife, Beth, for her love and patience through the entire process. I want to thank my kids—Bo, Chet, Elissa, and Abby—for their support through this entire ordeal. I want to thank my friends and family: Neal Vaughn, Jack Klem, Marty Von, Grant Beachy, Matt Olson, Brent & Lori Nelsen, Cary & Julie Smith, John & Dawn Kennedy, Wanda Mikhail, Jonathan & Sarah Bailie, John & Donna Ehrie, Martin & Kathy Whigham, Antone Goyak, Kevin & Laurie Priest, Mike Glanzer, Elliot & Jenny Figueroa, Jim & Edith Brooks, Bobby Wood, Dick Fellers, Amy Miller, Andre Gazal, Neal Cushman, Peter Sullivan, Hugh McCoy, Pete Hansen, Jim Bennett, Paul & Jan Magnuson, Neal & Carrie Angel, JP Sibley, Ray & Laura Godwin, Susan Wagar, Chris Metras, Paul Whitt, Dean Bryant, Anna Moore, Pete & Lisa Wehry, Brenda & Brian Ellison, and so many more who have contributed so much insight and love throughout the phases of this journey. I don't know what I could have done without such good friends along the way and all the crazy belly-aching and obsessive philosophizing they had to endure from me as I was trying to get through this journey and organize it into a book. I also want to thank my mom, Gail Whigham, most of all. She has always encouraged me to write. Without her prodding, I don't think I would have ever had the courage to face the blank page and get the project going.

AUTHOR'S
INTRODUCTION

"It is not one swallow or one fine day that makes a spring,
so it is not one day or a short time that makes a man blessed and happy."
—Aristotle

BEFORE 1860, ABRAHAM LINCOLN WAS, by all accounts, a failure. He sought
public office on eleven separate occasions and was unsuccessful nine times.
He was born poor. When he was a child, his family was kicked out of their
home. During those critical childhood years, young Lincoln had to work to
help his family make ends meet. Before his tenth birthday, his mother died.
The child Lincoln never received a formal education. He had to teach himself to read. In his twenties, he started a business. It failed. The next year,
he lost his job and was rejected when he applied to law school. A year later,
Lincoln borrowed money from a friend to begin yet another business, a grocery store. Within the year, he went bankrupt again. It took him seventeen
years to pay off the crushing debt. Just a year later, the love of his life, Ann
Rutledge, died of typhoid. She was only twenty-two. Shortly afterward,
the unemployed, heartbroken, and heavily indebted Lincoln suffered a total

nervous breakdown, entertained thoughts of suicide, and even confined himself to bed for months.

If we were to stop at this point in Lincoln's story, we would not see the successful, even iconic, president of the United States he ultimately became. We would only see a broken man with nothing but trouble engulfing him.

No matter where you find yourself at this moment in your story, the ultimate happiness, or blessedness, of your life cannot be fully told in the midst of the journey.

Nor can mine.

I tell you this for a reason. As you read this book, keep in mind that this is the chronicle of a journey. If you were to stop at any point of the story, you would quickly come to the same unfortunate conclusion as we would have in Lincoln's case. I purposefully chose to write this book in a general chronological order, taking every care to preserve each thought and feeling as it occurred to me in the moment—protecting each one from the dulling effect of applied hindsight. Therefore, my thoughts and feelings are raw and incomplete along the way.

The last third of the book is, in my opinion, most important. Yet the first two-thirds are necessary to appreciate it fully. The first part of the book is the black velvet cloth on the jeweler's counter. The latter part is the jewel. The jewel shines best when set on the cloth. So, I believe you will benefit most by reading the full account in the order as it is presented.

Concerning the discussion of various religions and philosophical traditions

I searched the great faith traditions of man and learned much from my journey. I also looked into great philosophical and scientific ideas through the centuries. If I tried, I don't think I could write all that I learned in this book. Even if I were successful in doing so, this book would be much too expansive to enjoy. I wrote what is necessary for the retelling of my particular journey.

When it comes to the great religions, I hope you will not think I am being too dismissive of, or too quick to judge, one religion or another. Quite the opposite. I hold to the three rules of religious understanding of Krister Stendahl, the late and great Swedish theologian and former professor at the Harvard Divinity School:

1. When you are trying to understand another religion, you should ask the adherents of that religion and not its enemies;

2. Don't compare your best to their worst; and

3. Leave room for "holy envy."
   (I understand him to mean that we should look for elements of that tradition we can admire and yearn to be reflected in our own religious traditions.)

If any of my discussions of religion, philosophy, or science stoke curiosity, I hope you will make it part of your own personal journey to find out more. I've included a book list at the end that served me well along the way. The search was worth it for me, and I am confident it will be for you. Because of my efforts to understand, I believe my life will be fuller as I continue to walk down my own path of being and purpose.

Twenty years from now, I don't know how I will feel about all that is written here. Twenty years ago, I could never have imagined thinking, feeling, and knowing what I do today. Yet, through all the spinnings, plot-twists, anguishes, ecstasies, and discombobulations, I have come to realize—no, better, *embrace*—that there is a real rest from all striving. It is a rest that extends beyond mere conciliation or assent, offering instead a rest of genuine knowing. Human anxieties do have an antidote. A blessed life is possible. As I've experienced, it takes time and a commitment to honest seeking to find it. Along the way, if your experience mirrors mine, you will not know yourself from one day to the next. You will morph. It will be shocking. And, if that change pushes you towards the good, well . . . then the shocks will be worth it in the end.

One swallow does not make a spring—nor one season of life, the man.

"O ME! O life! . . . of the questions of these recurring;

Of the endless trains of the faithless—of cities fill'd with the foolish;

Of myself forever reproaching myself, (for who more foolish than I, and who more
faithless?)

Of eyes that vainly crave the light—of the objects mean—of the struggle ever renew'd;

Of the poor results of all—of the plodding and sordid crowds I see around me;

Of the empty and useless years of the rest—with the rest me intertwined;

The question, O me! so sad, recurring—What good amid these, O me, O life?

Answer.

That you are here—that life exists, and identity;

That the powerful play goes on, and you will contribute a verse."

—Walt Whitman

Leaves of Grass

Chapter One

WHY AM I HERE?

SOCRATES FAMOUSLY SAID, "AN UNEXAMINED life is not worth living." I say, "An *examined* life is no picnic either!"

I see people all around, from the deeply religious to the stridently irreligious, streaming past every day, buying lattes and walking their dogs, people who appear to be perfectly happy not to examine their lives but, instead, seem blissfully content to take their current view of the world—and their role within that world—as a simple given. They don't appear to need to ask the big questions:

Why am I here?

What is this life all about?

What kind of a story am I in—if it's even a story at all?

I've attended dinner parties with these unexamined souls. I have participated in the mindless, pointless conversations of weather, sports, politics, and seamy gossip that led nowhere and accomplished nothing—while, within my overheated brain, a burning angst overtook me. I suddenly felt the urge to stand, slam my glass on the table, and burst out: *Stop all this! Don't we know what's happening? Do any of us really know why we're here???* (Only to have my reason restrain me from doing such a crazy thing and remind me that, if I were to speak so honestly, I'd quickly discover I'm actually the only one who's ever seriously entertained these questions, and I'd ultimately find myself standing there feeling naked as the day I was born.)

But my obsession with asking the big question, "Why am I here?" is more than a neurotic tic. It is also asking for the purpose to my life. It may sound silly, but *why* am I asking, "Why am I here?" Snickers, our family dog, seems perfectly content to live in the moment. She never seems to care one whit about her existence. Snickers loves to take walks, smell and pee on things, eat, and bark at squirrels she sees out the back window of our home. (Squirrels must be more evil than most of us think.) She possesses no teleological angst. Purpose beyond barking at squirrels is senseless blather to her. But for humans, I think there are many who carry this nagging notion that there is or should be a purpose to our lives. Call it our end game. It's something our life means. Something our life points toward.

There are others, though, who deny that life has any meaning at all. They believe the raw data of existence flies in the face of any reason to assume there is any meaning to our pointless, insignificant lives. Ultimately, we are all food for worms. And any notion of happiness or purpose is merely a mirage to help us cope with our otherwise hollow lives. They echo Macbeth's harrowing words:

> To-morrow, and to-morrow, and to-morrow,
> Creeps in this petty pace from day to day,
> To the last syllable of recorded time;
> And all our yesterdays have lighted fools
> The way to dusty death. Out, out, brief candle!
> Life's but a walking shadow, a poor player,
> That struts and frets his hour upon the stage,
> And then is heard no more. It is a tale

Told by an idiot, full of sound and fury,

Signifying nothing.

This idea of non-meaning is becoming more popular in Western culture these days. And this notion is increasingly peddled most by our intellectuals. This dark, deterministic, hopeless, and pointless moment of consciousness we ironically call "life" is simply a ruse. And the responsible way to deal with it is to call life what it is—a freak of happenstance where you squeeze a bit of pleasure out of it and then die. Looking at the evidence from a purely materialistic point of view, it only seems reasonable that this deterministic, even nihilistic, worldview cannot be anything but true. Yet, I doubt anyone who really believes this to be true honestly wants to believe it to be true. Most of us would rather deny it because of its being terribly depressing and un-motivating, whether it's true or not. To a man, we want to believe there is meaning to our lives. If there isn't meaning, most of us would prefer the nihilist to keep his mouth shut and let the rest of us live our meaningless days in our self-deluded bubble. *En masse*, we recoil from those who preach non-meaning, not because we are content with the absurdity of our lust for meaning, but because, deep in our heart of hearts, we cannot escape the notion that our lives are pregnant with significance and that, once birthed, that significance will satisfy the *sehnsucht* we all possess in our bones.

Viktor Frankl, the Austrian psychiatrist and Nazi captive, in his wrenching book *Man's Search for Meaning*, describes his discovery of the need for meaning in the brutal realities of Auschwitz. He quotes Friedrich Nietzsche at the start of his book: "He who has a why to live can bear almost any how." Frankl saw firsthand how those who held on to a deep sense of meaning or purpose in life were more likely to survive that hellish nightmare than those who did not. Therefore, if we take Frankl's word for it, meaning can be useful even if it may or may not be true. Meaning accomplishes things because it makes life better (that is, if a better life is something we choose to value).

Yet, the quest for meaning goes beyond serving as a psychological crutch. It has been a human obsession for as long as we know. Thousands of years ago in the Book of Job (which many scholars believe may have been the first book written in the Hebrew Bible), deep questions concerning meaning were penned. Even the great Greek philosophers Socrates, Plato, and Aristotle in the fifth and fourth centuries BCE wrestled endlessly with identifying the central meaning for the existence of man. And so have many obsessive thinkers ranging from Boethius and St. Thomas Aquinas to Mark Twain and Jean-Paul Sartre—all with varying ideas. But one conclusion most people in most cultures and in most times come to as the source for the highest meaning in their lives is religion—our relationship with the Absolute, whether it is a personal god (or gods), a universal life force, or an ideal. Religion is the choice for 98.5 percent of the U.S. population. Early in my life, it had been for me too.

The world is a deeply religious place. Peter Kreeft, a present-day philosopher, once said that "religion makes the greatest claims to be true. If those claims are true, they are the most important truths in the world. And, if they are false, they are the most important falsehoods in the world. Religion is either the world's biggest truth or the world's biggest lie."[1] All you have to do to prove his point is run a simple experiment. After you meet a relatively intelligent person for the first time, ask that person a pointed question:

So, what's your take on religion?

What do you expect his response to be? Discomfort? Devotion? Rage? Embarrassment? There is one response I know you won't get: indifference. Most of us in the politically correct societies of the West would initially receive a thinly veiled polite response. But, if you were to probe further, you

---

1   Kreeft, Peter; *Faith and Reason, Lecture 1; Modern Scholar Series*

would find that this person is passionate about his view on religion, God, and the afterlife—whether for or against—and that his passionate opinion on religion frames his entire worldview.

Most major events in human history have been catalyzed by religious faith—from the most bloody and senseless wars (like the Christian Crusades, the Protestant-Catholic conflicts in Ireland, present-day Somalia, and an entire array of terrorist jihads) to towering humanitarian endeavors (like Mahatma Gandhi's liberation of India and Martin Luther King Jr.'s leadership of the civil rights movement). There is no doubt that it would be impossible to disentangle religion from human history. I know of many who have lost their faith because of the ill effects religion has had on human existence. And, I must say, this fact played a significant role in my eclipse of faith as well.

Even if you wanted to, living a life completely divorced from the spell of religion is next to impossible. No human society in history has existed without it. Religion is more than the mere opiate of the masses; it's the Higgs boson of human experience—the thing that gives all other things mass or meaning. We humans have religion somehow hard-wired into our collective psyche. Whether religion—or, more fundamentally, God's existence—is fact or fantasy will not change its profound effect on our lives. But whether it is true, or not, haunted me. I do not want to live my life based on a lie. And I am confident most other thinking adults do not want to either.

But, how does a person know truth when he sees it? Pontius Pilate asked Jesus, "What is truth?" Isn't truth in essence a mysterious vapor of a thing that depends on a person's point of view? Most know what truth is; we just aren't sure what is true. Isn't truth relative to whatever angle you happen to view life from? While in some cases relative truth may apply (like which is better: blue or green drapes for your living room), it is wholly inadequate for most situations, especially to the deepest and most elemental dimensions of our existence—like 2+2=4; the speed of light; Planck's constant; the essence of self, God, and religion. Even though there are some tender-minded, pseudo-philosophers/psychologists who are in complete denial of the realness of reality and who prefer to base their lives on how they feel instead of expending the necessary energy for finding out what is real, it doesn't make truth any less objective. They are simply choosing to ignore reason and live in a self-aggrandizing fantasyland where they can play mayor for a day and make up all the rules as they see fit. To see this phenomenon in full bloom, go to any bookstore and observe the overstuffed shelves of self-help and free-form spirituality books that would be better labeled as emotional candy rather than true nutrition for the soul.

The most important things in life have a fundamental realness to them and are not subject to the fancies of a passing perception or a sideways glance. But it takes effort to absorb and identify the true essence of something. It's hard going. Truth is the understanding that best explains the total reality of the object in question, whether it is a brick, an emotion, a thought, or a transcendent being called God. Yet, we humans are mostly unwilling to do the heavy lifting to get to ultimate truth. We'd rather live by a pre-conceived notion or a gut reaction on scant data than meditate on the essential truth that is fully evident if we simply open our eyes and our minds.

I envy those who don't feel compelled to grapple with the truth claims of faith. Honestly, it seems like a less stressful way to live. And who am I to think I am any better of a person by pursuing these truth claims? My angst simply may be an unfortunate by-product from an overactive imagination gone terribly wrong. Or, I simply may be weak-minded of a different sort. Even so, the big questions came tumbling down upon me one day, and I didn't possess the certainty to shake them. They muscled their way into my waking thoughts. They mercilessly terrorized my dreams. Not just for a day, or even a month. They terrorized me for years.

Well, this is my story. It's a story about an examined life. And it's rife with ecstasy and agony, confusion and clarity. It's at its best a lover's quarrel with religion and the notion of an all-supreme being many label as "God." At its worst, it's the story of a soul falling blindly into faith only to see it become completely eclipsed in doubt.

So, if you choose to read on, do so knowing that what you are about to encounter can be rather unsettling. Scandalous questions are asked. Sometimes answers appear quite readily; sometimes they don't. If you choose to continue, you might want to pour your pleasant cup of coffee or spiced tea into a spill-proof mug. If anything, it will be a bumpy ride.

LUNATIC DOUBT

Strangely, the sun and the moon appear the same size in the earth's sky even though the sun is four hundred times larger than the moon.

In a total solar eclipse, the moon comes in between the sun and us, blocking the sun's light. Night overtakes day—only to leave a faint, glowing ring of light, like a promise ring empty of a finger, to mock us of that certain comfort which has gone missing.

So how does the moon hide the sun, a thing much larger than itself?
By being four hundred times closer.

Such is the nature of doubt.

Such is our dalliance with the Absolute.

Chapter Two

THE RISE OF FAITH

As a child. I thought as a child.

MY PARENTS CAME TO FAITH when I was in the third grade. It was spring in the sleepy town of Pascagoula, Mississippi. Back then, life was simple. For me, the big questions were "What's for dinner?" and "Will the St. Louis Cardinals make it to the playoffs this year?"

My parents entered a life of faith with a jolt. Before, my dad was a hard-working surgeon with a two-pack-a-day cigarette habit. My mom was a beautiful socialite with a fascination with the occult (which she came by honestly from a thoroughly modern mother who was also transfixed by the surreal and otherworldly). They were good Methodists: warm-hearted, tax-paying, and social-drinking. As I remember, they never were devout, but they were definitely upstanding, moral, and attended church regularly. I do remember as a child waking up on weekend mornings to find empty Old Milwaukee beer cans strewn around the living room after a grand night of partying. (I would go around and sip the leftover beer in the cans before my parents awoke.) From the evidence at hand, my parents knew how to have a good time.

The year preceding their conversion was pockmarked with personal tragedy. The year was 1969. Hurricane Camille mercilessly pummeled the Gulf Coast. Our house was right on the beach, barely ten feet above sea level, with only a handful of live and water oaks shielding it from the fury of Camille's storm surge. To make matters worse, shortly after Camille, our newly rebuilt and remodeled house was callously burgled and violated while our family innocently celebrated Christmas in Barbour County, Alabama, the childhood home of both Mom and Dad.

That Christmas was an exhilarating blur to me. My first cousins had just gotten a new go-cart for Christmas. I spent most of my holiday either racing around the back roads of Louisville, Alabama, in their go-cart or endlessly pontificating about go-carting to anyone so unfortunate to be within earshot. I had, in my opinion, very important questions to ponder: *How fast can a go-cart go if we took off the governor? What if we built a ramp? Think we could jump over the neighbor's cat?*

In contrast, that Christmas was a disconcerting blur to my parents. It was then they began to grope with "the really big questions." And it was shortly after that they found solace in the proselytizing message of the Christian charismatic movement.

My mom and dad went all in. In the parlance of the Charismatics, they were "gloriously saved." They were baptized in an Olympic-sized swimming pool (with a totally awesome corkscrew slide, I might add) and began attending church every time the doors opened. They began a torrid regimen of Bible reading and family devotions. And my dad, with his dizzying intellect, began to devour the Bible with a passion unpracticed even by the most ardent theologian.

After becoming more familiar with the Bible, my parents migrated from the seemingly shallow doctrines of the happy, slappy charismatic movement to the intensity of a fast-growing church brimming with independent, fundamental Baptists. And it was there in that church and in its newly minted Christian school that I began my journey of faith. The fiery messages from the pulpit of our church on the Gulf Coast of Mississippi ignited salvos of "Amen!" and "Glory!" and "Preach it, Brother!" from the otherwise mild-mannered congregation. And the polytonal voices of the faithful raised the rafters and our hearts heavenward while singing folksy Baptist hymns.

It was in this church with its fleet of twenty-plus Blue Bird buses (used by its lay leadership to pick up all manner of unfortunate souls for church) where I was taught to revere the Bible as God's Holy Word and to regard faith as the single most important aspect of life and existence. I had a red-letter King James Bible with my name stamped in gold foil on its cordovan-dyed calfskin cover. I knew every major Bible story by heart. I memorized whole chapters of Scripture. And I could walk a person down the "Romans Road" with the skill of a silver-tongued tour guide.

As a child, I had no reason to question my faith—or anything, for that matter. What I was being taught about God and my place in this world was totally fine with me, just as long as it didn't prevent me from playing baseball with my friends during recess.

So, I began the life of a devoted follower of Christ. I acted as a good Christian should—except for the occasional need to cuss every once in a while to "remain relevant" to my non-churchgoing friends or take the occasional peek at a dirty centerfold picture that my morally-deficient best friend kept stashed under his mattress.

My life was simple: fishing, playing baseball, swimming, and hanging out with friends. And so was my faith: memorizing Scripture, going to church, and passing out gospel tracts to poor people in the projects on sticky Saturday mornings during bus ministry recruiting.

As I grew stronger and taller from childhood to my teenage years, my connection to the Christian faith grew stronger too. Even though my thoughts now turned from childish things to more adult issues, doubt about my faith never surfaced. To my thinking, it was a given and indisputable reality: Jesus Christ is God's Son—the perfect representation of Creator God. Jesus, fully God, lived as a man on earth, shed his blood on a cross for our sins, and rose from the grave bodily and now lives in heaven at God's right hand. And for all of us who believe, we will enter heaven to live with him forever. For those who do not, they will die eternally condemned and separated from God's love in a fire-burning hell. Straightforward story. And I was totally okay with it.

I believed the Bible was God's inerrant, inspired, and definitive communication to man about himself and the life he desired all of us to live. And I treated the Bible with incredible respect and care. For in it, God spoke. In it, all of the meaning of life was fully explained. In it, life itself was revealed, neatly packaged into a codex of sixty-six Holy Spirit-breathed books. It was God's love letter to man, not man's fantastical mythology about the unknown. Snakes really could talk, and a man could live in the belly of a whale for three whole days. The Bible was a gift from heaven man should treasure. If ignored, it was at our own peril.

I was taught that man's reason was too broken by "the Fall"[2] to make sense of anything in this life apart from the Holy Scriptures. I could not trust my own thoughts—or the thoughts of others. Without the Bible, I had no capacity to understand anything with any degree of confidence. The Bible was my golden key to all life's big questions.

I was taught to distrust Catholics, that the Roman Catholic Church was the "Whore of Babylon" as described in the Book of Revelation, the final

---

2   "The Fall" is a reference to the biblical story in Genesis when Adam and Eve, the first human couple, ate the forbidden fruit and "fell" into sin. According to orthodox Christian theology, this was the beginning of sin, death, and suffering.

book of the Christian Bible. I was taught all other religions were pagan and Satan's great deception. I was taught that liberal "Christians" who did not believe in the divinity of Jesus were, even though well meaning, going to an endless eternity of hellish torture. And I was taught that there were many other supposedly devout believers in Jesus Christ who were poisoning the gospel (or "good news") story with devilish and dangerous doctrines and compromises. I was taught that Christ's true followers were on a narrow path headed upward to "life everlasting," and everybody else was on a broad path headed down to "destruction."

I was also taught to view new scientific theories like evolution as Satan's ruse to destroy the faith of the faithful. I was taught that the beginnings of our natural world are best explained using the first few chapters of the book of Genesis than with all the fancy gadgetry and intellectual blather of a God-hating scientific community. These so-called "scientists" were intent on attacking God with a sulphuric rage that the father of lies, Satan himself, had impregnated within their imaginations. In my mind, I could just see these soulless deceivers concocting rancid lies about God as they incanted blasphemies while huddled over strange fire that rose from their Bunsen burners. I was told this kind of deception should be expected. It's the signature move of a devil intent on discrediting the Author of Life.

All this made sense to me. And it explained a lot about the state of my world: why suffering existed, why bad things happen to good people, and why I had bad thoughts and desired to do bad things from time to time. My worldview was comprehensive and complete. I had no reason to doubt any of it—at least, not yet.

Chapter Three

SHADOW OF DOUBT

Lord. help my unbelief.

I GRADUATED FROM A CHRISTIAN university. One short month later, I married my best friend and high school sweetheart, Beth. Beth was everything I ever dreamed of, both as a girlfriend and as a wife. When I first met her, she was undeniably, without effort, the prettiest girl in high school. And that's not just bias talking. I had other guys, some of them my good friends, jealously tell me so. (Honestly, it kind of freaked me out when they did.) Beth was a cheerleader and class officer, and she possessed a smile that could melt the coldest of hearts. But her beauty transcended face and form. Inwardly, she was the most beautiful person I had ever met. She was truly "good." She and I did everything together. In the immortal words of Forrest Gump, Beth and I were "like peas and carrots."

We were a fresh-faced, newly married couple full of dreams and promise. We both went to graduate school. Beth worked on her master's in art. I got my M.B.A. We attended church regularly. I became a deacon and adult Sunday school teacher at a local fundamental Baptist church. Beth taught art at a local Presbyterian day school.

And it was during these salad days the doubts began to emerge.

You might ask, what could go so terribly wrong on a cool Tuesday evening in Georgia at a routine deacons' meeting? Good question. The obvious answer is nothing. But, to me, it was a fateful night, a terrible plot-twist that would send my world spinning out of control.

You'd think that a small local church would lovingly open its arms up to a group of Brownies who needed a place to meet every Thursday after school to do crafts and special projects. (Brownies are girls in the second and third grade in the Girl Scout program—the female version of Cub Scouts.)

They needed a place to meet for a few hours on Thursdays. Our church had plenty of rooms perfectly outfitted for the simple needs of a Brownie troop. We used the rooms for only forty-five minutes a week on Sunday morning. They were definitely available. Sounded like a no-brainer to me. But for our deacon board, it was far from that.

"What does it say if we associate with the Brownies organization?" one deacon bellowed. "Do we agree with the Brownies philosophically?"

And, at that question, a debate broke out.

You see, there's something you must understand about independent fundamental Baptists, generally. They have this teaching called "the doctrine of separation." The basic gist of it, as best I understand it, is that if you associate with a person who knowingly is doing, saying, or promoting ideas and/or behaviors that are contrary to sound biblical teaching/living, it is a sin to associate with them. And there are degrees of separation too. At the time of "the Great Brownie Debate," I didn't have a firm attachment to the way many Christians interpreted this doctrine and really wasn't a big fan of the way they practiced it. It seemed to me, at best, a twisted misapplication of scriptural teaching and, at worst, a passive-aggressive way to register your displeasure with another person or organization on grounds that are less than noble . . . or clear.

For example, if I, as a pastor, didn't particularly like rock music in my church service (call my church "Church A") because I believed God really prefers a good Bach fugue to a funky beat, I can freely stiff-arm Church B because they allow rock music to be part of the way they worship. I, as pastor of Church A, would simply separate from Church B. I would not invite their pastor to speak in my church, nor would I speak in theirs. Nor would I partner with them on anything. I simply would no longer "associate" with Church B. And if Church C, who also doesn't like rock music in their worship service, chose then to associate with Church B, I could also separate from Church C because they don't have the spiritual spine to separate as I so bravely did. And the real kicker is this: I could simply separate from them and never tell them I had actually done so. Nor would I ever feel compelled to confront them. Sometimes I might. But most times, I wouldn't. I'd just whisper my discontent to my friends and tell them I had separated from churches B and C and allow a good rumor mill to commence. My separation from Church B is considered first-degree separation. My separation from Church C is called second-degree separation.

If the whole separation/association issue makes your head hurt, you've got good reason. It's a confusing, bizarre idea. It's why many fundamental Baptists remain independent. Maybe it's because they have no choice. They've pretty much separated from everyone else.

So, back to the Brownie debate . . .

Of all five deacons present, I was the only one in favor of allowing the Brownies to meet in our church. Everyone else was completely against it—on the principle of negative association. The Brownies just weren't "biblical" enough (whatever that means!)

One chimed in, "What would the community think if we did allow the Brownies to meet in our church building?"

Another piled on, "Wouldn't they naturally assume we are aligned philosophically with the Brownies?"

By this time, I'd heard enough. Unwisely, I shot back: "What kind of a subversive philosophy can seven-year-old girls hold? Their only philosophical concern is whether the Elmer's glue is going to hold the macaroni noodles on the paper plate long enough to make it home so they can show it to their doting parents! We have nothing to worry about, philosophically speaking."

I think the other four deacons picked up on my less-than-subtle sarcasm. They were not amused. In their minds, I was too young and naive to understand. Obviously.

So, when the debate broke out, I felt something break inside me.

I thought, *If this is Christianity, I want nothing to do with it!*

The vote was one in support and four against. The Brownies' request was denied. Next item of business . . .

After a good night's sleep and a surprisingly tasty Egg McMuffin, I re-emerged into the world with my faith in Christianity restored, but with a telltale hairline fracture. The birds were singing. The sunshine poured down from the bright blue sky, drenching the Georgian pines in a yellow glow. In light of that particular glorious morning, the fracture seemed insignificant.

At the church, I was teaching a verse-by-verse study of the Gospel of John in Sunday school. I was thoroughly enjoying it. The portrait of Jesus in John's Gospel inspired me. It is in this particular Gospel that Jesus is most clearly identified as the divine Son of God. I had read many commentaries on the text and was getting a solid grasp of its major themes. I was overwhelmed with Jesus' love for others and His commitment to His cause of redeeming a fallen race of man. It's a beautiful, romantic story, full of intrigue and tension.

But when the pastor of our church would preach the Sunday sermon, I heard something completely different. From him, I heard about a Jesus who suffered terribly because of our sins and that the God of heaven was ever angry with our constant disobedience and rebellion. Our pastor (actually a good friend of mine) would routinely break into tears, begging the congregation to come forward and get right with God. All of us had sinned in some way during the week, and we needed to come forward and confess those sins. And we'd sing the hymn, "Just as I Am," over and over again, waiting to fill the front of the sanctuary with crying, broken souls begging for God's forgiveness. Occasionally, one or two people would come down for prayer with the pastor, but, more often than not, no one would come down, leaving everyone feeling terribly awkward and impatient.

I felt the heavy hammer of condemnation week-in and week-out. It was relentless. I felt beat up and bloodied after every service. I found myself dreading church. It just wasn't enjoyable anymore. And, to feed my neurosis further, I felt guilty for wanting church to be enjoyable in the first place. I must be the poster-child of hedonism to even have thoughts like that.

As I looked at the beautiful portrait of Jesus in John's Gospel and compared it to the sermons and the deacons' actions in my local church, I began to see an irreconcilable chasm forming. What I read in the Bible and what I was seeing lived out in my church were at odds with each other. This divide between what we experienced in church and how John's Gospel described Jesus' life didn't match up. The stress of the inconsistency wore at me. Was it our behavior that was wrong? Or did I misunderstand the Bible's teachings? I think most people would conclude that it was the bad behavior that was in the wrong, not the teaching. At the onset, so did I. But, as the shadows of my eclipse of faith began to elongate, my conclusions didn't remain there long, as you will see soon enough.

Even so, I began to have very sour thoughts about my church. I wasn't sure that my church was what Jesus and his apostles had intended the church to be. So, I began an intense period of searching for a church that better matched up with what I understood the Bible to be talking about. And, boy, was I in for a surprise . . .

AND SO IT BEGINS

First contact happens . . . the moon nicks the sun. Then, in short order, it takes a huge bite out of the sun's face. Yet the human eye sees no change in the intensity of the sun's light. Ten percent of the sun gets blocked. Then twenty. Then more, with little change in the radiance of the sun's light.

But something is happening. A change has begun. We begin to feel it in deep, indescribable places. And what has begun will not stop until it completes its course.

We can no longer call today an ordinary day.

Chapter Four

A CHURCH BY ANY OTHER NAME

Jesus wept.

GRANTED, THE BIBLE PORTRAYS JESUS as a perfect man. And granted, a church is made up of not-so-perfect people. I got that then. I get that now. That being said, there is a widespread phenomenon present in American-style Christianity. Self-pleasing religious pundits call it the "church hop" . . . a term I'm not fond of. The church hop is when people hop from one church to another because they don't like something in one church and they start looking for a more suitable church situation. And, yes, Beth and I found ourselves guilty of church hopping when we left our browbeating church in search of another.

During this period, I began to judge churches based on a set of acceptable criteria, not unlike I would use when shopping for a car or a box of cereal. There were certain features a church must have in making it more pleasing to my personal tastes. I began looking at churches with a list of desired features—some of which I was fully conscious of, others that were subconscious and ineffable. I tried to group the list into negotiable and non-negotiable issues. There were the negotiable features in a church like church decor, music styles, or whether or not they had a time to greet first-time visitors in the middle of the service. Then there were the non-negotiable features such as sermon quality, emotionalism, church service length, whether crying babies were allowed to stay in the service, and whether or not the church actually followed the teachings of Jesus Christ—an attribute that is not necessarily a "given" in today's church choices.

Ironically, if you were to ask me to admit to you my list of features for a suitable church, I wouldn't come completely clean. I wouldn't want people to know how shallow my criteria were. I also didn't want to admit to myself just how self-serving and consumeristic my church shopping had turned out to be. Naturally, I found myself never quite satisfied with any one church. I noticed I began to judge the entire church experience from a faulty perspective. As I talked with other Christians, those who are either conspicuously happy with their church of choice or those who are highly critical of their churches, I could sense the same faulty perspective too.

The idea of church is an interesting concept on its own. We don't read anything about "the church" in the Jewish Scriptures (that's the Old Testament if you are Christian or a Muslim). Yet, it appears rather regularly in the Christian writings of the New Testament. Historian Diarmaid Macculloch links this concept of "church" (the original Greek word is *ekklesia*) to the concept of the *polis* or pre-Christian Greek city-states, like Athens and Sparta. It appears to be a borrowed idea. It is quite reasonable and highly probable that the apostles of Jesus were using the Greek term in a purer denotive sense than we use it today. If that is the case, the original idea of the church as imagined by Jesus and his disciples might not be the exact idea most of us have in our minds concerning the church in our twenty-first century cultures. Maybe the concept of church actually could be simpler. Maybe it's more of a principle than a prescription. Yet, most of us moderns/

post-moderns assume our current mental picture of a group of people who meet in a building with a steeple every Sunday morning is the proper way to define church.

It might be worth examining this assumption more carefully. Christians have notoriously misunderstood and misapplied scriptural principles in the past. Concerning our conceptualization of what a church should be, is it possible we are doing it again? Just observe the Christian church's response to Copernicus, Galileo, and the other heliocentric scientists of their time. Some leaders of the church tried to squelch their newfangled scientific theories that contradicted the church's reading of the Bible. Consider the flat earth champions of the medieval church era. How can a world that has four corners—a literal reading of Isaiah 11:12—also be a sphere? Impossible, they reasoned; therefore, the earth must be flat with definite outer borders. Anyone thinking otherwise was a heretic. Thankfully, over time, these church leaders recanted and accepted both the heliocentric reality of our solar system and the spherical shape of planet Earth.

If we are misunderstanding what the church fathers meant by their use of the term "church," it might explain a lot. It may explain my disillusionment with church specifically. It might explain why even some devout Christians are routinely frustrated with their current houses of worship and voice their complaints to family and friends. It might also explain why many well-meaning, spiritually minded people are turned off by the church and no longer view it as relevant to their pursuit of spirituality. Maybe we're asking the church to be something Jesus and his immediate followers never intended for it to be.

For instance, who decided a local church needs to have a building? I've talked with many Christians over the years about this, and most are adamant that a church needs a building. (I follow with "Why?" All I ever get back is "Because.") Who said a church must meet three times a week—on Sunday morning, Sunday evening, and a mid-week service? Who said a church needs a fleet of paid pastors? Who said a church needs to have Sunday school? Who said a church needs to have an organist and a choir—or, for that matter, a praise band? Who said it is better to dress up in our finest just to go to a worship service? Who said we have to sit like quiet zombies in padded pews for the requisite hour or so and listen to things that terribly bore every one of us (that is, if we're willing to be honest enough to admit it). Who gave us all these ideas? Strangely, the Bible doesn't prescribe these. Are these traditions we are either too lazy or too scared to question and change? Inquiring minds want to know.

Something was deeply disturbing Beth and me about church, and we couldn't seem to pinpoint it. Instead, we floundered in this melancholic marinade of disassociation and discouragement. We endured and kept going to church because it seemed like the proper thing to do. Out of respect for the church and its teachings, we made the assumption that the problem resided within us and not within the church.

Over the course of the next ten years, we jumped among an assortment of churches: Baptist churches, Presbyterian churches (two types), a Church of Christ, a non-denominational church, and a Bible church. We spread these church hops over three different cities. Some of our church experiences were simply delightful, but others were disastrous. And, to add to the fun, we had four children along the way.

In the midst of all these life-changes, my business failed. And we found ourselves swimming in a sea of debt. During our recovery time (which took seven years), we began worshipping with a group of believers in the inner city of our hometown. The spiritual fervency of this church was intoxicating. Even though the congregation was a motley crew of misfits, the members of this church loved each other deeply. We had recovering drug addicts and drug pushers coming to this church. We had former prostitutes.

We had the homeless come. We had a mix of blacks and whites attending and holding church offices together. It was an amazing menagerie of the botched and bungled that, I could sense in my heart of hearts, brought an amused smile to Jesus' face.

Now, this felt like Christianity to me. As I began doing much of the Sunday morning teaching of our ragtag congregation, I could feel a wave of fatigue slowly overtaking many of our more stable families. No doubt, the ministry was taxing, both financially and emotionally. We were wearing out. I could feel the exhaustion metastasizing deeply into the marrow of my bones. We weren't strong enough to keep it going. We needed help.

We had, on average, about thirty to forty extremely poor people who attended our services regularly. They were the forgotten of our town. Uneducated. Unskilled. Unwanted. As our church began to crush under its own load of needs, the leadership had to look for answers. We turned to church after church, only to receive pity before being pushed away.

Finally, one small church approached us and said they were interested in helping. They had wanted to start an inner-city ministry and thought they could come alongside us and help. We talked merger with them. They enthusiastically agreed.

There was help. There was hope.

We began to encourage our families to attend services with us at the new church. Most came along. Some didn't. Now, we had many poor, black children who came along with us. They had been with us from the very beginning. And we wanted to continue to minister to them. Most of these children came from broken homes, many of which didn't know where—or even who—their father was. They were not the nicely scrubbed middle-class children already attending this church.

You know you're in trouble when you get reports back from some of the middle-class white families that the inner-city children are routinely "dropping the F-bomb" and getting into the occasional scuffle during Sunday school. These middle-class families were not happy. They demanded our kids not come to church until they could behave properly. Neal Vaughn, one of my best friends, had been ministering with me in the inner city, and he was the person most connected to these kids. He was the one who told me about the growing problem.

The church elders got involved. In a meeting, Neal and I were told not to bring these kids back to this church until their behavior improved. I thought the church was an ideal place to bring these kids to help them grow and become better behaved. The elders disagreed. They were concerned that all the middle-class families would leave the church if this problem was not rectified.

So we had no choice. If the children had to go, so did we.

The hairline fracture in my faith became a crack that day.

Over the course of the next few years, Neal tried to find a permanent home for these kids. Church after church would get excited with the thought of helping, offer help, and then abandon the kids as soon as the ministry became messy and inconvenient. This happened time after time after time. Young middle-class mothers would chide us for the behavior of these kids. A cloud of discouragement and anger began to billow in my heart. All these kids needed was to feel accepted and to be loved. These moms only saw children that were unruly, unlovely, and unworthy of love.

The distance between the portrait of Jesus in the Bible and what we saw in the churches of our city was growing.

Where was the love that Jesus talked about? Where was the concern and care? I saw church after church, congregations who were busy voting on multi-million dollar expansions to their worship auditoriums and family life centers, turn a cold shoulder to these kids. I saw the posh pews, modern sound systems and lighted stages, the fancy industrial-sized kitchens, but with nothing to offer those who couldn't pay their rent or feed their families. I saw pure, unadulterated narcissism sneering in the face of dire need while billing itself as the true disciple of Jesus, the Christ of God.

When I heard that one of the largest mega-churches in town shunned our kids, I became incredulous, frustrated, and embittered. I wanted to puke. They talked a good game, but their only interest was in their own personal comfort and the nicely padded, safe, and pristine social circles.

If this is Christianity, I want nothing to do with it!

After a fitful night's sleep, I awoke feeling not better, but angrier than ever. Let those hypocrites roast under the hot lights of their fancy worship services decked out with Hollywood-style showmanship! Let them choke on their freshly brewed espressos purchased in their church foyer! Let them suffocate under the weight of their own self-indulgence and selfishness! Let them . . .

I jerked myself out of my poisonous spin, sat down on the side of the bed, and took a deep cleansing breath.

This is not the Christianity Jesus talked about. This is *not*. In fact, this is not Christianity at all. Jesus purposefully mingled and spent large blocks of time with the disenfranchised and despised. The religious elites of his time took him to task because of it. But these Christians (meaning "little Christs") in my hometown, unlike Jesus Christ, intentionally tried to protect themselves from these unsavory creatures. So how could these judgmental, pious people call themselves Christians? It seemed like a bad joke—or, more accurately, a brash conspiracy to practice deceptive advertising. I concluded at that moment that it was impossible to find real Christianity in any church anywhere. So I was going to stop looking.

Starting right now.

So I gave up on church. For a time, I stopped going to church altogether.

When radical Islamists call the United States "the Great Satan," it used to offend me. Now, I tend to see their point. What we've been offering the world as a means of culture and morality is nothing like the teachings of the historical Jesus I saw in the Bible. Yet, we proudly call ourselves a Christian nation. But the world only sees our Christianity as a reflection of our culture: a feeding frenzy of greed, pride, sexual irresponsibility, and violence. The Islamists are in effect saying, "If this is Christianity, I want nothing to do with it!" What they see is a terminal case of a morally corrupt societal malignancy. And, if we were truly honest with ourselves, we should join their protestations.

During this time, many disappointments with God began to pile up. More financial troubles. Health issues emerged. Good deeds done in good faith that exploded in my face. I would do things I thought Jesus commanded his followers to do, like giving generously to the poor and helping people in need. For all my good intentions, all I ever received back was a bitten hand and a heart-stopping load of unwanted stress. There were situations on which I asked God for guidance and wisdom only to receive nothing but silence in return. I put out the fleece. I prayed often. I prayed with fervency. I asked others to pray too. I even reduced myself to bargaining with God.

Silence.

I felt abandoned. Where was God in all this pain . . . this chaos? Were my prayers just a pathetic psychological crutch? Were they a horrible waste of time and energy? I found myself withdrawing from anything that had the name of God or Jesus attached to it.

My wife became concerned, naturally. As I looked around me, all I saw were religious charlatans feeding on the fears and insecurities of an unsuspecting public—spiritual puffery with no life, love, or noble value. Had I been part of this cynical farce? Had I been feeding similarly on vapid souls for my own emotional benefit and self-aggrandized identity? I felt betrayed. And dirty. I felt as though I was given a raw deal from a deity I tried hard to honor and serve.

I became Asaph, but without the terminally sunny disposition. And Psalm 73, at least the first part of it, became my credo. Was I wasting my time trying to be devoted to a God who didn't care? Or, if he did, was it that he just didn't care that much for me? So many others who cared not a whit for things spiritual seemed to be well adjusted and happy in their lives. They had no regard for the God of the Bible. And their lives seemed to be going along quite well without him.

Maybe I misunderstood God. Maybe I had created a completely unrealistic portrait of this otherworldly being. Maybe all the people I had been listening to all my life were no more right about their view of God than the man curled up in the corner of a padded cell thinking he's the next incarnation of Batman. Maybe the people I had been listening to, although sincere, were simply operating off bad information. Possible.

I remember having this blasphemous thought: maybe God isn't what we thought him to be at all. If not, then what? Maybe God is something entirely different than I have ever heard. Maybe God isn't the pure soul as I had originally thought. Maybe he is more capricious than that. Maybe he is more like a mad scientist toying with the lives of his creatures just to see what kind of response we'd have if he were to subject us to an odd assortment of painful situations and stimuli. Maybe he has me in this petri dish with my name coded as a 13-digit sample number scribbled on a torn piece of masking tape stuck to its side. If that were true, it would explain a lot.

Maybe God is something less cynical but yet equally unpredictable. Maybe God is better understood as a playful, simple-minded toddler. And one of his favorite toys just happens to be this third rock from the sun. Occasionally, he gets interested in it, picks it up, slobbers all over it, and then shakes it randomly and violently, squealing with glee. As he innocently does this, he totally shakes up the lives and dreams of all of us here on earth. Maybe we are the "Whos of Whoville," and he is our Horton—sans the sympathy and good-natured intent. Maybe this understanding better explains the data.

Maybe we've falsely re-characterized God in the way the Bible describes him (and the way we hear people describe him today) because it makes us feel better about things. Maybe we're just hedging the truth somewhat in order to protect our fragile sanity. Maybe the truth is just too outrageous to seriously entertain it as a possibility.

How can we really know for sure? Is it even possible?

Then, when you get to this point, it comes down to the epistemology of our experience as humans. How can we ever know anything for sure? The basis of my faith was in the unwavering confidence in a source document I could always run back to for definitive answers. And when that foundation fails to hold, the entire structure shakes and falls. And what a felling it will be.

A silent voice within the emotive center of my brain began to accuse me. It bathed the rest of my consciousness with panic-inducing chemicals. Its source was unknown, but its tenor was all too familiar. *Had I crossed over into heresy? Had I broken through into the rarefied but damning realm of blasphemy?* Like a junkie flushing drugs down a toilet at the sound of a police raid, I frantically stuffed these thoughts deep within my subconscious hoping that God, if he were aware enough to observe them, would simply overlook them, or at least empathize enough to forgive. I mean, Job kind of went there in his tirades against God's justice. Maybe God would remember his history of tolerance when he considered my case.

At that point, I began flirting with a new level of doubt I never thought I would ever entertain. And it truly scared me.

Chapter Five

CRACKS IN THE FOUNDATION

The truth will set you free.

MY ANGST RAN MUCH DEEPER than just Christians behaving badly. I began to see the very foundation of the Christian faith as suspect: the Bible. No matter if you are Catholic or Protestant, the Bible has always served as the foundation of the Christian faith. Christians, Muslims, and Jews are all known as "people of the book," meaning that their faith is bolted to a collection of writings that is the touchstone of all necessary truth for life and godliness. All church creeds, doctrine, liturgies, and behavioral norms are built on what Christians mine from the Bible. The meta-story of the Bible is the story of God's redemption of man through his Son, Jesus Christ. The Bible calls Jesus the very Word of God, the *Logos*. The Bible also calls itself the Word of God. In the orthodox traditions of the Christian faith, believers see Jesus as the incarnate Word of God and the Bible itself as the written Word of God. Both are foundational to the Christian faith. Jesus is the hero of the story. The Bible is his portrait, the means of making his story known.

What if the Bible is not completely reliable?

For all my Christian experience up to this point, I never questioned its veracity. Did a snake actually carry on a conversation with Eve in the Garden of Eden? Did Moses part the Red Sea with his staff? Did Jonah live in the belly of a great fish for three days? Did Jesus actually walk on water? Did he really feed five thousand people with only five loaves and a couple of fish? These are strange stories that are way beyond the scope of our everyday experience. If viewed apart from faith, they seem ridiculous and fantastical.

Man has always had a flair for the imaginative: Homer's *Odyssey* . . . *Beowulf* . . . Lewis Carroll's *Alice's Adventures in Wonderland* . . . George Lucas' *Star Wars* . . . even Dr. Seuss' *The Cat in the Hat*. These stories have taken our minds and hearts to places not yet known—and even to the improbable. Could we be guilty of an overactive imagination in Christianity too? Could the stories from the Bible be more moralized myths, making it possible for us as sentient beings to function within a pointless reality? It's a question worth asking.

An overactive imagination has always been an electrifying force for mankind. It has the power to effuse some of the most exhilarating joys while, at the same time, unglue us with indescribable terrors. It is the currency of Hollywood. And we cannot get enough of it.

But the active imagination also goes beyond the occasionally good movie. Man's imagination has had a significant impact on the course of human history. What drove Europeans to seek new pathways to the Far East but wild stories of Marco Polo and the pipe dreams exchanged along the Silk Road? It was the power of the imagination. And how did the Americas become colonized but by the imaginative reports of cities of gold and the inflated accounts of profits from trading exotic spices and treasures found among the natives of the New World? And how did Adolf Hitler convince an otherwise Christianized nation that eugenics and the wholesale eradication of the Jews were not only in the best interests of Germany but were also in the best interests of all humanity? Again, the imagination.

In his *Pensees*, Blaise Pascal argued that the imagination "is that deceitful part in man, that mistress of error and falsity, the more deceptive that she is not always so; for she would be an infallible rule of truth, if she were an infallible rule of falsehood. But being most generally false, she gives no sign of her nature, impressing the same character on the true and the false." The imagination has been the favored tool of leaders and dreamers as well as tyrants and deceivers—those unable to persuade mankind to their way of thinking with reason alone. It has been and continues to be the prevailing conspirator of politicians and religious charlatans.

Part of Pascal's argument against the imagination states clearly that it is not always deceitful. Imagination can be a force for good, if pointed with good intent at a worthy target. The imagination of man has created some of the most magnificent ideas, music, dance, literature, architecture, and art—the kind of creation that stirs within you the sweet, pleasing pain that can only come from a direct encounter with beauty. The imagination has given us glorious cathedrals and unraveled some of the greatest mysteries of the universe, like Einstein's Theory of General Relativity. Imagination is one of the great crowning distinctions of the human race. We, as a species, appear to be lavishly endowed with it, compared to all other forms of animals. Yet, with its great powers to inspire and improve, the imagination has a seedy, dark side.

When you think of all the crazy notions that have endured through the years, ideas like Satan worship, the Cold War, disco, racial discrimination, beauty pageants, or that wealth ultimately leads to happiness, you can see that the ill effect of the imagination plays a key role in their propagation. Even today, we see the effect of an ill-pointed imagination in the extreme conservative and liberal movements in American politics. So, just because a good story tweaks my imagination and foams up within me strong passions does not necessarily mean it is tapping into a buried vein of truth.

I have always been amazed at the power of the stories in the Bible. For me, they have always had a ring of truth to them. But does that mean they are true? As I descended to this level of doubt, I began looking for answers. I asked the question, "How did we end up with this collection of writings, this canon of sixty-six books, as the 'Word of God'?"

I began hearing of others who had asked this question and were looking at other possibilities. There was a whole host of apocryphal writings that were circulating during the first couple hundred years after the death of Jesus that new crops of biblical scholars were reconsidering. They had been rejected as dangerous and heretical. The most famous of all these works was the gnostic *Gospel of Thomas*, a part of the Nag Hammadi library, a collection of fifty codices discovered in Egypt in 1945. Today, it is growing in popularity among both scholars and the laity.

As the early Christian church began to grow in the first century of the Common Era, there were many colorations of teachings and practices of the Christian faith. Many were very similar. Some were directly opposed to each other. It was a kind of free-for-all, may-the-best-debater-win environment. What was the true Christian faith? People began writing books and letters, trying to best explain the Christian faith. That's how we came across the writings that Christians now consider the New Testament. All of the twenty-seven source documents that, together, form the New Testament canon were letters and books written by people to capture the essence of Jesus' teachings in order to standardize the Christian faith.

That's how we get the term *orthodoxy*. Orthodoxy is the agreement of generally accepted, or "right," teachings among a community of believers. It became evident early that an agreed upon collection of writings was important to standardize the Christian faith. The sixty-six books of the

Protestant Bible became widely accepted rather early in the process. The eighty books of the Roman Catholic Church include an additional collection of fourteen semi-canonical books that were clearly categorized as apocryphal by the Catholics themselves. They are included by the Catholic Church for their spiritual richness but not for their authority as the other canonized books are.

But who made these decisions? And did they consider all the evidence before making a completely informed decision? Was it even possible for the early Christians to make such a decision with the restricted access they had to all Christian thought scattered across the known world at that time? In other words, can we trust these "guys" (is it appropriate to call the church fathers "guys"?) who made the decisions that would so profoundly affect the faith of millions, even billions, of people two thousand years into the future?

Are we basing the Christian faith on the right foundation?

Even with a fairly standardized body of spiritual writings, today the Christian faith is fragmented into a huge menagerie of sects and cults. From the one parent Catholic, or "universal," church governed by the bishop of Rome, the Eastern Orthodox tradition splintered off in the eleventh century over a variety of doctrinal disputes. Then, in the 1520s, the Protestants exited from the Catholic Church under the fiery leadership of Martin Luther and the reformers. Martin Luther, John Calvin, Huldrych Zwingli, and others were intensely concerned with the perceived un-Christian or—if you take their writings and sermons at face value, the *anti*-Christian—leadership within the Roman Church's Holy See. They viewed the church as an unholy mixture of paganism and the pure teaching of Jesus and his apostles. They wanted to return the church to *sola scriptura*, a Latin catchphrase for "the Scriptures alone," in order to scrape off the pagan accretions and return to the one true, original orthodoxy of the Christian faith.

Yet, even with this surge of reformational energy, the church became not more unified, but less so. These protests against the church led to our current experience with Christianity: 38,000 different Christian sects and cults. The Christian church has broken apart into a variety of self-defined dogmas and ideologies. You have your Catholics, your Anglicans, your Eastern Orthodox, your Baptists, your Presbyterians, your Methodists, your Pentecostals, your Maronites, your Seventh Day Adventists, your Christian Scientists, your Mormons, your Nazarenes, your Mennonites, your Congregationalists, your Four-Square Gospelists, your Episcopalians, your Amish, your Non-denominationalists (whatever that means), your . . . and the list goes on almost infinitely. Most have a lot in common. Others don't even recognize each other as authentically Christian.

In John's Gospel, Jesus prays his "High Priestly Prayer," as the church calls it. It was obviously a spoken prayer that the disciples must have over-heard on the very same night (but just before) Judas Iscariot betrayed Jesus and conspired to have him arrested. In the minds of many theologians, this prayer is one of the most intimate portraits of Jesus' heart. He prays for his disciples. And he prays for those who will believe in him and his message in the future. The one poignant part of his prayer is when he prays for future believers. Jesus prays that "all of them may be one, Father, just as you are in me and I am in you. May they also be in us so that the world may believe that you have sent me. I have given them the glory that you gave me, that they may be one as we are one: I in them and you in me. May they be brought to complete unity to let the world know that you sent me and have loved them even as you have loved me" (John 17:21–23 NIV).

Jesus doesn't pray that "all of them may be 38,000, Father, just as you are . . ." But yet, here we Christians are, all fragmented and barely speak-ing to one another. I began to wonder whether ecumenism (or religious unity) was honestly an evil thing and something no good, Bible-believing

Christian should ever talk favorably of. It seemed to me that Jesus was promoting ecumenism in that passage of Scripture.

So, the point remains. We have so many people completely devoted to the Christian faith, using the same foundation (the same body of writings, the Scriptures), and yet coming to an insanely variable, even contradictory, mix of conclusions. It just makes you wonder: how good is this foundation . . . really? Are the Scriptures the problem? Or does the problem lie somewhere else?

Faith apparently needs a foundation. It needs something bigger than itself from which to draw its strength. Faith, at its essence, seeks to exercise control and meaning over forces that seem most out of control and beyond our understanding. That would explain the scientists' tendency to remove as part of faith any phenomenon that can be rationally explained by scientific means. Scientists also tend to relegate any inexplicable data to the intellectual backwoods of the "God of the gaps." Because of this, many scientists dismiss any knowledge of God as only that which has not yet been fully explained by the scientific method. Given enough time, some scientists predict anything that is inexplicable now but believed (which they temporarily categorize as "faith"), will ultimately be explained through natural, deterministic science and be re-categorized as "knowable" and, therefore, freed from the ignorant realm of faith. In time, as science marches forward, there will be no more gaps in knowledge and, therefore, no more need for faith or a "God of the gaps" to help us explain the currently inexplicable. Since the faith of most Christians is based on Scripture, if this collection of writings can be better explained naturally, as opposed to supernaturally, then maybe the seeming mystery of faith, God, and Jesus can also be re-categorized and freed from its current ignorant tyranny called Christianity.

So, if the foundation of faith, the Christian Scriptures, were to be shaken, does faith itself shake? For some, it might not. But for me, it began to.

I first stumbled across the scholarship of Dr. Bart Ehrman through my public library. Desperately seeking answers, I found a series of lectures Dr. Ehrman gave on the writings of the New Testament on compact discs. For several months, I listened intently to Dr. Ehrman's lectures driving to and from work. His deep intellectual honesty and willingness to deal with the prickly issues of the Christian faith endeared him to me. Through his lectures, I could tell he had followed an investigative path into his faith in much the same way I had. And I eagerly listened to his lectures and began to read his books. I had a lot to learn.

Bart Ehrman, at the time of this writing, is the Chair of the Department of Religious Studies at the University of North Carolina at Chapel Hill. He has been widely interviewed by a variety of media concerning the Christian faith. What is most remarkable about Dr. Ehrman's work is his deep research into the reliability of the Christian texts, in particular the New Testament writings. And, ironically, his academic work moved him from being a devout, Bible-believing Christian fundamentalist to an agnostic. Through his research, Ehrman found he could not accept the fundamentalists' view of the inerrancy and infallibility of the Christian Scriptures. And, because of that, it loosened the bolts of his faith. He found he could no longer rely on the foundation of the Christian faith—at least not in the way in which many evangelical Christians were defining the faith.

Not to recount all of Ehrman's work, but the evidence that shook me most was the variations among the resurrection stories of the four Gospels. There were significant details of the story that were at odds with each other. One of the Gospels talks of just one angel being at the open tomb. Another talks of there being two. There were discrepancies between who actually came to the tomb that Sunday morning and how many. Also, where did Jesus, post resurrection and in bodily form, first appear to the disciples? Was it in Jerusalem? Galilee? Somewhere else? The resurrection accounts in the four Gospels of the New Testament don't appear to line up.

They may seem like little pieces of data that don't amount to much, but one must understand that, for many Christians, the accuracy of the Scriptures is of prime importance to the reliability of the truth claims of the faith. The Scriptures were God-breathed, according to the Apostle Peter's first letter. Christians everywhere see the Scriptures as not written by man, but believe that men wrote the very words as they were revealed divinely to them by the Holy Spirit himself, the third person of the Trinity. According to the most devout, this is why there is so much life-changing power in the Bible. All you have to do is read it to appreciate its divine inspiration.

When I began to grapple with the possibility of the Bible not being as inerrant as I first was taught, a sick feeling overtook me. I didn't want the foundation of my faith to be shaken. This was shaking it. Before, when I was disgruntled with the behavior of Christians in contrast to what I read in the Scriptures, I could point my finger at people as the problem. Now, I began wondering if I needed to point my finger at the faith I so relied upon for the basis of my life. I didn't want to question the Scriptures. If the Scriptures were riddled with errors, like a collection of fantasy writings manufactured in the mind of man, could it really serve as the basis of faith? I found comfort in thinking that the Bible was without error. With an infallible source for truth, my life had a touchstone. Without it, then everything is up for grabs.

I felt nauseated.

I found myself in spiritual vertigo. I was losing my sense of balance and perspective. The whole world whirled around me with no sense of direction. I began to feel light-headed—and floating. I was at once giddy with a newfound sense of freedom, but then, in an instant, found myself plunging into an abyss of debilitating fear. My chest crushed my lungs. I felt the air rush out of the room, leaving me gasping for oxygen. Extended periods of deep depression set in like a choking fog.

I wondered if any of my Christian friends ever had the same doubts as I did. I invited them for a cup of coffee, a quick breakfast, or a lunch "catch-up" meeting. I eased into the question, not knowing what kind of reaction I was going to cause. Only a few had ever asked the question. And among those who had, none had followed through to seek an answer. Some were taken back. Others were mesmerized. Overall, I felt like a sinister force of evil—a heretic.

I began to wonder if I was truly being honest with myself about my doubts. Was I trying to be different just to get attention? I had a history of doing stupid stuff like that. Was I having a knee-jerk reaction because of my current disappointment with God? Was it a combination of both? Or was it neither?

After a few months of confusion, I began to see evidence of both motivations driving me to the place where I was. I liked the attention of being the resident cynic in an otherwise uniform clique of believers. I fancied myself as having secret knowledge. I had become gnostic with knowledge not illuminating but scandalous. I was like the character Dr. Robert Langdon in *The Da Vinci Code*. I was uncovering a two-thousand-year-old conspiracy of church deceit and cover-up. It was the classic story of the rogue intellectual who bucked the powers that be and exposed the manipulation of innocent people toward nefarious ends. I felt a sudden rush of adrenaline. It gave me purpose.

But I also sensed in my motivation an ugly bitterness. I was angry with God. Why not? I had reason. I had devoted myself to him and denied myself many things in order to please him—only to be ignored. The fact that I now had evidence that the God I had followed for so long might not be the all-wonderful God I had constructed in my own mind gave me the opportunity to marginalize him and push him aside. I could manage him better. If I wanted to, I could even ignore him. Return the favor, so to speak. And, now, I could reconcile his lack of response with his seemingly inability to be the God I had learned about in Sunday school: the God who gave mankind a marvelous gift of perfection, his divinely inspired Word. But now, it seemed that God had gone away. He had literally packed up his royal diadem and "caught the last train for the coast" as described in the strange and poignant lyrics of Don McLean's *American Pie*. And it felt that way. It truly seemed like "the day the music died."

I became an alien and an outsider among the faithful.

I could not imagine a faith where the Bible was not free of error. I did not even want to think in those terms. Inconceivable. If it were wrong on one point, how could it be trusted for all others? The Bible stories I had taken for granted as demonstrably true were now suspect, open for critical analysis. All the verses I had memorized and assumed to be flawless diamonds now needed to be carefully scrutinized under a textual critic's loupe to expose inclusions, scratches, and other imperfections. This seemed like dirty work to me. Unholy work. Work that smelled of sulphur and smoke. And it turned my stomach just to think on it.

Was I wrong to have thought of the Bible as inerrant? I had heard so many pulpit-pounding preachers rant and rave about the inerrancy of Scripture, about how vital it was to the faith. Anyone who denied the inerrancy of Scripture was in effect sabotaging Christianity. Deniers were in effect sweaty-toothed agents of Satan luring the faithful away. I accepted an inerrant Bible as a seminal doctrine—the perfect revelation whereby all tenets of Christianity were conceived. It had to be so. It simply had to.

Or did it?

The Bible itself never claims its own inerrancy, but it does emphatically declare its own authority and infallibility. Up until the mid-1800s, inerrancy of Scripture has never been an issue for Christians. During this time, German higher textual criticism emerged as mainstream, and Darwinism broke onto the scene, challenging the literal reading of the first few chapters of the book of Genesis. Intellectuals began asking hard questions about the historical accuracy of biblical accounts and the authorship of texts. I was led to believe that these "wolfish scholars" schemed to unravel, thread-by-thread, the interrelated accounts of Jesus' life. They inoculated the potency of the Bible by rebranding the original authors' writings as mere works of literature written independently of other books in the Bible. They proposed that each book actually had a specific intent and point of view. Imagine that! The Gospel of Mark had a specific theme and point of view, as did the Gospel of Luke. And they were different from each other. This challenged the more traditional approach of lower textual criticism, which sufficed itself to compare biblical texts to other biblical texts, regardless of the originality and specific intentions of individual authors. It's easy to understand why many evangelical theologians would be very comfortable with the lower textual criticism approach because, according to their presuppositions of the authorship of the original texts, all Scripture originated with God anyway. Therefore, every book of the Bible is by divine design perfectly interrelated and intertwined.

As I was exposed to this level of thinking about the Scriptures, I began to long for the days when I used to say, "God said it. I believe it. That settles it." Simpler times, for sure. It was as if I had just learned that Santa Claus wasn't real. So much of the mystery of life had ground down to a mere mathematical algorithm. Sure, it had its own elegance, but in my mind, it has lost its mysterious eloquence. The wonder and wildness of a faith in a magnanimous, heavenly Father had been reduced to the mechanistic writing of a research paper.

I resigned from leadership in my local church. I quit leading the Bible studies I had been leading. I pulled away. If this book, this Bible, were merely a collection of good writings that were not all that special except for their ability to tweak the imagination, I didn't see the need to obsess over them as I had in the past. They obviously played a major role in the course of human events, but they didn't necessarily need to dominate my life as they had.

If the Bible were not inerrant, could it still be authoritative and infallible? I chose to leave that possibility open. But its lack of inerrancy gave me reason to consider some of the arguments by some that Jesus, albeit an important historical character, may have been just a really good moralist and teacher but not the divine Son of God as I had been taught. If that is a possibility, then the unique stature I had in my mind concerning Christianity had to be called into question. How do I know that God, whoever or whatever he is, is to be found in the Christian faith particularly? Could the over two billion professing Christians alive today be wrong in thinking so? What about those of other faiths? Could they be holding on to a better understanding of who God really is?

I began praying to God apart from the normative Christian teachings. I began to appeal to him as simply Creator God and asking him to help me find his true self. Could I have been looking in all the wrong places for God for all these years? What sent me reeling was an odd little conversation I had on a Friday afternoon in Jerusalem with a man named Wael.

THE SUN-EATING DRAGON

The ancient Chinese feared the solar eclipse when, according to legend, a vicious, black-clawed dragon would appear in the heavens to eat the life-giving sun, thereby threatening to plunge mankind into a future of darkness.

To chase the dragon away, the ancients would bang gongs, cymbals, pots, and other noisemakers. "The louder, the better!" they reasoned, hoping loud distractions would foil the dragon's scheme. And, as they did so, the sun would re-emerge from the dragon's mouth and fill the sky with brilliant light again. The future was spared!

Like the ancients, how less unnerving it is for us moderns to fill our souls with the noisy distractions of life than to risk our futures being darkened with uncertainty from an eclipse into doubt.

Chapter Six

LOOKING FOR GOD IN ALL THE WRONG PLACES

Seek and you will find.

IT WAS THE SUMMER OF the 2006 Israel-Hezbollah War. In Lebanon, they preferred to call it the July War. My niece, Natalie, was getting married to a delightful Palestinian man, Yusef, in Ramallah within the West Bank just a few miles from Jerusalem. There was another man with the same last name, totally unrelated to Yusef, who was making headlines across the globe that summer: Hassan Nasrallah, the religious and military leader of the Islamist Hezbollah Movement in Lebanon. During this fateful summer, Hezbollah militia was launching rockets into the border towns of Israel. Israel, in response, launched massive air attacks and staged an armed invasion of portions of Lebanon. Plumes of dust and smoke created by strategic Israeli bombing raids rising from Lebanese cityscapes became the lead images on the evening news across the world.

But this same July was Natalie and Yusef's wedding. Before the war broke out, my mother and I had purchased plane tickets to attend the wedding. I was excited about the trip and had decided to take my kids along. I had never been to the Middle East and always wanted to go. But that was before the bombing began. And when it did, our plans began to change. So many people from the United States who were planning on going to the wedding decided it wasn't very smart to enter a potential war zone. Neither did the U.S. State Department. So, everyone in my family who was planning to go cancelled their flight reservations—except my mom. She was undaunted. She was not going to miss the wedding of her granddaughter. After much reasoning and pleading for her to stay, the family gave in to her will. But, I couldn't let her go over there by herself. I agreed to escort her to the wedding—but without the kids, just in case there was going to be trouble over there.

As we left U.S. airspace and jetted toward Ben Gurion airport in Tel Aviv, I knew we were going against conventional wisdom. The Delta plane from the United States was, at best, twenty-five percent full. No one was headed to the Holy Land. The name "Holy Land" sounded even more ironic than usual to me. When we arrived in Jerusalem, very few of the holy sites were open to the public. Many were chained up. In several of the shrines, we had to bribe people with some cash just to unlock the doors so that we could see them. Nothing seemed to be happening in Jerusalem. Shops were empty. The restaurants were lightly active. The street vendors in Old Jerusalem were struggling with boredom as so few tourists passed by their confectionaries, clothes, and leather goods displays. Everyone was solemnly hunkered down, waiting for the conflict to pass.

My brother-in-law, Charles, Palestinian by birth, secured rooms for us in a hotel in the Arabic section of Jerusalem. It was a delightful hotel. Small by American standards, but very clean and quite comfortable. The owner of the hotel, Wael, a childhood friend of Charles', treated us like royalty. He was devout Sunni but carried himself in a Westernized, cosmopolitan sensibility.

The hotel was only partially filled with guests. Most were workers and officials from the United Nations. I think my family and I were the only guests who were not with the U.N. Wael took great care of us, and I thoroughly enjoyed the times he spent with us. In typical Arabic fashion, he did everything he could to make us feel welcome and comfortable.

At one point during the week we were there, Wael asked us to dinner at his house. The wedding was on Thursday night. Saturday we were leaving to go back to the States. So, he offered a dinner at three on Friday afternoon at his house. Excitedly, Wael promised that his wife would cook us a traditional Arabic meal. He told us to come hungry. We felt honored and looked forward to it.

At the time, it hadn't dawned on me that Wael had asked us to break bread with him on Friday, Islam's holy day. I'm quite sure he was aware that our family was Christian, so I was more impressed with his invitation after thinking about his gesture of hospitality. I'm not sure many devout Sunni Muslims would have been so eager to eat with infidels in their own home on their holy day. So, I treated the invitation with an extra level of respect and honor.

Wael's wife filled the table with food: stuffed grape leaves, yogurt and fruits, the biggest plate of rice I had ever seen in my life, vegetables, and, most importantly, sheep's neck. It was the most wonderful meal I think I had ever had the privilege of eating! Everything was so tasty. The sheep's neck was a delicacy. I had never heard of people eating it, but the flavor and the texture was so delicious that it still ranks in my book as one of the best cuts of meat I had ever eaten. My mouth is watering right now just thinking about it.

But the conversations before, during, and after the meal were even more delightful. Wael had just come back from prayers at the local mosque. Due to the stress between the Jews and the Palestinians because of the war, the

Jewish government that particular Friday had banned any Palestinian man who was under the age of thirty-five from going into a mosque for prayers. The Israeli government explained that it was for security reasons alone, that terrorists were using the mosques to plot all kinds of mayhem. The Palestinians interpreted the Israeli crackdown as another form of harassment and spiteful subjugation. Just the day before, I had seen Israeli soldiers carrying machine guns, leaning up against an armed vehicle in the Palestinian sector of Old Jerusalem. Their demeanor was menacing and obviously intended to provoke a response. About a half dozen Palestinian teenage boys taunted the soldiers with verbal insults and inflammatory hand gestures, circling the soldiers and the vehicles in the warm, mottled late-afternoon sun. And, just that morning, I walked past several hundred Muslim men gathered in the main square of Bethlehem reciting prayers while being led by an imam chanting verses of the Qur'an through a cheap loudspeaker. In unison, the men recited prayers and bowed their foreheads to the ground. It was an astonishing sight.

I asked Wael how he came to be a Muslim. He didn't answer right away. He thought for a moment, stroked his chin, and then answered plainly. His father was Muslim. He grew up in a neighborhood of Muslims. He went to a Muslim school. He married a Muslim girl. He had simply always been a Muslim.

When he talked of his faith and his recounting of answers to prayer, I could swear I was talking with another Christian at a typical Bible study back in the American South. Wael spoke affectionately of Allah the same way most evangelical Christians talk of Jesus. It surprised me. At the time, I didn't know why it did. Or whether it should. But it did. I wasn't expecting a Muslim to have the same type of relationship with Allah as I had seen with fellow Christians. That's not the picture my pastors and Sunday school teachers back in the overwhelmingly Christian United States had painted for me. Could Wael really be in that kind of personal relationship with God? Is it even possible? Could he know God intimately in a religion that I had considered all my life to be false and manufactured? What was I misunderstanding here?

The flight back to Atlanta from Tel Aviv was packed with all kinds of people. Everyone in Israel seemed eager "to get the heck out of Dodge." I had a very open, very obvious, gay Jewish couple seated beside me on the plane. They were chatty and wanted to ask me all kinds of questions and involve me in their conversations. They were delightful people, warm and engaging. Unfortunately, I was in no mood for mindless chitchat. I was all torn up inside, thinking about that meal experience with Wael and its impact on my worldview.

Had I been Christian because I grew up in a Christian home . . . or because I lived in a Christian community . . . or because I went to a Christian school . . . or because I married a Christian wife?

Wael was Muslim because of the influences surrounding his life. Was I Christian simply because of my environment? Had I simply taken the path of least resistance and, by default, become a replica of all that is around me? What if I had grown up in Ramallah as Wael did? Would I have chosen to become Muslim because of everybody else? Or would I have chosen another path to God, a truer path, the Christian path? Or was the Christian path even the true path? Did I come to faith in God through Jesus Christ because I was compelled to do so and because I was fully persuaded of the truth claims of Christianity in light of all other truth claims found in other religions? Or was I just spiritually lazy? My heart chilled at the thought. I didn't have a good answer.

Just a generation ago, the default religion in the United States was Christianity. Nine out of ten Americans back in the 1970s considered themselves Christian. Now, at the start of the twenty-first century, that number has dropped to somewhere between seven or eight out of ten. Christianity is still the dominant religion in the United States for now. Presently we are seeing more and more religions showing up across the country. Buddhism, Islam, and free-form spirituality are on a rapid rise. The U.S. is becoming ever more pluralistic and variegated in matters of religion. The newly rising Millennial Generation (those born in the 1990s and later) is more religiously plural than any generation in American history. This has caused some evangelical Christians to panic and predict the fall of the United States as a world power because America, as a culture, is leaving the Christian God for other gods. Therefore, God has been, is, and will continue to pull his blessing away from us even to the point of preparing us for a wrath-filled, divine intervention of biblical proportions. I guess only time will tell if these apocalyptic prognosticators are correct.

When I landed back in the States that fateful Saturday morning, not only was I physically tired from a fourteen-hour flight, but I was spiritually exhausted. I knew I had taken a very big leap intellectually and spiritually while I had been gone. And it was a leap I think most people find a way to avoid for most of their lives. But for some strange reason, I was about to go down a different path as a result of it. Though I had landed physically in Atlanta, Georgia, metaphysically, I had no idea where I had landed or would ultimately land. Where faith was concerned, I was airborne, circling an unknown terrain with no idea of my arrival destination—or arrival date.

SO, YOU'VE GOT FAITH, BUT IN WHAT?

Depart from me into everlasting darkness. For I never knew you.

IF GOD IS WHO I had always assumed he was, then I might be standing on shaky ground. Here I was, a very limited creature, putting God, by definition an obviously unlimited Creator, on trial. Who was this God? On what basis can I know him—or her? Had I been unwittingly sucked into this universal deception disguised as ultimate truth? Had I fallen for the worst scam in the history of man? Atheists would think so. As would Muslims. Definitely Scientologists.

Being overly self-possessed as I was and tempting a Creator God by peppering him with pointed questions made me nervous. I felt as if I were juggling open vials of nitroglycerin blindfolded. It was an explosive undertaking fated to leave one horribly maimed . . . or worse.

I remembered the story of Job from the Bible. The Book of Job is actually a script for a play written in poetic form. It is a beautiful book that addresses one of the most troubling topics facing humanity: suffering. Job is a wealthy landowner with ten kids, each with their own house, plenty of livestock, and servants. Job is the main character of the story. God has a speaking role too. And even the dreadful Satan makes two rather dramatic appearances. There is also a supporting cast of Job's four friends, Job's wife, and some servants. But the plot of the story begins with Satan's approaching God and asking God to allow him to inflict Job with some good old-fashioned trouble to see if Job's faith in God could be crumbled. After some negotiations, and in the unexpected and seeming unholy form of a wager, God allows Satan to have his way with Job. Satan kills off Job's children. Satan arranges for all of Job's livestock and servants to be pillaged by foreigners. Satan even causes Job to suffer physical pain by covering his body with painful boils. It's a terrible travesty and, after Satan does everything but kill him, Job simply wants to lie down and die. During this period of suffering, God does not tell Job what is going on or why he is suffering so terribly. Job is left on his own to guess why.

Four friends come by to encourage Job. They do everything but that. The things they tell Job are the typical rationalities and moralisms that most people give for the explanation of "why bad things happen to seemingly good people." Many of the points these friends make sound oddly reminiscent to many sermons I've heard over the years from preachers—even to some of the sermons and teachings I've delivered in my past. Job's rudeness to and irritated attacks against what his friends say to him is shocking. He gets ticked off at his friends, telling them to shut up and go away. Job then turns his attacks against God directly. In the most bold and honest of prayers, Job pleads with God to leave him alone as well. It is a painful spiritual meltdown. Job's friends warn Job to watch what he says about God and show more respect. Job ignores their advice and coughs up complaint after complaint to them and to God, almost as if he raises his fist toward heaven and challenges God to a duel.

But the kicker of the story is when God finally shows up in chapter thirty-eight. God puts Job in his place first and says to him, "Where were you when I laid the foundations of the world? Speak, if you know." Job wisely chooses to keep his mouth shut. It proves to be a good move. God then praises Job and severely reprimands Job's so-called friends for their ridiculous comments. Job is justified and restored. God condemns and pushes aside the four friends.

Job's story encourages me in an odd way. Not because of the suffering. I hate suffering. I'd rather be an anesthetized hedonist than be inconvenienced even in the mildest way. I don't possess the stamina of Job. But the encouragement comes from God and his attitude toward Job. He is willing for Job to question, fume, accuse, and whine. But the entire time, Job is simply trying to figure God out. And Job talks very openly and passionately to God. God seems to be fine with the anger and doesn't seem annoyed by Job's accusations. God seems to appreciate Job's willingness to talk straight. Strangely, it is Job and Satan who are the only characters in this story who directly engage God in conversation-prayer. Job's wife and the four friends only talk about God conceptually.

I'm hoping God's tolerance for frank discussions among his creatures is a universal attribute of God's character. I'm hoping he will treat us with the same degree of forbearance when we step forward to ask the hard questions. If God's patience with Job's questioning was just a dispensation for Job only, then I'm feeling quite vulnerable now. Most of us are too timid, too conventional, to ask God to help us understand the really tough questions. Maybe there's actually wisdom in conventional wisdom. Maybe not. I'm praying that if God does care enough to pay attention to my questions, he will allow me at least a tiny degree of grace in the process.

But back to where I was . . . about to take a big leap.

Calling into question one's childhood faith is disorienting. It's more than just choosing to move from the country into the city or choosing to wear this shirt over another. It is a tectonic shift of values and perspectives that rearranges the entire landscape of experience. It loosens all the bolts and allows everything to float free. It's as if gravity has been ruled unconstitutional and ripped out of the law books. Everything in life that had an ordered arrangement had been lost, tossed into chaos. So, where does everything go? How to make sense of it? All the things we previously thought were important must be analyzed individually with no reliable means for analysis.

I began looking around me, and I noticed how disaffected most American Christians are with their faith. Even though there are a small percentage of exceptions, most appear to be frustrated. What's causing this universal angst? It feels like a stifling blanket of malaise thrown over the religious community. Could there be a sense of need to question assumptions that was throttled into silence by an unspoken convention of fear in doing so? We are creatures desperately seeking safety within community. Challenging communal mores makes us feel the threat of alienation from the pack. So, maybe we swallow our angst concerning our faith in a self-preserving guise of community. We protect the pack by not allowing variant thinking to slip into our communities of faith. We suffer from group-think. As our lack of questioning protects us from disaffection, it exposes us to the real risk of living a lie. We live that lie not because we are stupid or morally insipid. We live that lie because we value communal acceptance more than we value truth. Tangible human relationships tend to trump abstract principles. A warm hug from and a conversation with another human being feels more real to us than a cognitive understanding of the nature of an unseen Creator God whom we cannot hug or a divine voice we cannot hear.

When I think of Socrates and his rejection of the polytheism of the ancient Greek culture, I wondered if he, on a personal level, ever mourned his loss of faith. I don't see much in Plato's dialogues to give me a definitive answer. But Socrates' willingness to defy the common beliefs of his day, risk alienation from his community, and seek other explanations as the inspiration for goodness, truth, and virtue must have been a nerve-racking enterprise. It ended up getting him killed. Even so, his seeking after truth caused him to deviate from the cultural norms of his day.

Additionally, I think the large majority of us are captivated by cultural norms. Because the notion of the supernatural has such power over the human psyche, it contributes to the fear of calling into question those norms. It takes a bit of courage (some would go so far as to call it hubris) to buck against a commonly accepted deity and think you have arrived at a level of enlightenment that has completely evaded scores of otherwise intelligent people for generations. If you think about it, it's somewhat cocky to believe you have the rare ability to see a false reality that has bamboozled everyone else.

Yet, that's where I found myself—alone and at odds with my faith and at risk of breaking faith with commonly held beliefs within my circle of family and friends. And I'm praying that God, if he's paying attention and is the same God I am in the process of disowning, will find it within himself to forgive me if I find myself having to come back groveling.

So, then, what were my options? Another manifestation of the Christian God? Maybe the God of the Jewish religion? Or Allah of Islam, maybe? I became a tourist of the monotheistic religions and ventured out to see the world through a different religious lens. But, the hardest part was the beginning. I wanted to divorce myself from what I'd known completely and view the transcendent from a new point of view. I made the decision not to rely on Christians to educate me on the faiths of others. I wanted to learn from those others directly. And that is exactly what I did.

EKLEIPEIN

To the early Greeks, "ekleipein" meant abandonment: when something, or someone, of importance leaves with no certainty of return.

It's where we get our word "eclipse."

With a solar eclipse, the sun's light momentarily leaves us. But we are certain of its return. Science and history confirm this. After a brief moment of devilry, the sun re-glorifies the sky.

No abandonment.

But with faith, I fear a true ekleipein—a leaving with no certainty of return. This numinous light, so inveterate in my past, steadily darkens.

But will it . . . or can it . . . or should it . . . ever return?

Chapter Eight

ANOTHER CHRIST

Who do you say that I am?

C.S. LEWIS WAS A STAGGERING intellect. In his most influential book, *Mere Christianity*, Lewis tried to strip away all the sectarian differences within Christianity to explore and articulate the "mere"-ness, or basic essences, of the Christian faith. Former atheist, Cambridge professor, and a writer of more than fifty books, C.S. Lewis wrote during World War II and its immediate aftermath. That period of history must have been a wrenching time for deep thinkers, because the rawness of existence was exposed and brought to the foreground. War, death, injustice, evil, faith, the afterlife, and meaning were topics that were sparking with electricity like a broken, active power-line dancing in the middle of the road. What can be made of all the inhumanity and destruction? What to do with the cruelty and unchecked power-rush of world leaders like Hitler, Stalin, Mao, and Mussolini?

But it was searing thinkers like C.S. Lewis, J.R.R. Tolkien, Viktor Frankl, Dietrich Bonhoeffer, and others who pushed humanity through the darkness and helped the generations following to make sense of the chaos. And it was during that time when C.S. Lewis seemed to give Christianity its clearest voice since the times of Thomas Aquinas and St. Augustine. In *Mere Christianity,* Lewis very effectively identified the core of the Christian religion as it has been practiced throughout its history since the disciples of Jesus were first called Christians, or "Little Christs," in Antioch. Lewis described "mere Christianity" as a hall from which all Christian sects can be thought of as rooms that can be entered from that hall. What Lewis is attempting to describe is the central orthodoxy of Christianity. But there have been other manifestations of Christianity that are not best classified as orthodox. Orthodoxy classifies these aberrant forms of Christianity as heresies (based on a Greek root word meaning *choice* or *to choose*). Could there be truth about Christianity that was not considered orthodox but that had been forcefully blocked by a disillusioned majority? Could it be that the more enlightened and truth-seeking minority had been wrongly labeled as heretics? Sounds like the makings of a good plot for a Hollywood movie.

I've been around long enough and around enough people to know that just because something is commonly believed to be true does not necessarily mean that it is. Common belief, or consent, is generally good evidence that there's a high probability of something to it and that we should take that belief seriously. But common consent doesn't mean it's a slam-dunk lock on truth. So, my question is this: is it possible that orthodox Christianity has been backing the wrong horse all these centuries? This point of view would assume a huge conspiracy of epic proportions and a massive squelching of truth. If the Christian God were as powerful as Christians say he is, how then would he allow such a deceit to continue unchecked in his name? It doesn't fit with the way all Christian sects appear to describe him: an all-knowing, all-loving, and all-powerful God. It's possible there's a conspiracy, but highly improbable.

But I wanted to make sure not to leave any stone unturned in my search, so I opened up to the potential of a different, "heretical" Christianity that may be the real truth of the Christian faith but that might have been bullied and marginalized by common consent. So, I poked around for a time in the worlds of Christian Gnosticism, Mormonism, Jehovah's Witness, Universalism, and the like.

I remember sitting on a plane next to a young Mormon devotee as he and I were both heading for Salt Lake City. He was heading there for a religious studies program, and I was headed there to go skiing with my wife and another couple. During the entire flight he sat in his seat, dutifully reading the Book of Mormon, highlighting passages, and taking notes as he did. I was struck most by his earnestness.

Not long after that trip, I remember browsing through a bookstore where I stumbled across a dense commentary on the Book of Mormon that was easily over two thousand pages long. I cracked open the commentary and looked for the name of the author. He had two doctorates in philosophy, one from Brigham Young University. He had devoted his entire life's work to the understanding of the Book of Mormon—a book which most orthodox Christians believe to be manufactured by the overactive imagination of Joseph Smith, not of divine origin. I wondered at that moment how a man of obvious intellectual capacity could spend so much time, care, and scholarship on a book that was of lesser spiritual value—or so I thought from my prejudicial perspective.

Throughout my life, I have known people who have been part of the Mormon faith. For the most part, I've not seen anything but good people associated with Mormonism. Apart from the occasional news story about some fundamentalist Mormon who marries an underage teenage girl as his fourth sister wife in an already dysfunctional plural marriage, most of the good people who follow the Mormon faith are just that—good. They are law-abiding, monogamous, and tax-paying. They keep their yards mowed and are polite in checkout lines at the supermarket. If the end game of a religion is to produce good, moral people—or saints—then I think of all the Christian sects active today, it'd be hard not to argue that Mormonism has the better track record. Just line up any Southern Baptist or Anglican congregation against a Mormon congregation family-for-family and look at any selection of moral attributes you deem as important to moral upright-ness, and I'm fairly sure nine times out of ten, the Mormon congregation will win easily.

But this phenomenon is found not just in Mormonism. There are very devout and wonderful people who are attached to other divergent, unorth-odox colorations of Christianity. The Jehovah's Witnesses are easy to poke fun at because of their door-to-door evangelism techniques, but many of the people in those communities of faith are also highly moral people. You will find them to be very respectful and caring. And Jehovah's Witnesses also appear to be quite happy as a general rule—again, more so than many "orthodox" sects of Christianity like Methodism, Lutheranism, and even Pentecostalism, just to name a few.

So, what was I to make of this exploration? I began reading the Book of Mormon and its doctrinal statements. I listened to their sermons and their intellectuals talk about their faith. I also did the same with Jehovah's Witnesses, the Quakers, and the Universalists. All in all, I could see within each vein of these religious expressions a bit of important insight—a unique spark, a fresh perspective.

This got me thinking. What is the end game of religion, anyway? Is religion a part of us to promote morality, or right living, as its foremost objective? Or is there something more? Is religion here to add happiness to the lives of its adherents? Or is there something more? If morality were the *summum bonum*, then I think a case could be made against those Christians who say, "We are the orthodox ones!" Baptists, Presbyterians, Catholics, and Charismatics all have a rather poor performance record in producing decidedly moral church members. Some of the "unorthodox" sects appear to do a much better job with morality.

Let's look at happiness. If happiness were the *summum bonum*, as Aristotle reasoned, then Orthodox churches don't seem to excel in this category either. Divorce, suicide, family violence, and depression are just as rampant in most orthodox circles as in the general population. Yet, it appears some of the unorthodox sects are not as plagued with these obvious signs of unhappiness.

Should the promotion of morality and happiness be the end game of religion? If you listen to most religious leaders pontificate, those two supreme ends seem to be the end game. But, when I got to thinking about it, I wasn't sure it was so. To look at its denotation, religion can have two meanings. Religion means either "to bind, or reconnect" or "to revere the bond between mankind and the sacred and/or divine." Both have in common the idea of connection: in essence, the religious man in relationship with what he perceives as God. So, how does morality and happiness fit into this idea of religion? They fit in more as secondary issues rather than primary issues. The primary issue is in establishing a connection. According to many, that connection requires a certain level of morality, or sinlessness, to be present. And, according to many, happiness is a pleasing outcome for a reconnected soul to the divine. But, can morality and happiness be present without reconnection to the divine? It's quite possible. So, if I find that religion is not best connecting me to the divine—no matter how much morality or happiness it is producing within me—I'm not being true to religion at all. If there is a God, and his idea of human existence depends on religion, or reconnection, then that is the primary test of whether a religion is the best mode to truth. Among the overwhelming majority of religious thinkers throughout known history, whether that thinker was a skeptic or a true believer, religion has most to do with man's attempts to connect with the divine, not to promote morality alone or to induce happiness alone. If you think about it long enough, it makes all the sense in the world. When I came to this realization, I found this part of my journey to be wholly dissatisfying.

I never found any of those unorthodox Christian worldviews convincing. Their structure of belief didn't explain my reality any better than orthodoxy: who I am, who God is, and the ultimate meaning of life. There seemed to be something missing with each: a concreteness. Those heresies seemed to be more of a means of forcing a reconciliation of ambiguities rather than a complete codification of truth. In the worldviews of those peculiar forms of Christianity, there seemed to be very specific *corrections* to Christianity that the founders of those forms were trying to make. The early formulators of those sects observed problematic points within either the orthodoxy or orthopraxy of Christianity that didn't seem to make sense to them. So they tried to patch it with a new cloth of understanding in an attempt to mollify the incongruities observed. The Mormons went as far as manufacturing additional canonical writings, *The Book of Mormon*, to support their redefinition of Christianity. No matter what form it came in, the patchwork of those heresies, however, seemed to me to distort both the underpinnings of why the Christian faith existed in the first place and the experiential observations it tried to reconcile. From my analysis, it was as though by trying to build a bridge between the two, those non-orthodox theologies actually destroyed more than they built. So, I found myself leaving them alone to move onto other things.

G.K. Chesterton, a tenacious seeker of truth, set out on a similar yet more rigorous path in his thinking concerning orthodoxy. In his book titled, quite obviously, *Orthodoxy*, Chesterton ultimately concluded, "I did try to found a heresy of my own; and when I had put the last touches to it, I discovered that it was orthodox." Time had definitely tempered the orthodox faith. Christian heresies, from my review, lacked the necessary gravitas to be more true than the orthodoxy they chose to distinguish themselves from. Superficially, they're gratifying. But when it came to the deeper complexities of religious experience (concerning God's nature, man's nature, the problem of evil, and the reconciliation of man to God), I found them to be wholly inadequate.

I settled in my mind that the historical orthodoxy of Christianity is the soundest representation of the Christian faith—and the most beautiful. That's what disconcerted me most about my drift into doubt. The historical portrait of Jesus is a thing of gleaming beauty: an engaging, loving, gentle, strong, resolute, fiery, patient, even peaceful Creator God. I recently heard an interview on the radio with the comedian Samantha Bee, where she talks about having a "crush" on Jesus from the paintings she saw of him when she was a girl. She liked the paintings of Jesus with the piercing blue eyes and silky hair. She imagined being married to Jesus. Naturally, the paintings that exist of Jesus are only imaginative interpretations of artists. But I understood where Samantha was coming from. Not in the same sexual way Samantha was referring to, but, like her, I wanted Jesus to be my God. The Christian faith portrays him in such an attractive way. But just because I prefer God to be portrayed this way doesn't mean that it is the most truthful representation of God. Heaven help us if absolute truth should be held captive by such unstable and emotional preferences!

Here's a thought: what would you prefer, to worship a God you liked best but suspected wasn't the true God or worship the true God you didn't like so much but felt most confident was God? I found myself wanting to revert back to the Christian God simply because I liked him so much. If there were a God I could respect and relate to, it would be Jesus. But, deep inside, I could not just settle for Jesus based on sentiment alone. I needed to know if Jesus was truly God or not. That would require me to be willing to let go of my preferences for Jesus and openly consider the alternatives. I needed more data.

So, I turned to the other monotheists . . . Judaism and Islam.

Jewish and Muslim scholars would hedge a bit on calling Christianity a purely monotheistic religion (meaning a "one-God religion") due to its Trinitarian doctrine of the Godhead being comprised of three persons: the Father, the Son, and the Holy Spirit. The Christian theologians say it's really only one God, and the persons of the Godhead are not separate Gods, but one unified Whole. If you are confused by this doctrine, join the Jews and the Muslims. They don't see it, nor do they acknowledge it. In fact, throughout the history of Christianity, there have been followers of Jesus who haven't completely understood it, either. The "heresy" of Unitarianism is an example of Christians who couldn't subscribe to the doctrine of the Trinity. And then there are others, notably the Modalists, who take the doctrine of the Trinity a bit too far according to orthodox traditions. The Modalists do see distinct persons in the Trinity who act in a unified purpose. This makes most Christians nervous because it smacks of polytheism, an idea Christianity claims it wants to avoid.

Are these arguments over the Trinity just semantic differences, or are they substantial differences? Sometimes I wonder if these types of arguments are just ways for insecure people to flaunt their theological acuity rather than demonstrating a real love for truth. I've been around people who draw swords on seemingly infinitesimal distinctions in doctrine. As a whole, I sense an overall dryness in their relationship with God as they speak so exacting of God. Quite honestly, these people bore me terribly. Sure, the doctrine is important, but I just don't see these nit-picking theological pundits as having much of a craving for intimacy with the God they are so intent on protecting. But that could just be me.

But, this time, launching into the study of Islam and Judaism felt differently than before. In the past, I'd been curious about these faiths and had read the occasional book or accidentally watched the PBS special report about them when there was nothing more entertaining on the television. But being intellectually curious about it differs dramatically from looking into the faith for the possibility of encountering transcendence. This time around, these faiths I instantly re-categorized in my mind from being interesting novelties into something much more visceral. I looked at them for understanding before; now I looked into Judaism and Islam for life. And that change in perspective caused me to grow weak in the knees.

I decided to look into these faiths from the point of view of those who wholeheartedly were devoted to the faith I was exploring. I didn't want to read about those two faiths from Christians trying to make sense of them. I wanted to get the information firsthand from those who trusted in it for the salvation of their souls. So, I read directly from the rabbis and the imams. I wanted to see their God from their perspective with no filters.

Concerning Islam, I had read several books on the faith by Christians. Since the September 11, 2001 attacks in New York and Washington, a flood of books about Islam, particularly fundamentalist Islam, has overwhelmed the market. They were selling fast. Everyone wanted to know what motivated these terrorists to attack with such wanton callousness for human life. TV news show after TV news show interviewed seemingly knowledgeable people quick with an explanation. But the way they described Islam made it virtually impossible for any sentient being to be duped by a religion that promoted such insane atrocities as *jihad*–or at least the Westernized understanding of *jihad*. I think the West simply wanted a pure, black-hearted villain to rage against. Maybe the motives of those terrorists were tainted, but I couldn't imagine 1.2 billion people throughout six continents of the world being so duped by such insanity. Islam must be about more.

So, I began listening to lectures by Muslim clerics and Jewish rabbis to get answers directly. I read books. I sought out opportunities to talk with devout Muslims and Jews to understand them better. I wanted to know why they were in the faith they were in. What did they see that helped them understand God, humanity, and the ultimate meaning of life? How must I approach this study to see these faiths clearly without prejudice?

As I began exploring these other faiths, a panic overcame me. My palms actually got sweaty as I picked up a new book about Islam or Judaism. I cared enough to know the gravity of this step. I was about to do what so few devoted religious people ever do . . . deviate from their original faith. As I thought about it, I realized that I did have friends go from devout to doubt. And I knew others who doubted and then became devout. But that was all movement *within* the Christian faith. Personally, I didn't know anyone who went from Christian to another faith altogether. All of the sudden, the radical nature of my next step intensified.

What was I doing?

Was I about to step into a world that could unhinge everything I thought to be true?

Was the true God to be found somewhere else?

Chapter Nine

THE FAITH OF ABRAHAM AND ISAAC

The Jews answered and said unto Jesus. Abraham is our father.

JESUS WAS A JEW. ALL his disciples were Jews. And so was the Apostle Paul. All these men, these founders of the Christian religion, were born into Judaism. Most of the people they interacted with and shared the gospel of Jesus Christ with were also Jews who believed that, by blood, they were children of Abraham—and that they worshiped the God of Abraham, Isaac, and Jacob, the patron fathers of the Jewish faith.

The only difference between Jew and Christian was what they made of this Galilean, Jesus of Nazareth, who lived around the years 4 BCE to 29 CE. The historical realness of this Jesus has never been seriously disputed by either Jewish or Christian scholars over the past two thousand years. He did live in Palestine during those years and was known as a religious leader. Except for a few instances, the early Christians worshiped peacefully alongside the Jews in temples and synagogues during the first century or so after Jesus' death. That's how similar the faiths appeared to be to the first couple of generations of Jews and those who were loyal to this new Jesus, the self-proclaimed Messiah. Many Jews did believe that Jesus was the Messiah, but not all. Some still remained skeptical.

The Jewish religion has in its writings, especially in the prophecy of Isaiah, this notion of the Messiah, the Anointed One, coming to earth to re-establish King David's monarchy. When Jesus came to preach, he talked of a kingdom too, but nothing like the rabbis of his time had pictured it. Jesus spiritualized his kingdom. Jesus explained to them that his kingdom was not of this world. This definition of the re-establishment of David's kingdom was at odds with the prevailing wisdom and prophetic insight into the concept of the coming Jewish Messiah. This troubled many of the more learned rabbis. They had a difficult time accepting Jesus' claims as Messiah, even though this Jesus was quite a spectacular teacher who seemed to cause everyone to stop and take notice. To put it more directly, Jesus was not the type of messiah the more religious Jews were looking for. Maybe they had a point.

Jesus' claim to messiah-ship was not unique. There had been many others through the years before and even surrounding Jesus' life who had claimed to be a messiah too. There were some who appeared after Jesus' death. So, could Jesus have been just one more in a steady stream of misguided persons with self-delusions? Yet, his claim to be the Messiah wasn't the ultimate deal-breaker for the religious Jews. The real disconnect for many Jews was in his self-proclamations to be divine—to be the great "I AM" of the Jewish Scriptures.

According to Jewish rabbis of the time, the expectation of *The* Messiah was not that he would actually be divine as Jesus and his followers claimed him to be. The Messiah was to be a man born quite naturally and not supernaturally. He was to take King David's throne and lead the Jewish nation into the age of perfection as prophesied by Isaiah, Hosea, Amos, Zephaniah, and Jeremiah. In essence, the title of messiah is a Jewish term used for anyone who is anointed with oil, which included both kings and priests. So, this notion of the Messiah as elevated by Jesus of Nazareth is a twisting of the prophecies. Therefore, according to Jewish scholars, Jesus could not have been *The* Messiah the Jewish nation was looking for. Why? Because the Jewish sacred writings described a messiah of a different sort.

To say that the Jewish faithful are a "people of the book" is a gross understatement. The Jews' fidelity to the Torah, or law, is intense. Many of the most devout Jews of Jesus' time were Pharisees. The Pharisees were a class of rabbis totally devoted to the Torah. They knew it inside and out. The tradition of interpretation of the Torah was that the Messiah would come and lead the nation into a full and complete observance of the law. Jesus of Nazareth did anything but that. The New Testament is littered with instances when Jesus would break the rules of the Torah, like healing people on the Sabbath (in Jewish terminology, the *Shabbat*), and the Pharisees would call him out on it.

As a Christian, I used to be hypercritical of the Pharisees because of their reaction. Here's a situation where Jesus clearly does something entirely mind-blowing and supernatural and yet, in light of this incredible miracle, the Pharisees would stand there, huddled together with their copy of the Torah, and condemn Jesus on a technicality. *Bad form, I say!* No wonder Jesus accused them of straining their drinks for gnats, but swallowing camels. The only explanation for the behavior of these Pharisees was that they were idiots. Or so I thought.

But the Pharisees' devotion to the Torah was relentless on purpose. They were told that in it was everything needed for life and the understanding of the mind of God. They were told that charlatans would come and try to steal their faith with devilish signs and wonders in an attempt to get them to break faith with the very Word of God. And here was one, this Jesus of Nazareth, born of a simple Galilean woman with a scandalous story to mask his obviously illegitimate birth, asking them to ignore what they knew to be clear commands from God. Maimonides, the great medieval Jewish philosopher, once wrote:

> The Jews did not believe in Moses, our teacher, because of the miracles he performed. Whenever anyone's belief is based on seeing miracles, he has lingering doubts, because it is possible the miracles were performed through magic or sorcery. All of the miracles performed by Moses in the desert were because they were necessary, and not as proof of his prophecy.

> What then was the basis of [Jewish] belief? The Revelation at Mount Sinai, which we saw with our own eyes and heard with our own ears, not dependent on the testimony of others . . . as it says, "Face to face, God spoke with you . . . " The Torah also states: "God did not make this covenant with our fathers, but with us—who are all here alive today" (Deut. 5:3).

These words of Maimonides, even though written in the twelfth century CE, were not a new progression of Jewish doctrine during a later time, but a crystallization of a doctrine common throughout the history of Judaism, even back to the Judaism of Jesus' day. No wonder the warning flags went up for them when Jesus spoke against the Torah.

The supposed virgin birth was also troubling for Jewish scholars of Jesus' time. First off, Jews did not see the passage in Isaiah 7:14 as a prophecy of a virgin birth, but only that a young woman would give birth. They claim the Christians have misread the Hebrew Scriptures (as Christians seemed to often do, in their opinion) in order to defend the claims of Jesus and his followers.

Another aspect of the teachings of Jesus and his followers that concerned the Jewish leaders was the seeming dualistic portrayal of reality: of one kingdom of this world and another kingdom of heaven. Jesus and his followers seemed to marginalize the material world with all its pleasures and experiences as being predominantly evil in favor of a more spiritual world where God was most pleased to dwell. The Jewish leaders frowned on this sense of dualism. The divide between Jew and Christian only increased through the years to follow as the ascetic practices of the early and medieval churches became more pronounced. Denial of the flesh became a code of honor among the early Christians. Self-flagellation, monasticism, priests forbidden to marry, etc.—these practices and others caused the Jewish rabbis to view the Christian faith as anti-material. In their mind, Christians were quick to declare things that are good creations of a Good Creator as being sinful and ugly.

The Jewish theologians and historians were not as bothered with Jesus' role as a good moral teacher. Many of Jesus' teachings they already knew because they were very similar to the rich, moral traditions of the Pharisees. Even many of the apocalyptic teachings attributed to Jesus resounded with the influence of the Essenes, a mystical, messianic sect of Judaism popular during Jesus' time. So, there was not too much concern about Jesus' teaching or his role as a teacher. But, the Jews had problems with Christianity when the growth of this "Jesus cult" sought to deify and portray Jesus as the very Son of God. This worried Jewish devotees the most.

As I looked into the relationship the Jewish tradition has with other religious traditions, especially that of Christianity, what surprised me most was the complete lack of proselytizing Jews were encouraged to do. Comparatively speaking, Jewish people have limited interest in sharing their faith outside their own ethnic identity. If you are a Gentile and were to walk up to a devout Jew, he or she would not be eager for a chance to share the Jewish faith with you. Their faith is theirs. And they simply want to worship God in their way and, for the most part, be left alone. Most wouldn't be belligerent about it, but proselytizing would not be much of a priority or issue. Their God is the God of Abraham, Isaac, and Jacob (the Jewish patriarchs) and not the God of Augustine, Aquinas, and Luther. God is seeking a relationship with his chosen people primarily. Those not chosen, not Jewish, are not a serious concern, religiously speaking.

This is quite unlike the Christian and the Muslim faiths. The Christian and the Muslim faiths are all about conversion and winning over the world in order for that soul to attain eternal life. It's hard not to be hit up with a proselytizing Christian when you go into a major metropolitan area. I've been handed so many gospel tracts in my lifetime that they'd be virtually impossible to count. Christians talk openly about their intent on sharing the gospel with you. Jesus is even credited with giving his disciples a Great Commission that commands them to go and make disciples of all nations. That's why, in recent history, there have been so many missionaries sent out from Great Britain in the eighteenth and nineteenth centuries and from the United States in the twentieth and twenty-first. It's also the reason why we are seeing a surge of Christian missionary activities emerging from newly Christianized countries like South Korea and, even more recently, China.

In Islam, the pressure to proselytize is equally strong, if not more so. Much of the growth of Islam during the early years of the faith was done not only through persuasion but also through intimidation and the sword. The need for a society to be Muslim is such an important part of the Islamic faith that conversion of many, if not all, has always been of supreme importance. But before I paint a cartoonish portrait of Islam, there has always been a degree of tolerance of other "people of the book," primarily Jews and Christians. Muhammad and his immediate followers were not so radical at first in their proselytizing that they did not allow for the freedom of religion for others.

But back to Judaism. For non-Jews—or as Jews more commonly label them, *goyim*, or, in biblical terminology, *Gentiles*—conversion to faith in the Hebrew God is not necessary. In fact, Gentiles can simply adhere to the "Seven Laws of Noah," also called the Noahide Law, and a Gentile will be just fine. I found this Jewish doctrine initially refreshing. It kind of sits well with my natural bend toward tolerance and "can't we all just get along?" sentimentality. But, when really thinking on it for a while, I began to grow troubled by it for two reasons. The first was in the very character of the Creator God that the Jews revere.

Here is God who created humankind "in his own image," as the first book of the *Tanakh*, Genesis, recorded. His first human creation was Adam and his wife Eve. From this divinely created couple, the entire human race emerged. And from these two, almost seven billion humans roam this wide world as "little image bearers" of the Creator God. From the language of the Hebrew Bible (the Christian Bible's Old Testament), God was quite fond of these human creatures. He spoke longingly about their value to him even though he occasionally wiped out entire communities, even civilizations, because of the human race's maddeningly stubborn tendency to trample on core life principles God highly valued, like charity, truthfulness, unselfishness, generosity, sexual propriety, and so on. God's anger, when stoked, was of . . . well . . . *biblical* proportions.

But God's affection for humanity appears unconditionally deep and wide. He called out to people to repent of their stupidity and stubbornness. He spoke lovingly of his willingness to forgive and forget and to become their God. Even so, the Jewish faith portrays its God as marginalizing large swaths of his image bearers, the Gentiles. Gentiles just didn't need to be concerned that much with the things of God. According to the Jewish faith,

God was portrayed as totally fine with a majority of his Gentile image bearers not concerning themselves with him nor needing to live a life of awareness of him. The commands God gave his chosen people, the Jews, which God passionately affirmed as being important to him, had no bearing on the rest of humanity. This seemed odd to me. In effect, God had his handful of chosen people, and that was enough. The rest of us could go on with our lives, completely oblivious to the need to connect with the metaphysical. When I look around at the spiritual hunger of most Gentiles, they desire to know God just as eagerly as the Jewish people do. The fact that the Jewish faith didn't address this problem seemed disingenuous to me and entirely too convenient—even contrived. Their religion compartmentalizes God and makes him appear to be an exclusive Creator God with little concern to the non-Jew who still hungers to be connected to him. I think the Jewish faith in practice and the holy writings that this faith claims to use as its basis for faith are at odds with each other. And, therefore, my ability to accept the Jewish religion as the one that best aligns itself with the nature of reality began to weaken.

The second reason the Jewish faith troubled me was the person and work of Jesus of Nazareth. Granted, the Jews thought the followers of Jesus romanticized this person so much that it's hard to know fact from fiction, but to minimize Jesus the way the Jewish faith does puzzled me. If they are right about Christians' creating a divine mythology around a good rabbi, then you still need to appreciate this rabbi for what he said and taught. Either that, or totally try to wipe his memory off the face of the earth because of his blasphemous teachings. Our response should be anything but lukewarm about him. The people who met Jesus when he was alive were astonished at his teachings and his demonstrations of miraculous power. There's never been a religious leader in history—Moses, Buddha, Zoroaster, Lao Tzu, Confucius, or Muhammad—who electrified the world with his teachings as Jesus did. Historical records tell us of Jesus' early followers being persecuted terribly for their faith in Jesus Christ. Human history has never seen that degree of devotion to an obvious charlatan and fraud.

Maybe it's because of my Christian upbringing, but I became unconvinced with the Jewish interpretation of Jesus and the treatment of non-Jews. I didn't think the Jewish faith was for me. I desired so much to know God that I couldn't fathom his not being interested in me because of the lack of Jewish blood coursing through my veins. The Jewish exclusivity claims were enough to turn me away from Judaism. As a Gentile, it is as though I have little choice anyway. The Jewish God doesn't seem that stoked about having a direct relationship with me. I came to the conclusion that if I had to choose between Judaism and Christianity, then Christianity won. It makes more sense. It explains more reality, especially about all my angst. Most importantly, the character of Jesus is just too intriguing to marginalize and dismiss. I like him too much. And maybe that's just my childhood comfort-food talking. Maybe it's my Gentile-ness. But whatever the cause, I knew I wasn't able to dive into Judaism as the solution to the ultimate religious answer. Judaism was far too limited and anemic for me.

I know I have painted with a very broad brush when talking of Judaism the way I have. Quite a few sects within Judaism give this faith interesting colorings and intrigue. From reformed Jews, to Orthodox Jews, to Kabbalah, to Hasidism, and to even atheistic, secular Jews. All of which can be splintered in a variety of ways themselves. But even within these unique manifestations of the Jewish faith, I found no comfort, no home. The Jewish community and their portrait of the Jewish God don't seem bothered that I am left out of the relationship. The Jews and their God didn't have room for me. I knew I couldn't become a follower of the Jewish faith with any degree of authenticity.

I do not mean to paint Judaism as a lesser or thinner form of religion. Quite the contrary. There is a stunning tapestry of transcendent and beautiful truths within the Jewish faith. One of the most amazing spiritual epiphanies I ever had along my path was in encountering the thoughts of Emmanuel Lévinas, a twentieth century Jewish-French philosopher who wrote so compellingly about the ethics of "the Other," where our encounters with those outside ourselves, whether other people or God, becomes the self-evident principle of all ethics and philosophy. Lévinas' reorientation of philosophy as not being the "love of wisdom" but the "wisdom of love" is striking, not only in its lofty sentiment, but also in its connection to all the deepest longings within the human soul. To argue toward this first principle, as philosophers are wont to do, seems absurd. Yet, to begin all argument with this "revealed" idea as an *a priori* truth gives us a tool to explain so much about reality, our desires as humans, and our irrational addiction to heroic expressions of self-emptying, other-focused love. Lévinas, as a Jewish contributor to religious thought, does not stand alone. Don't forget about Maimonides or some of the other great Jewish religionists of the twentieth century. The humanitarian perspectives of Martin Buber and the unifying relationships between God, man, and the universe as explained by Franz Rosenzweig are religious ideas every person should wrestle with, Jewish or not.

Just as important, I must say that the warm friendships I have had throughout my life with both devout and secular Jews have been of incalculable value to me. I will always cherish them on a human level, whether or not I can ever enjoy them on a spiritual level. I've never experienced a strain of indifference from my Jewish friends, even though I realized their religion seemed to show a mild form of indifference towards me, if not neglect. The Jewish God as described in the Jewish Scriptures can be enigmatic to the Gentile. Sometimes he showed incredible mercy and forbearance with us, but other times this Jewish God showed a seemingly blind rage against the Gentile to the point of launching wholesale pogroms against entire Gentile civilizations. But this is a perspective from a jilted Gentile who desires nothing more than to know his Creator personally and hopes that this same Creator shares the sentiment. Sadly, I don't see it in the Jewish faith, at least not in how it is represented by that community of faith's spiritual leaders. So, I guess my search must continue since the God of the Jews seems to be rather reluctant to accept my request to know him on a personal level.

But, there was another sister-faith that has captured the wildest imaginations and conjured up the deepest fears of the Christian West: Islam, which just happens to be the topic of my next chapter.

ONE LIGHT THAT
DROWNS OUT ALL OTHERS

The stars of the nighttime sky are always present. They can't be seen when the sun is in the sky because of its dominant closeness. The sun drowns out their light.

During a lunar eclipse, the sun's light gets blocked momentarily. And when the sun's light is blocked, all the other stars that have always been there get to be seen during the day.

Our source of enlightenment can behave the same way. Because most of us have one dominant light in our lives (the religion and worldview of our family and our culture), we may never get to see the other sources of enlightenment in the distance. We would only see one source for light and never look beyond it into the greater universe of thought.

How much lesser of a worldview we possess because our primary light has never been eclipsed by doubt!

Chapter Ten

THE FAITH OF ABRAHAM AND ISHMAEL

Surrender to the will of the One God.

CONSIDER THE CRACKS IN MY faith now as chasmic. My faith has splintered so far away from my heritage that I'm now free-floating. I've gone away from the known and the comfortable and now plunged myself into the exotic and surreal.

In a post 9/11[3] world, especially in the United States, seeking the truth claims of a religion that seems to have a bloodlust to destroy your culture is, at its most modest level, bizarre. At least that's the way most people that I talked to would classify it. Some thought I was just trying to be novel and countercultural. Others thought I had been paying far too much attention to the news about all the clashes of culture electrifying the world's headlines from Dallas to Djibouti. Still others said I was just going through a phase—I had been reading too much for my own good.

---

3   Referring to the attacks on New York City and Washington, DC, on September 11, 2001.

During a routine garage sale, my wife cleaned out our house and tried to sell a bunch of clutter to the unsuspecting public. Quite honestly, I hate garage sales. I cannot stand to go to them. I cannot stand having them. All the work it takes to sell $200 of worthless knick-knacks at the crack of dawn on a Saturday doesn't do anything for me. I'd rather be $200 poorer, take all the junk either to recycling or the Salvation Army, and enjoy my Saturday with a good book and a piping hot cup of freshly ground coffee. Single source Kenyan will do just fine.

But my wife, bless her heart, is willing to do the yeoman's work of a garage sale. I must say, she does a magnificent job. My only problem is that she cannot go at it alone. In her economy, a garage sale must be organized and done as a couple. It's all about teamwork. We must work together in total coordination, or the venture will fail miserably. Just the thought of a garage sale screams failure to me—team or no team. I wish she knew how painful it was for me to do all that organizing, putting tiny price tags with tiny prices on infinitely invaluable junk, dragging it out into the driveway, and watching all those strangers traipse through our yard and garage to haggle over a quarter or two.

But it was at a garage sale where a fine, upstanding Christian woman summarized my current state of religion: confused. Some of the books I had purchased, read, and quickly grew tired of were out on display that Saturday—a wild menagerie of philosophies, religions, and political perspectives. What she saw gave her the impression of a dangerously deluded mind. It made her uncomfortable. Among my bargains were books by the Dalai Lama, Christopher Hitchens, John Calvin, Maimonides, Thich Nhat Hanh, Sam Harris, Karen Armstrong, Jean-Paul Sartre, John MacArthur, and Mother Teresa. When my wife reported the woman's comment back to me, I was simultaneously flattered and offended. Flattered that I was able to shock someone whom I deemed to be narrow-minded and limited.

Offended that what I was going through could be dismissed as neurotic and passed over. She didn't know my inner struggles, tears, depression, and sleepless nights terrorized by uncertainty.

How could she be so dismissive? Had she never worried about the trustworthiness of the truth claims of her faith? Did she know she might be living a lie? Did she know she might be criticizing someone who may be making significant strides toward truth that she didn't even know existed? Obviously not.

But my offense was also rooted in my discomfort. Talking of Christianity and Judaism was easy. They are so closely aligned. But Islam . . . now *that* was taking my spiritual journey into another realm. I had left the comfort of the Christian Scriptures I knew and began looking outside into new texts and teachings that were foreign to me and to everyone I cared most about: my family and my close friends.

But I had to know.

My thoughts about my conversations with Wael came rushing back to me. And, I began looking for ways of talking with Muslims whenever I could find the point of connection. But, more than anything, I engaged in a rabid regime of listening to recorded lectures from respected imams, reading commentaries on Islam, visiting Islamic websites and blogs, gathering news from *Al-Jazeera*, and reading the Qur'an itself.

To Muslims, the Qur'an is the ultimate authority. Everything in life is built upon it. All religious teaching—all ethics, societal laws (which they call Shari'a law), and even when it is appropriate to make love to your wife—find their basis in the Qur'an. Muhammad did not write the Qur'an. That's because Muhammad did not know how to write. It is believed that the Qur'an is Allah's words, not Muhammad's. Muhammad was only the messenger and final prophet of Allah (Arabic for "God").

The Qur'an is a collection of revelations that Muhammad claimed he had experienced when God spoke to him directly in dreams and unexpected trances. Muhammad recited these revelations word for word to his growing band of believers in the early 600s CE on the Arabian Peninsula. They were committed to memory by Muhammad and his followers. And it wasn't until after his death in 632 CE that these divine revelations were written down.

The Arabic language was standardized by the Qur'an. Muslim children are taught to memorize long passages from it. There is still a tradition within Islam where people strive to be able to recite the entire Qur'an by heart. A person who is able to do this is called a *hafiz*—and it is a requirement for admittance to certain Islamic religious schools.

The Qur'an is everything to the Muslim. It is eternal as Allah himself is eternal. Therefore, according to Islamic doctrine, it is a dangerous thing to attack the Qur'an or to treat it lightly. To do so is to endanger your soul. Among faithful Muslims, there is great reverence for the Qur'an because of these teachings. Scientific, textual analysis like higher criticism is definitely not allowed. You might remember when Salman Rushdie, now an avowed atheist, criticized the Qur'an in *The Satanic Verses* in the late twentieth century, leading many Muslim clerics to call for him to be hunted down and killed for his infidelity.

As an outsider to the faith and considering it for the first time, I found the Qur'an to be a very beautiful and engaging collection of religious writings. Reading it in a second-tongue translation and not in its original Arabic probably dulls its literary quality some, but hopefully not its message. There are great, towering thoughts in the Qur'an. And there is an unbelievably high exaltation of Allah all throughout the book. Some of the teachings are very specific and concrete. Others appear to be intentionally ambiguous in order to incite discussion and contemplation. All in all, there is something special about this book. It is easy to see why people can become enraptured if not obsessed with it. So, I figured that the Qur'an was the book that I needed to get to know in order to see if this is where to find God if not in Christianity or Judaism.

First, being a very practiced Christian and quite versed in both the Old and New Testaments, I began my readings of the Qur'an quite unavoidably in comparative mode. How is this like the Bible? The same? Different? If so, how? And why? I guess it's expected for a person so well indoctrinated in one faith to have a rough time objectively analyzing another. And, I must admit, I found myself struggling as well.

I remembered a series of lectures I had listened to on comparative religions. The professor, Dr. Charles Kimball, talked about a debate he participated in during his doctoral training at Harvard Divinity School. The debate was centered on whether it is advantageous to be personally religious or personally nonreligious in the study of comparative religions. Naturally, there are two sides to this debate and great points can be made from either point of view. But I began to question whether I could be truly objective and forthright in my investigation of Islam.

I knew I wanted to get to ultimate truth. And I knew if God were a part of that truth, that I'd ultimately find him, or her, when I got to that point. And if I found that ultimate truth is simply a fantasy, then I would have my answer as well. Thankfully, Islam makes it easy. There is nothing undergirding the faith but the very words of Allah/God. And those words are found in the holy book, the Qur'an. Therefore, truth should be there. And if God wanted me to find him in Islam, I'd best find him there.

So, my question became, if God were to write an open letter to his creatures to tell them all the things they should know to enjoy the life he created for them, what would he write? What would it look like? What needed to be in this letter? For the Muslim, that open letter is the

Qur'an. For the Christian, that open letter is the New and Old Testaments. For Jews, that open letter is the Hebrew Scriptures (the Christian Old Testament). For the Muslim, Islam has the widest umbrella because not only does it include the Qur'an but also alludes to and builds on the stories in the Christian faith and the Jewish faith. The Christian has the Christian stories and the Jewish stories. And the Jewish faith has just its stories alone. But is that a fair way to analyze the value of God's revelation? Is it the largest, most rich, as the Islamists claim? Or, is it the simplest and purest, as the Jewish scholars argue?

If it is the simplest and purest, then it's the Jewish Scriptures that are best. There have been many false writings trying to market themselves as God's words that have waxed and waned through the generations: Gnostic Christian writings, Apocryphal Jewish prophecies, Sufi mystical writings within Islam (more on that later), and so on. And, if God's words are the supreme arbiters of divine intent for man, then the answer to these questions become central.

What has God said?

And how do we know it when we see it?

The most obvious way is to read the texts of each faith and see which one is most God-like and seems to exemplify God best. Well, by doing so, we're assuming that we finite beings are capable of such an analysis. That presents a problem. Are we capable? It's definitely a showstopper if we aren't. However, there's another side to that problem. God created us finite beings. If he wanted to communicate with us through an open letter, he would definitely be aware of our finiteness and would work around that problem in order to make his will known. A very reasonable assumption. Because of that, I'm willing to risk a slight measure of hubris in this area, relying on God's genuine desire to be known.

Another inherent risk in this analysis is in our ability to figure out truth from fiction. What if there are texts so well written that they sound like God but really aren't? Are we discerning enough to be able to make such a distinction? Another great question. However, I must run back to God's intent to communicate. If God wants to communicate with us, I think he can figure out how to distinguish his truth from a lie. I cannot imagine a Creator God worried that we can outwit him with clever writings that sound more like him than himself. That's intense cynicism of the first order.

All three monotheistic faiths are built on two key doctrines: (1) that the Creator God has revealed himself through sacred Scripture and (2) that the Creator God has as core to his personality a desire to commune with his creation. If both of these doctrines are true, and assuming that finite man can know the difference between truth and falsehood, then we should be able to accomplish this task. It may be naive, but I'm willing to step forward in faith. I'm willing to accept these premises and push forward toward a quest for truth. And I will use sacred Scripture to do so.

Since I grew up a Christian, I am already quite familiar with the Christian and Jewish Scriptures. Now I needed to make sure I had a good understanding of the Qur'an. So I bought a copy of M.A.S. Abdel Haleen's translation of The Qur'an by Oxford University Press, critically acclaimed as highly understandable in modern English and true to the authentic Arabic scripture.

The very opening *sura*, *"Al-Jatiha,"* of the Qur'an sets the stage. This particular *sura* is recited in daily prayers several times each day.

> In the name of God, the Lord of Mercy, the Giver of Mercy! Praise belongs to God, Lord of the Worlds, the Lord of Mercy, the Giver of Mercy, Master of the Day of Judgment. It is You we worship; it is You we ask for help. Guide us to the straight path: the path of

those You have blessed, those who incur no anger and who have
not gone astray.

There is a world of information about the Islamic faith in this short
recitation. It shows the Muslim's understanding of the supremacy of God as
Lord and Master, deserving of our worship. It characterizes God as being
merciful and helpful—that God is our ultimate Judge and Guide. It describes our life as being on one of two paths that man can choose: one ending in blessing, the other in apparent divine anger.

And in one of the most significant *sura*, named "Purity," M.A.S. Abdel
Haleen gives this introduction: "Because of the importance of this theme in
Islam, the Prophet said that this *sura*, despite its brevity, was equal to one-
third of the Qur'an."

In the name of God, the Lord of Mercy, the Giver of Mercy,

Say, He is God the One, God the eternal. He begot no one nor was
He begotten. No one is comparable to Him.

In this passage of the Qur'an, we see the absolute nature of God as being
eternal, the Creator God, and totally apart from creation, very much like
the doctrines of the Hebrews and Christians. It rings of the central teaching
of Judaism, the *shema*, found in Deuteronomy 6: "Hear, O Israel, the Lord
(is) our God, the Lord is one."

Yet, in the Qur'an's Purity *sura* and in the Jewish *shema*, we see where
both the Jewish and Islamic faiths' overt statements of the oneness of God
collide with the Christian's Trinitarian view of God. The Muslim asks,
"How can three be one?" It defies the most fundamental point of logic:
the law of noncontradiction. And, therefore, the Jews and Muslims reason, a three-person God cannot be in the remotest way true. In fact, it is
blasphemy and is a bastardizing of the true nature of God's oneness and

completeness. If the Scriptures are the ultimate statement of faith, which is the assumption these faiths tell us to take, then the Christians have a whole lot of explaining to do.

In the *sura* named "Mary," we see the Qur'an speaking clearly against the possibility that Jesus was God's Son, a direct attack against Christianity's central claim about the divine nature of Jesus:

> [But] he said: "I am a servant of God. He has granted me the Scripture; made me a prophet; made me blessed wherever I may be. He commanded me to pray, to give alms as long as I live, to cherish my mother. He did not make me domineering or graceless. Peace was on me the day I was born, and will be on me the day I die and the day I am raised to life again." Such was Jesus, son of Mary.
>
> [This is] a statement of the Truth about which they are in doubt: it would not befit God to have a child. He is far above that: when He decrees something, He says only, "Be," and it is. God is my Lord and your Lord, so serve Him: that is a straight path.

Overall, the Qur'an itself is not a daunting work. The language in it is very straightforward. It has a pleasant, flowing, poetic quality to it. It is relatively short. Even though there's the occasional literary ambiguity, it is essentially consistent among its major themes and teachings. There's not a whole lot to worry over concerning its literary quality. It feels very solid and substantial as you read it.

But it can get very specific and practical from time to time, almost excruciating in detail. We can sense the level of prescription for certain societal mores in the Qur'an in the following *sura* named "Women":

> Concerning your children, God commands you that a son should have the equivalent share of two daughters. If there are only daughters,

two or more should share two-thirds of the inheritance; if one, she should have half. Parents inherit a sixth each if the deceased leaves children; if he leaves no children and his parents are his sole heirs, his mother has a third, unless he has brothers, in which case she has a sixth. [In all cases, the distribution comes] after payment of any bequests or debts.

And this particular prescription for behavior continues much more deeply for quite some time. It has the feel and structure of a standard legal contract. This is where the Qur'an begins to appear lesser of a communication than a decree from God. Its level of prescription is highly convoluted and feels forced and manufactured. The transcendent God that the rest of the Qur'an talks about seems to be reduced to a petty contracts attorney or a compliance office of a major corporation. The transcendence doesn't come through. This is where the gravity of the writing of the Qur'an turns into something that smells of a less glorious human design. Compared to many of the rich passages of the Hebrew and Christian Scriptures, my spirit does not get "whisked up" into the supernatural reality of an Absolute Being. If anything, it started to appear, quite honestly, a bit petty.

But my saying these things creates a huge problem for me. Other parts of the Qur'an speak against my rashness with a holy vitriol. In the "Prophets" *sura*, we hear these words from Allah:

We did not create the heavens and the earth and everything between them playfully. If We had wished for a pastime, We could have found it within Us—if we had wished for any such thing. No! We hurl the truth against falsehood, and truth obliterates it—see how falsehood vanishes away! Woe to you [people] for the way you describe God! Everyone in the heavens and earth belongs to Him, and those that are with Him are never too proud to worship Him, not do they grow weary; they glorify Him tirelessly night and day.

Have they chosen any gods from the earth who can give life to the dead? If there had been in the heavens or earth any gods but Him, both heavens and earth would be in ruins: God, Lord of the Throne, is far above the things they say: He cannot be called to account for anything He does, whereas they will be called to account.

And in the *sura* named "Ripped Apart," we get another flavor of the brash attacks against anyone who doubts the authority of Qur'an:

In the name of God, the Lord of Mercy, the Giver of Mercy

When the sky is ripped apart, obeying its Lord as it rightly must, when the earth is leveled out, casts out its contents, and becomes empty, obeying its Lord as it rightly must, you humans, toiling laboriously towards your Lord, will meet Him: whoever is given his record in his right hand will have an easy reckoning and return to his people well pleased, but whoever is given his record from behind his back will cry out for destruction—he will burn in the blazing Fire. He used to live among his people well pleased. He thought he would never return [to his Lord]—indeed, he will! His Lord was watching him. I swear by the glow of sunset, by the night and what it covers, by the full moon, you will progress from stage to stage.

So why do they not believe? Why, when the Qur'an is read to them, do they not prostrate themselves [to God]? No! The disbelievers reject the Qur'an—God knows best what they keep hidden inside—so give them news of a painful torment. But those who believe and do good deeds will have a never-ending reward.

The Qur'an makes a sweeping statement: anyone insane enough to question the Qur'an has hidden reasons for questioning. Doubt cannot be the result of an innocent concern over whether God actually spoke these words to Muhammad. This passage, then, is basically saying, "This is God's word. Question it and you are at risk of 'a painful torment'"—which can only be a less-than-discreet allusion back to the whole damnable burning in "the blazing Fire." No sane, self-preserving person wants to face that.

And in the *sura* named "The Cow," we see a gauntlet being thrown down, challenging anyone to question what's written in the Qur'an:

> If you have doubts about the revelation We have sent down to Our servant, then produce a single sura like it—enlist whatever supporters you have other than God—if you truly [think you can]. If you cannot do this—and you never will—then beware of the Fire prepared for the disbelievers, whose fuel is men and stones.

This reading breaks faith, in my opinion. Why would God, the Ultimate Truth, have to be so defensive and mean-spirited about this? It doesn't match up with the other ways his character is described in the Qur'an. It makes you not respect him, or, for that matter, like him. So, I rapidly concluded that Islam didn't present the most flattering—or convincing—picture of God.

But, if that's the case, then why do so many people choose to follow Islam? It's at 1.2 billion and counting, mind you. I think, at the outset, the Qur'an was exactly what the Arabic tribes needed in 620 CE. And Muhammad was a gifted military leader and administrator. He also apparently had the heart of a poet, much like King David in the Hebrew Scriptures. I bet he was infinitely engaging, charming, and persuasive. Not only did he unite a disunited people, he also gave them a reason to trade in the polytheistic religion of their forefathers for a new, monotheistic one.

As Muhammad's command over the Arabic tribes matured, his vision and hegemony intensified. Ironically, so did the tenor of the Qur'anic revelations he received. In the earliest Qur'an texts, we hear whispers of a more accommodating and peaceful Islam, paralleling the early years of Muhammad's life when Muhammad was trying to be accepted by the leaders in Mecca. Islamic scholars break the Qur'an into two sections: the Meccan revelations (those received earliest when Muhammad was still in Mecca) and the Medinan revelations (those receive later in Muhammad's life when Muhammad had moved to Medina and established a full-blown theocratic state). In the later texts, we hear a more war-like voice in the revelations. And, because of the change in tone, some of the Meccan and Medinan passages conflict with each other. As a result, Islamic scholars have concocted a doctrine called *al-Nasikh wal-Mansoukh,* the doctrine of abrogation, that affords scholars a way to reconcile competing teachings within the Qur'an. If there is a conflict between verses, the later written verses supersede the earlier revealed verses. We find that teaching in the *sura* named "The Cow":

> Any revelation We cause to be superseded or forgotten, We replace
> with something better or similar. Do you [Prophet] not know that
> God has power over everything?

This doctrine of abrogation allowed the prophet to intensify his teachings in order to create a war-like state. Yet, it also shows a fracture in the Qur'an that smacks of human invention. If Allah is as all-wise, all-powerful, and all-knowing as the Qur'an testifies, then why would Allah have to update the message he gave his people just a few years earlier? It doesn't make any sense. It creates a cloud of doubt as to whether these revelations received by Muhammad were truly divine or not. But, during the early years when Muhammad was building this new community of faith, Muhammad was able to draw people together and organize them in such an amazing way that I doubt anyone really thought about these inconsistencies enough to call him out on it. It would be a task left to future leaders and scholars of Islam to sort out and make sense of.

Yet, Muhammad contributed more to the Arabic tribes than simply a new revelation of faith. Muhammad was obviously a master at rallying warring tribes around a common cause. And, because of that, Arabic pride became commingled with the Islamic faith. Muhammad was able to create a nation out of a common cause that involved a more systematic, organized, and essential statement of faith. And, after a bit of persistence on Muhammad's part, the Arabic people accepted it enthusiastically. They needed someone to unite them. And they took this newly founded strength in numbers and created a sense of communal Arabic pride. The Arabic tribes were united not only in tongue and commerce, but now also in religion and a systematic social contract, the *Shari'a* law founded on the teaching of the prophet.

The spread of Islam came by the end of the sword as the Arabs swept through the Middle East, North Africa, Persia, and Eastern Anatolia. With the conquering Arabs came the new faith of Islam. As the Rashidun Caliphate was spreading geographically, this "Rightly Guided" Four Caliphs also deepened the Islamic faith by establishing orthodoxy and committing the Qur'an officially to writing. Even though the Islamic conquerors were open to other people practicing their own faith, each new territory formed its governments based on *Shari'a* law, making it the official government and code of ethics for the Caliphate. This turned people quickly to Muslims. And, in very quick order, the Islamic faith became integral to a variety of people groups. And it remains so to this day.

Because there is not much encouragement for open discussion and criticism of the Islamic faith, it has become ever more difficult for the cultures indoctrinated in Islam to break free and question its truth claims. But, don't get me wrong. I'm not saying that many Muslims are sadistically forcing people to be Muslims. Actually, forced conversions are forbidden in Islam. But the culture Muslims live in is intolerant of any open discussion. Therefore, since most people like to run from pain and run toward pleasure, sometimes it's just best not to try to stir things up—especially if the religious leaders in your community are saying you will burn in a blazing fire if you choose to question things. Best to go with the flow.

Another point of consideration is the level of violence promoted through Islam. Before I go down this path, I must say I am fully aware of the history of violence every major religion has been guilty of, such as Islam's early bloodlust against all its neighbors under the cunning sword of Khalid ibn al-Walid; Christianity's unholy "holy" crusades intent to recapture the Holy Land; and the Buddhist-monk-slash-Japanese-prince Asaka Yasuhiko's oversight of the 1937 Rape of Nanking. All of which were violent atrocities ill fitting for a religion that should bring out the best in mankind, not its worst. It just goes to show you how a few can cloak evil in a veil of righteousness in order to deceive multitudes that they are on the side of the angels—that they are "fighting the good fight."

I believe we live in an age that should be more enlightened than in generations past. So much history, so many lessons. That being said, I take great offense to a religion that has spawned so much hatred and wanton suffering as radical Islamic fundamentalism has done in recent years. And it goes beyond the suicide bombings supported by fringe groups like al-Qaeda, Hamas, and Hezbollah. It stretches beyond the violent expansionist rhetoric of the Wahhabis, the Jihadi Salafis, the Mujahideen, and the followers of the ideology of Sayyid Qutb. When you look at the rank insanity of Islamic factions like the Taliban in Afghanistan and, even more horrifying, the al-Shabab movement in Somalia (that bans music, gold teeth, and bras—go figure!) as a way of living true to *Shari'a* law, then it's obvious that something is terribly amiss. In Somalia, ritual butchering still remains widespread for minor infractions of *Shari'a* law. The public cutting off the hand of a thief for minor offenses is still practiced today. To hear the stories of young teenagers fainting from excruciating pain as both their left hand and their right foot are sawed off with dull knives for stealing chills my blood. The public stoning for adultery still happens. Al-Shabab has been recruiting and continues to recruit young men from all over the world in order to wage a global jihad—from Europe, the Middle East, and America. Blind hatred abounds. And these jihadists are the ones who are extracting from the Qur'an and the traditions of their faith a clear teaching to support these atrocities. For these brutal religious zealots, anything associated with the modern world is suspect and violates *Shari'a* law—that is, anything modern except the terrorizing blast of a fully loaded AK-47 assault rifle. For these people to call Allah "the merciful, the beneficent" is an affront to the meaning of those words. A religion that can give birth to this level of inhumanity has a fundamental moral flaw. If Allah promotes this kind of evil, or even if he through his indifference tacitly condones it, I did not see how the Islamic faith could stand on the overall premise of being a religion of peace and goodwill with a clear conscience. If the god described in the holy writings of the Qur'an is the supreme creator of the universe, then all of man's moral sensibilities are completely out of line with its creator. Our moral compass is not just pointing in a different direction; it is broken beyond use.

The Qur'an takes this hatred even further. In *sura* 98, named "Clear Evidence," the words of Allah are:

> Those who disbelieve among People of the Book and the idolaters will have the Fire of Hell, there to remain. They are the worst of creation.

We see a real antipathy for "People of the Book," a particular reference to Jews and Christians in the Qur'anic revelation. These teachings (that must be understood by those who are commanded to take the Qur'an as the literal words of Allah) hammer the wedge between Islam and the other Abrahamic faiths. A moderate Muslim—which, thankfully, most are—has to ignore, even defy, the pure teachings of the faith to live at peace with the rest of the world. The Qur'an builds a systemic prejudicial attitude toward the faith of others. And it is more than simply prejudice; it smacks of animosity. This is a terrifying reality that I wish were not present in this faith of 1.2 billion people around the world.

But this antipathy goes beyond mere attitude. It manifests itself in the Qur'an in the form of aggression and violence in the *sura* 9 named "Repentance" where we read:

> Fight those of the People of the Book who do not [truly] believe in God and the Last Day, who do not forbid what God and His messenger have forbidden, who do not obey the rules of justice, until they pay the tax and agree to submit. The Jews said, "Ezra is the Son of God," and the Christians said, "The Messiah is the Son of God": they said this with their own mouths, repeating what earlier disbelievers had said. May God confound them! How far astray they have been led!

These verses came very late to Muhammad (631 CE, one year before the prophet's death and considered as his last received revelation) when Muhammad was in Medina building his theocratic state and spreading his faith through violent hegemony. The entire ninth *sura* talks directly of conquest and killing those of other faiths. In fact, it is this last revelation, making it the most authoritative passage in all Islam because it is not subject to the doctrine of abrogation, where we find the famous "verse of the sword":

> When the [four] forbidden months are over, wherever you encounter
> the idolaters, kill them, seize them, besiege them, wait for them at
> every lookout post; but if they return [to God], maintain the prayer,
> and pay the prescribed alms, let them go on their way, for God is
> most forgiving and merciful.

Even the *Hadith*, which are collections of Islamic holy writings collected throughout the history of Islam that are used as commentaries and detailed religious teachings, support, even glorify, this innate aggression. Here is a significant passage from Sahih Al-Bukhari. It is from Volume 4, Book 52, *Hadith* 53, a Sunni collection that most Muslims consider as the most trusted collection of *hadith*, second in authority only to the Qur'an:

> The Prophet said, "Nobody who dies and finds good from Allah (in
> the Hereafter) would wish to come back to this world even if he were
> given the whole world and whatever is in it, except the martyr who,
> on seeing the superiority of martyrdom, would like to come back to
> the world and get killed again (in Allah's Cause.)"

> The Prophet said, "A single endeavor (of fighting) in Allah's Cause
> in the afternoon or in the forenoon is better than all the world and
> whatever is in it."

Because of all that, I cannot get comfortable with Islam. I couldn't find a compelling reason to believe it offered anything better, or different, than the other two monotheistic religions, except for the differing level of intolerance and violence that waged *jihad* against the very core of my sense of morality. My sense of morality, however, is not some romantic notion, mind you. It is a sense of morality that is present within the hearts of every human I have ever met along the way. I see it in the cries of children playing when they exclaim, "That's not fair!" to a playmate who has violated an unspoken moral code. I see it in every piece of literature and movie that speaks of some "other" good that needs to be righted when wronged. My sense of morality is not a perspectival morality, but one that runs deep into the heart of every one of us. It is so universal that it hardly needs to be defended. It is present in every form of religion except for these particular passages in the Qur'an. It is a code hard-wired in us that must have become that way because it adheres to manufacturer's specifications from our Creator. Because of this, I began to become deeply skeptical whether the truth about God resided in Islam, either. There had to be something better.

But I was surprised by one aspect of Islam, and that was Sufism. It's a sect of Islam that has a transcendent beauty. One of the most storied poets of the Sufi tradition is Rumi, who was a Persian in the twelfth century CE. It is beauty of the highest order, and it is irresistibly imaginative and persuasive.

In the *Masnavi*, Rumi writes:

> Lover's nationality is separate from all other religions,
> The lover's religion and nationality is the Beloved (God).
> The lover's cause is separate from all other causes
> Love is the astrolabe of God's mysteries.

Also, Rumi writes:

> I died from minerality and became vegetable;
> And from vegetativeness I died and became animal.
> I died from animality and became man.
> Then why fear disappearance through death?
> Next time I shall die
> Bringing forth wings and feathers like angels;
> After that, soaring higher than angels -

What you cannot imagine,
I shall be that.

Also, Rumi writes:

We are the flute, our music is all Thine;
We are the mountains echoing only Thee;
And movest to defeat or victory;
Lions emblazoned high on flags unfurled—
Thy wind invisible sweeps us through the world.

The beauty of the poetry and the yearning for communion with God inspires and evokes deep-seated longings even in the stoniest of hearts. It echoes of the great words from St. Augustine in his *Confessions*: "Thou hast made us for thyself, O Lord, and our hearts are restless until they find their rest in thee." Rumi's yearning for God is achingly beautiful. It just goes to show that there's a God-shaped hole in all of us.

But the longing for God must be buckled to the truth about God, not our own imaginations. With all the beautiful devotion of the dervishes, I felt for the dear souls who so long for the spiritual but were misguided by the underpinnings of their own faith. As I hear the longing in Rumi's words, I fear he was, to quote a famous country song, "looking for love in all the wrong places." This is tragic. I do not espouse the philosophy that, as long as you have the right intentions, everything will be fine. A nice sentiment, but wholly wrong. There is truth out there. And if there is truth while there are also irreconcilable ideas on what truth is, then there must be falsehood. Rumi, even though a deeply spiritual man, is a good example of faith affixed to falsity.

I have met many moderate Muslims, like Rumi, who do not espouse the harsh, intractable teachings of their faith. They have found ways of working around the troubling teachings and, instead, have given birth to a more moralistic, peaceful, and beautiful portrait of Islam. I hear their glowing stories of celebrating Ramadan (the holiest month of the Muslim calendar, where all devout Muslims refrain from eating or drinking until the sun goes down). Their stories include deep times of prayer and worship of Allah, sweet moments of fellowship with family and friends, and opportunities to practice *zakat* (the giving of alms to the poor). The way they speak of Ramadan's specialness is quite appealing spiritually. Ramadan gives Muslims the opportunity to fully engage in worship and not be distracted by more base appetites. It has been the experience of Ramadan that has won over many non-Muslims to the faith.

In the United States in particular, we have seen how Islam has helped many in our black communities develop a sustainable moral fabric within a newly formed family of faith. I remember working in and around a Muslim gathering in the inner city of Greenville, South Carolina. I saw how this community of faith was able to help many troubled young males who seemed destined to be marginalized along the fringes of society establish a disciplined approach to life and overcome overwhelming obstacles. The work of many of these highly devout Muslims has improved entire communities for generations to come.

I must admit, there is beauty in Islam. Unfortunately, this beauty is partnered with an inherent ugliness and inhumanity that cannot be reconciled with the public portrait of a merciful, peace-filled Allah that many moderate Muslims wish to portray to the infidel. For the sake of world peace, I hope these moderates do overtake and minimize the dark side of Islam. But that being said, it can only come with a fundamental redefinition of Islam at its core: the Qur'an. I wish I could say otherwise, but I am not optimistic.

I do not see enough truth in Islam to convince me that Islam is where God is best found. The Islamic faith may be practiced by many. Some fully submit to the teaching of the Qur'an in its purest sense. We call them fundamentalists. Other Muslims practice a more peaceful and tolerant rendition of the faith. Even though there is an earnest desire to follow Allah in most Muslims, their earnestness doesn't mean that this particular faith contains the truest path to God.

I am not willing to live a lie. I'm not willing to be so impressed with the earnestness of my own desires that I blindly base those earnest feelings on an untruth. I do not think anyone should live this way. As I expose my mind and heart to Islam, I find that it is a great ethical system with many reflections of truth within it, but I find it, as a whole, unconvincing.

Yes, I do feel empathy for the earnest devotees to Islam. I am convinced they are sincere. They believe they are jealous for the very truth of God. But the truth Islam espouses has the quality of truth acquired as opposed to truth that is authentic. I knew I had not found a home in Islam. When looking at devout people of different faiths, I wish God would make it more clear to his creatures. It seems bordering on cruel to see 1.2 billion people chasing after a portrait of God that is, at best, a forgery. Great mystics and theologians talk of God as being unknowable. His nature is beyond knowledge. If that is true, then why is there such a hunger across the globe and the ages of frustrated men wanting to know this God? Why are we forced to live our lives with all this uncertainty? What good is there in that?

While in China, I heard a Chinese English professor ask this question, "If God exists, why can't I see him?" Excellent question. And definitely one worth exploring.

Chapter Eleven

BEYOND MONOTHEISM

One who knows the truth that underlies
all things lives in this world without danger.

ABRAHAM LEFT HIS MARK ON this world. He was a patriarch who lived some 3,500 years ago in modern-day Iraq. And it is Abraham who is credited for bringing the idea of a single and supreme Creator God into the consciousness of the world. Jews lay claim to him as being their Father. So do Muslims. And the Christians, though not by bloodline but instead by common belief, count themselves as children of Abraham too. The total sum of souls alive today who hold some connection to Abraham and his idea of a personal, all-knowing, all-powerful, all-wise, self-existing, all-loving Creator of all things is more than fifty percent of everyone alive today.

Even the great Greek philosopher Socrates rejected the idea of many gods and posited the concept of a single God behind creation. We even see flashes of monotheism in the *Tao Te Ching* by Lao Tzu as he describes the ultimate Nature of the Tao.

But the question is this: Is there really only one all-supreme Being behind all that we see and know? Or is that just a convenient way to summarize all the data in this world we currently do not understand, just like a constant

133

in a physics equation? Is there an idea of God because there is something unknown present, but we know not what? Is the idea of one all-supreme Being a temporary measure to make the world we have no knowledge of seem just a little less spooky? It's worth at least a passing thought.

From this point on, I am entering a part of my search that I didn't really reveal to people. I knew they would think I had simply gone mad. So, I'm warning you now, I was determined not to leave any stone unturned in my search for truth. That meant I had to explore some parts of human experience that most are unwilling to explore. And it is this exploration that is the subject of this chapter and beyond.

At this point, I had come a long way from my days of a simple acceptance of the Christian message. I looked back at my thoughts and understanding of the world, and I realized how narrow of a world I had been living in. Most of us walk through life with blinders on. We block information from our view because we do not want our gentle minds disturbed. There are some parts of our existence we simply want to assume are bedrock true so we never have to challenge them. We'd prefer not to do the heavy thinking required to process a worldview so alien to our own. It is much easier to accept what we know, make slight adjustments if we must, and label those nudges as radical leaps. To fully tear down and reorient our thinking is intensely stressful. Pablo Picasso once wrote, "Every act of creation is first of all an act of destruction." And for us to create a new perspective of ultimate truth requires a sledgehammer, a strong back, and a Teflon-coated stomach.

Both excitement and anxiety rose in my chest as I considered walking down this path. The excitement was the result of the insertion of the new and unknown. It was as if I were embarking on an adventure to a faraway, exotic land. The anxiety was in leaving what was known—the unmooring of a mind that was once at peace with its understanding of truth. I felt the struggle of warring energies. I felt my heart ripping into two. At times, I wanted to run back to what I knew, climb on Jesus' lap, and sob uncontrollably, sorry for betraying a comfort that served my childhood so well. Then at times, I wanted to blindly dive into something new and gulp a lung-full of a fresh new reality atomized with the intoxicating scent of the unexplored. I never knew which feeling would overtake me—or when.

I knew I was crossing over a significant threshold. If I recanted, I wasn't entirely confident the God of Abraham would allow me to cross back over into monotheism if, somewhere along my tour of truth, I determined I had made a wrong turn. Was this my spiritual Rubicon? I didn't know, but it sure felt that way. Sadly, the God of Abraham I knew in my youth chose not to intervene. I wasn't sure if he was even aware of what I was up to—or, just as probable, capable of being aware.

So, here I was—on my own in a foreign land with no clue of the language, landscape, or the local customs. I was the most ill-prepared explorer of the Absolute in the history of skepticism. Yet, in true American fashion, I threw myself into the midst of it, assuming I would figure it all out along the way.

The next stop on my trip: polytheism.

I must admit at the outset, polytheism (meaning "many gods") was extremely hard for me to accept as a possibility of ultimate truth. How could it be? The cosmology contained in polytheism breaks down with only the smallest effort in reasoning. The origins of the gods, the cosmos, and man portrayed in the great polytheistic religions seemed wildly fantastical. Polytheism's cosmology creates more problems than it solves. I can see why Socrates was willing to deny the reality of polytheism to the death because it simply makes no sense whatsoever. And I'm not just talking about the historical Greek and Roman gods; I'm also talking about even the grab bag of religions we conveniently lump together as Hinduism. The sacred stories of Shiva and Vishnu, Krishna, Kali, Durga, Parvati, and Ganesh, et al. are fascinating and reveal a lot about the human experience, but they simply lack the compelling essence of ultimate truth. Overall, the philosophies, poetry, and rich symbolisms of the stories of Hindu divinities may pique the imagination but do little for the intellect.

On top of that, the concept of reincarnation is a strange doctrine indeed. We, as all sentient beings (whether human, toad, or cockroach), are caught up in this endless circle of do-overs called *samsara* that cause us to live our lives over and over until, somehow, we figure out how to get it right. I've heard amazing stories whereby some people confess they have received knowledge of, or experienced, their former lives. In some situations, I hear that people are able to recall particular information from former lives that would give you the impression that reincarnation is true, like the location of buried treasure, etc. The facts they report could only have been known by someone who actually lived during a specific time in the past. These stories are definitely intriguing and mysterious. And it does lend credibility to their claims.

A recent re-packaging of reincarnation has come in the Church of Scientology, a popular new religion revealed to the world through the writings of the quintessentially charismatic science-fiction writer L. Ron Hubbard. Fresh from the Second World War, Hubbard wrote a seminal work called *Dianetics* that explored a scientific approach to what it means to be human and how we can best navigate this life. I have family members who are deeply entrenched in this movement, so I have had ready access to this strange and highly misunderstood world. Scientologists are deeply caring people with a high regard for personal ethics and community involvement. In a weekend encounter at the house of actress Kirstie Allie while I was on a business trip in Los Angeles in 1991, I had the opportunity to engage this new faith directly. It was a fascinating encounter that piqued my curiosity into Scientology.

Famous Hollywood stars have converted to Scientology, and they claim that the teachings and practices of the Church of Scientology have had a huge impact on their success. Not only is Kirstie Allie a Scientologist, so are Tom Cruise, John Travolta, Anne Archer, and a number of others. A recent defector from Scientology, Paul Haggis, the writer/director of the Academy Award-winning movie *Crash*, also benefited richly from his many years in the practice of Scientology. According to Haggis, initial exposure to the teachings, or the "technology," of Scientology can be quite comforting. As Haggis explained in his article in the Scientology magazine *Celebrity* in 1986, "What excited me most about the technology was that you could actually handle life, and your problems, and not have them handle you . . . I also like the motto, 'Scientology makes the able more able.'" This is quite a powerful drug for many who are seeking a "leg-up" in a business that is as cutthroat and competitive as Hollywood is. In 2010, Haggis broke faith with the church and began to ask hard questions. As he executed his enquiry, he found the answers to be troubling.

Through the normal course of "auditing," a core activity of Scientology that is a process of self-discovery that reaches back into previous lives that may be occluding the faithful from becoming "clear," Haggis learned about some unsettling teachings. Through the process of becoming a third-level "Operating Thetan," Haggis was first exposed to some of the cosmology of the church that gave him pause. Hubbard's teachings about the genesis of humankind, the story of the despotic ruler of ninety planets, Xenu, and Teegeack (the name for the planet Earth seventy-five million years ago), created all kinds of intellectual confusion for Haggis, as it has with many disaffected, former Scientologists. The basis of Scientology seems more like a science-fiction fantasy plot in a penny novel than the actual history of our species.

Scientology goes so far to say that, if you do not "go through" its program of auditing, you can never achieve full spiritual immortality. Anyone who does not go through their process will be condemned to living and dying in a never-ending loop of ignorance. You will never achieve eternal life, and you will never learn of your true spiritual nature. Scientology's teaching of reincarnation has obvious echoes of Hinduism and, therefore, is suspect to the same withering scrutiny that challenges Hindu cosmology.

Whether Scientologist or Hindu, I find it amusing that most people today who believe in reincarnation can only remember being someone famous in a past life. Since the Hindu goal of *samsara* is to be free from *samsara* through the realization that we have become one with the collective soul, the Atman, then it's telling that all famous people in the past end up devolving into regular Joes today. I guess famous people in the past were just as likely to be un-enlightened as famous people are today.

And how did this wheel of birth and rebirth ever begin in the first place? When did someone, or something, trigger the need for *samsara* anyway? Hinduism, Scientology, and native religions appear more like human manufacture than divine. They have the air about them of stories concocted by someone a long, long time ago as a convenient diversion on a boring night around a community fire. Or worse, they are the illegitimate children of a clever prankster who maliciously told these stories as a practical joke one day in which gullible people in subsequent generations recalled and took too seriously, turning them into a religion. It's one of the few plausible explanations for why some far-fetched stories become myth and how myth becomes dogma.

With all the wild stories associated with many religions, I have always wondered how these stories came about. There seems to be a pattern of evolution. It usually starts with a touching story or a simple cause that tweaks the imaginations and/or pulls on the heartstrings of people. People are moved by it. That story becomes veneered as a primary moral axiom. Self-proclaimed "wise" men (often referred to as sages, prophets, ayatollahs, or patriarchs in various religious cultures) then begin to pontificate about that story and read into it a host of moral teachings and codes. Those moral teachings and codes are picked up by administratively minded religious bureaucrats (often called theologians, priests, imams, and preachers) who then systematize the moral teachings into a codex of belief and right behavior. And then those moral systems are picked up by a "community of faith" that tries to take over the world in the name of this religion. The stories proceed to take on a whole new meaning, and people are willing to kill each other over them. It's what I affectionately call the "Path to Religious Insanity."

We see it everywhere. An abbreviated example of it is the Islamic group, al-Shabab, in Somalia. Al-Shabab started off with a simple notion of trying to rid their homeland of invading Ethiopians. It was all about tribal protection: a simple, somewhat noble cause. But, in just a few short years, al-Shabab morphed their cause into a perverted version of Islam that positioned itself as a righteous defender of pure *Shari'a* law. They have convinced themselves that the gore and terror they employ are useful, Allah-directed means to establish a right-living society. Ironic, huh? And now they see Allah as commanding it and, in turn, pleased by it. Hence, we see the path to religious insanity.

I've heard atheists say, "See? Religion's the problem! You insert religion into anything, and it gets totally messed up!" As much as I'd like to disagree with the atheist, I must agree in principle. There's enough evidence throughout human history to prove emphatically how man has used religion to slake his thirst for blood and power. That being said, I think the atheists' argument falls short. It's only half of the story. Just as man has used religion to justify terrible things, man has also done some of those same terrible things in the name of atheism—or anti-religion. Just look at Hitler and the millions he slaughtered. Even though he sought to justify his hatred by using Christianity early in his career, his anti-religious venom became his defining characteristic. What about Pol Pot and the killing fields of Cambodia? What about Chairman Mao Zedong in China and the unnecessary 36-million plus deaths during his failed policy of *The Great Leap Forward*? And what about Joseph Stalin, a theology student at one point? His regime activated the coldhearted banishments of dissidents to Soviet gulags and the wholesale slaughtering of millions of his own people during the early years of the Soviet Union. If you could add up all the murdered millions upon millions just from the four mass murderers mentioned above, I bet it'd easily exceed the total number murdered in the name of religion throughout all of human history. So, there's no cause for atheists to claim superiority concerning religious zealots and try to take the moral high ground. There is no moral high ground. There's only a pigsty of man-initiated depravity.

It seems to me that religion is not the common denominator for sick behavior. Lunatic man is. The heart of man is dark and sinister. It is totally selfish and self-destructive. Karl Marx, the co-author of *The Communist Manifesto*, tried to right the world with communism—aiming to expel all environmental influences that seemed to explain best why man behaved so monstrously. Marx' *Entfremdung*, or "Theory of Alienation," is a brave attempt to find ways of transforming societies into just and equitable communities. His ideals were spot-on, but his assumptions were unfortunately wrong. Marx held too high a regard of human nature. He thought humanity would improve if properly planted in a good society. Marx faulted human systems as the culprit of suffering when the fault of alienation rested in the devilish heart of man. In a god-free, capitalist-free, communistic society like Lenin's Soviet Union and Mao's China—both built upon Marxist ideals—atrocities of enormous proportions still occurred. The fact that we have anything close to a civilization today may be the best evidence we have of a benevolent deity overseeing the affairs of man than anything else. We humans, as a race, are terribly screwed up. We seem incapable of *not* killing each other.

But, looking at religions beyond monotheism did lead me to a wonderful encounter with a religion that brought me the most happiness and peace during my journey. And it is a religion that's even hard to peg as a religion because God is not really all that involved in it. And that religion is Buddhism.

Siddhartha Gautama, known as the Buddha, lived in the sixth and fifth century BCE. Historians refer to this time as the Axial Age. During this time, some of the greatest thinkers of religion lived. Not only did Buddha live then, but so did Confucius and Lao Tzu in China. So did Zoroaster in Persia and the great Hebrew prophets Isaiah and Jeremiah. It was during this time where some of the greatest religious thinking of all time occurred.

Siddhartha Gautama was from a wealthy, warring class of people in Northern India. As a young man, even after he was married and had a child, Gautama had a gifted mind and an insatiable curiosity. As a young man, Gautama saw the suffering of all beings, from birth through sickness and ultimately in death. It touched him deeply. He developed a keen awareness of the universality of suffering all throughout life. And it was this understanding that shaped his thinking and led to his teachings that became the basis of Buddhism.

Under the famed Bodhi tree, Siddhartha Gautama sat in a state of deep meditation. He vowed while sitting under that tree not to get up until he had attained enlightenment. That was when Siddhartha Gautama woke up and became the Buddha we refer to today. For the Buddha means "the man who woke up." And Buddhists believe the Buddha to be a person who is fully free of all faults and mental obstructions. The Buddha's awakening is from the sleep of ignorance, and his mind is capable of being fully compassionate, completely impartial, and able to embrace all living beings with no discrimination. Just imagine living with that state of complete consciousness. How wonderful would that be! And I think that's what makes Buddhism so magnetic to so many. Imagine having that kind of worldview and openness. Imagine if everyone did. Don't you think we could conquer so many of the world's ills and solve many of its problems? Well, that's what Buddhists believe. And that's what the Buddha stands for.

Shortly after his enlightenment, the Buddha began to codify his teachings that began with his turning the first *Wheel of Dharma*, which included the Four Noble Truths. The word *Dharma* actually means "protection," and it is used intentionally in Mahayana Buddhism to describe Buddha's teachings as protection against suffering, problems, and ignorance. According to the *Dharma*, our quality of life is not dependent on external forces or the material world. Our quality of life is dependent on the inward development of peace and happiness. Outer peace begins through attaining inner peace first. Therefore, world peace must begin within the hearts of every human. This sounds so elementary, yet it addresses so many issues. We can only imagine how wonderful our world would be if only we humans were at peace with ourselves. Imagine how many moral evils could be done away with: evils like pride, jealously, selfishness, greed, and lust, which cause the most profound suffering in the world, even more so than natural evils like storms, earthquakes, and diseases. Buddhism deals with this most damaging form of suffering—the suffering created by human passions. The Buddha's antidote to suffering sharply contrasts to Karl Marx's ideas of a relief from suffering through societal reform. And, from all I can see, it has the potential to be much more effective.

There is much to Buddhist doctrines that I will not be able to go into deeply. If you are curious about Buddhism, there are some great people out there who have written liberally and beautifully about the Buddhist practice of *Dharma* and how to live the Buddhist ideal in a thoroughly modern world. A Vietnamese Buddhist by the name of Thich Nhat Hanh and the Tibetan exiled leader the Dalai Lama both have had major influences on my thinking. These two are wise men who have written well of Buddhism and the health of the mind.

If you look into the basic teachings of Buddhism, you can see the general Platonic optimism coming through about man's overall moral condition, that so much of the suffering of humankind has to do with ignorance. If we can only train our minds to the benefits of a peaceful, compassionate way of life, then so much good can be done.

The general premise of Buddhism is that all humanity seeks happiness and wants to avoid suffering. It is the root motivation behind all human psychological behavior. It is empirically true and has been supported by psychologists, philosophers, even theologians through the ages. It explains the most about how we act, react, and behave. If truth is that which best explains reality, then this Buddhist principle of humans seeking happiness and avoiding suffering is paramount.

I found many parallels between Buddhism and other teachings, especially the teachings of Jesus Christ. In fact, Thich Nhat Hanh wrote a wonderful little book called *Living Buddha, Living Christ* that juxtaposes the two religions. In it, we see Hanh's analysis of many similarities in message and means between the two religious leaders. And in many other of Hanh's writings, I could see a clear connection between many of the values within Christianity I learned as a child and those similar values within Buddhism becoming clear and connected. It was a deeply refreshing time and a confirmation for me that many of the longings within my heart were deeper, more universal longings that broke free of the confines of the Sunday school room. It was deep calling to deep. And I didn't know how reaffirming this connection would be during a period when my world was becoming confused.

As I opened up my mind and heart to Buddhist teaching, I felt a surging warmth and beauty overtake me, because Buddhism is truly a beautiful and intensely satisfying worldview. As I spent time meditating on Buddhism, my occidental mind still struggled, but my spirit soared. My mind was like a disorganized room filled with piles and piles of half-read books and with no logical order. And the disorientation was much greater than I even realized at the time. But the beauty of the Buddhist message calmed and centered me.

I went ever deeper into the teachings of Buddhism. It opened up a whole new world of possibility for me. I was transfixed with the psychological balm it was able to dispense. Yet, my intent still ran back to truth. Even though Buddhism made me feel good about my potential as a person, was it true? Did it explain reality best over all other religions I had encountered?

Buddhism talks of reincarnation, or *samsara*, just as Hinduism does. It is a circle of birth and rebirth that continues until something significant happens. In Buddhism, the end of *samsara* is when one achieves *Nirvana*—when the fire of experience goes out. Reincarnation as a concept has always been troubling for me. It doesn't explain human existence to any convincing level. Also, the claim that we do not have a self (which Buddhism claims is an illusion) and yet all of *samsara,* suffering and, ultimately, enlightenment occurs at the "self" level, makes absolutely no sense. Inside Buddhism are many contradictory doctrines and statements of belief about beginnings, God (if any), and the ultimate purpose of existence. Much of it, when looked at rationally, leaves you feeling quite unsatisfied and stumbling over irreconcilable inconsistencies.

I found my heart longing for Buddhism to be true, but found my intellect not able to accept it as truth. There are many things within Buddhism that are right and helpful, but as a system of belief and conduit for ultimate truth, it has significant and insurmountable problems. From Buddhism, we can learn more deeply about the inner life of man, but cosmologically, it makes no sense. Also, Buddhism still doesn't fully explain the insanity of man's actions. Ignorance is not enough to explain the intense cruelty and evil that is present. Just look around you. You will find people who know right from wrong who choose wrong many times, even though they *know* intellectually that what they are doing is wrong. Consider the Bernie Madoff Ponzi scheme of a few years back. Or, more commonly, look at spouses who cheat on their mates for a momentary thrill of sexual and/or romantic indulgence with another. The result? Suffering—terribly wrenching suffering for both the victimized spouse and the offending spouse. Very few of these choices were made because they didn't know that cheating on one's spouse is a bad idea. They knew. But they did it anyway. Moral insanity, not ignorance, best describes the situation. So, there's a bit of an incomplete solution within Buddhism itself in describing reality.

One part of Buddhism that freed my thinking was that it was a religion that did not need to involve a god. The presence of God in religion had always been an expectation for me. I had just assumed that God had to be in the picture. Buddhism doesn't make that assumption. Buddhism deals with the here and now. The knowable and the existential. And this opened me up to a new world of possibility: existence without God.

Throughout my life, I had a deep reverence for God. I had assumed that anyone who questioned God's existence was a blind idiot and was rebelling against God for many reasons beyond reason itself. As I started considering atheism for the first time, I realized my prejudices were wholly unfounded. Maybe I had been too close-minded to see the obvious truth.

Maybe religion was simply an opiate of the masses that completely clouded my ability to see reality clearly.

I knew I couldn't rest until I had at least considered a world without God. So, in typical fashion, I decided to find out on my own about this weird world of non-God . . . of atheism. To say my faith had crumbled to nothing is an understatement. I looked up into the sky of my worldview and saw my faith now becoming completely eclipsed with doubt. I could still see a ring of light around the edges, but I didn't know if that represented more blind hope than legitimate faith still trying to break through.

BAILY'S BEADS

When the darkened backside of the moon slips into eclipse position, covering the entirety of the sun, that brief second or two before total eclipse, a tiny sliver of sunlight clings to the edge of the moon, giving us a feeling of a fit of resistance against the darkness. The sunlight sparkles on the edge of the moon's black disk in the form of brilliant beads . . . Baily's beads. They are the last flashing of light before complete envelopment of darkness. And, once the beads are finally snuffed out, the eclipse becomes total. The face of the sun disappears completely from sight.

Chapter Twelve

BEYOND GOD

It is a tale told by an idiot,
full of sound and fury, signifying nothing.

MOST PEOPLE WHO CLAIM TO be atheist did not come to atheism by rational means. Usually, something triggers it. And, instead of proving atheism to be true, they simply drift away from whatever faith first claimed them and enter a world untethered by "the substance of things hoped for, the evidence of things not seen."[4] In my case, I must admit, it was the same. Even though I ended up looking into atheism rationally, it wasn't the true motivation behind my search. I had a trigger too. It was inexplicable suffering. And it ultimately caused me to question my faith.

When things go wrong, so much can happen to our perspective. People of faith are taught to look to a benevolent, other-worldly being for assistance and understanding to help us deal with the upset in our lives. If I'm a Buddhist, I realize that my upset has been triggered by passion that needs to be overcome. If I'm Jewish, Christian, or Muslim, I look to a heavenly Father who has a grand plan and is working things out according to his

---

4   The definition of faith as found in Hebrews 11:1.

perfect timing and benevolent intervention in my life. And this reliance on faith is where most humans live when dealing with suffering.

A few brave thinkers wondered if this concept of faith in the supernatural or mystical is nothing but a psychological impulse. They posit that when people of faith don't understand something, they suppress their worst fears by creating a fictional alternate reality they call God to help them deal with their out-of-control situation. For many, this notion of God serves as a bubble of comfort they simply would prefer not to have burst. These critics of faith reason that the meaninglessness of our existence is too much to bear. We need comfort. And one of the most comforting memories we have as people is that of a loving parent figure. Therefore, to comfort us from the obvious void of our existence, we psychologically create a "heavenly father" to shelter us from the emptiness and meaninglessness of existence. This, in their view, is the motivation behind religion. This is what gives the religious opiate its charm. With a mind released from the mind-altering effects of the opiate, what then could be discovered?

As I looked deeply into atheism, not from a reeling emotional reaction to suffering but from an intense intellectual desire to understand, I saw searing, logical arguments emerge. I decided to open my mind to the new atheists like Christopher Hitchens, Richard Dawkins, Sam Harris, Lawrence Krauss, Daniel Dennett, and even to Bill Maher. I was intrigued by what they had to say. They were aggressive and articulate about their atheism. They had spent time investigating the evidences and came to compelling conclusions. And I wanted to know more. I wanted to know the truth. And if they had it, then I wanted to find it. I wasn't interested in having a simple rebellious tryst with a dangerous, blacklisted worldview like atheism as some accused me of. Yet, I must admit, I did see some attraction to being a bit countercultural. But being countercultural wasn't enough for me. I really did want to know the truth.

So, I let these new atheists have a fair shot at me. I read their writings carefully and openly. I listened to Podcasts of the HBO show, *Real Time with Bill Maher*. And I really enjoyed Bill's banter and the religious tirades he launched from time to time. I listened to lectures by leading philosophers on atheism. Maher, Hitchens, and Dawkins made so much sense. And they gave me many things to think about.

Atheism is the belief that God does not exist. It differs from agnosticism in that an agnostic has come to the conclusion that it is simply impossible to know with certitude whether there is a God or not. "So why sweat it?" some reason. Agnosticism seems like such a reasonable way of looking at the situation. We simply come to the conclusion that the idea of God is unknowable and we should just get on with our lives. In light of all the confusion, agnostics argue that admitting our curse of ignorance is the only responsible thing to do. Maybe I'm stubborn and merely shouting into the abyss, but I am not convinced that ignorance can simply be the end of things. I cannot be convinced of the agnostic position that since I think that ultimate reality is unknowable, it is not there. How do I really know I exist? That's a crazy notion, but when you apply pure reason to the question, you quite rationally wind up wondering if my existence is so. But yet, I'm here, or at least I feel that I'm here. For me to think I'm not here but yet know that I'm not here seems problematic to me. I think Descartes was onto something when he said, "I think, therefore I am." Yet, some still disagree with Descartes' conclusion. Therefore, I cannot stop at agnosticism. I think it's a bit of a cop-out. It's like running a four-lap race around an oval track and stopping just shy of the finish line and saying it's simply not doable. Terribly unsatisfying.

Atheism, in particular, has become increasingly popular in the West over the past century or so. With the recent explosion of scientific thought and inquiry, the modern mind has put faith in God to the test. But, what does it mean to be an atheist? And what is the ultimate meaning of life if there is no God? If there is no God, then there is no eternal soul. And if there is no soul, then there is no afterlife for the soul. What is here is all there is.

The implication of atheism cuts deep. If there is no God, then what becomes of our common belief that there is something special about the human race? Jean-Paul Sartre came to the conclusion through his acceptance of atheism that there really is nothing special about mankind. And we are no more important in this world than any other piece of matter. If this is the case, then all my searching for meaning has been a monumental waste of time and anxiety. I should just get along with existing and try to find as much happiness from these stolen minutes from this senseless existence as I can and stop fretting over trying to determine meaning. Because, in reality, there is none. And, if I can gain anything from the angst I have put myself through, it may be this: that I've been able to articulate it to others who are also obsessing over meaning and allow them to free themselves from all this unneeded anxiety. Religion then can be moved out of the realm of philosophy and relegated to the soft science of psychology. Because the reason people believe in God is not based on truth claims but on psychological benefits.

An underlying thought behind atheism is that the only thing in existence is the material world. There is no good—neither ontological nor moral. And if no good, then no evil either. The only evil that can exist is physical evil: a hurricane that destroys a community and kills people, an earthquake that leaves thousands financially ruined, a terminal disease that ravages a young child's body. These are physical evils that have nothing to do with moral evil, the resulting effects caused by the will of man.

If atheism takes all good and evil away, it also strips bare the soul-nourishing, uniquely human behaviors that give rise in the light of the spiritual and that serve to comfort us when terrible things happen in our lives that are beyond our control. There is no need for daily prayer. For what is there to pray to? There is no longer a point to meditation or any of the religious aspects of Buddhism. For what within needs to be explored beyond our natural desires for survival and personal pleasures? Ultimately, we end up with Friedrich Nietzsche's proposition that we can live "beyond good and evil." So, then the question becomes, "Why be good? Why not be evil?"

Based on the scholarship of philosopher Peter Kreeft, there have been cataloged twenty questions that appear to require the same exact answer: "Therefore, it is more reasonable to say, 'God does not exist.'" It's worth taking a look at these questions to see how they affect our acceptance or denial of atheism. For a more thorough and exacting philosophical discussion of these arguments, I would highly recommend Peter Kreeft's excellent lectures on Faith and Reason through the Modern Scholar Series and the book he wrote with Ronald K. Tacelli entitled *Handbook of Christian Apologetics.* My comments that follow are impressions from a layperson and do not strive to attain the philosophical precision of Kreeft's analysis. If you want to delve into these questions with full energy, you won't be able to find a better guide than Peter Kreeft. That being said, I will be so bold as to give you my impressions concerning some very important, very weighty matters. So, let's dive in.

QUESTION #1
Can an all-good. all-powerful God co-exist with evil?

CALL THIS QUESTION "THE PROBLEM of evil." It is the one argument that atheists say with certainty that, if answered honestly, proves that God cannot exist. And, most assuredly, it is the most troubling of all the questions for the theist to answer. Here's how it goes . . .

According to all three monotheistic faiths, God is both infinitely good and infinitely powerful. Without exception, it is clearly articulated in their creeds, their holy writings, and within their practice of faith. God's goodness and power are essential to the nature and character of God. It is what makes God holy, or "wholly other," and deserving of man's worship and eternal devotion. God's absolute goodness and power are the cornerstones of all meaning and purpose to all that has ever been created or happened. The monotheistic faiths cannot be imagined without these two immutable, incommunicable attributes of God present. In early forms of polytheism and in many of the Hindu traditions, these two attributes of God are not needed, but in Christianity, Judaism, and Islam, they most assuredly are.

Here's the logic of the atheists' argument in its most complete form: if all four of the following premises are stated properly, then only three of the four can be true at the same time . . .

1. God exists.
2. God is all-good.
3. God is all-powerful.
4. Evil exists.

So, which three are true and which one is false? If we start with the theist's perspective, we do not compromise on the first three. They must all be true. But, then evil exists. So, what can we make of it? Without a doubt, evil exists. How can a God, who desires nothing but good and has all power, allow suffering and evil to be present? How can an all-good, all-powerful God allow a five-year-old little girl die in pain from leukemia? How can an all-good, all-powerful God allow Germany's Third Reich to systematically murder over six million innocent people in the ovens of Auschwitz, Treblinka, and the other concentration camps during the Holocaust? How can an all-good, all-powerful God sit back and idly watch the devastating 2004 Boxing Day Tsunami claim the lives of 230,000 people in 14 countries? And, to add insult to injury, why then does this all-good, all-powerful God allow so many people to commit such evil in his name, like the terrorist *jihads*, the Spanish Inquisition, the Christian Crusades, and the blood-thirst of al-Shabab in Somalia? Why did this all-good, all-powerful God directly command the Jewish people under Joshua to completely annihilate entire communities–including women, children and livestock—in the Bible? Seems terribly excessive and lacking in any quality that hints at the way most would understand "goodness."

If God is who theists say he is, then why does evil exist?

I don't think any sane person would try to argue away the existence of evil. We may quibble over the shadings of its definition, but the presence of evil is irrefutable, whether it is perpetrated by a moral evil resulting from the depravity of man or is a natural evil that simply happens in life, like with an earthquake or a hurricane. Evil is a fact complete with empirical proof.

Well, maybe it's the logical argument itself that's the problem. Maybe the argument that only three out of four of these premises can be true at the same time is inherently flawed. Theists have approached this argument from this angle throughout history. Yet, if we are defining "good" and "powerful" in the most universal sense of the terms, then the logic of the argument must stand. If any of us were God and could make anything happen (we were "all powerful") and were infinitely good, wanting all of creation to be complete and happy, would we then allow suffering and evil to bludgeon our creatures to the point of complete disillusionment and despair? If God exists, then why does he allow such things? It must mean he is either not good (which has been argued as well) or not all-powerful (which also has been argued). Yet, the theists are unwilling to retreat from these two necessary attributes for the God of their religions. From about every angle, the logic of the three-out-of-four-can-only-be-true is quite reasonable. Then

God, if he is all-good and all-powerful, cannot exist if evil exists. Yet, evil exists. So then, maybe God doesn't really exist.

The famed Greek scholar Epicurus once penned, "Is God willing to prevent evil but not able? Then he is not omnipotent. Is he able but not willing? Then he is malevolent. Is God both able and willing? Then whence cometh evil? Is he neither able nor willing? Then why call him God?"

Therefore, it is more reasonable to say, "God does not exist."

QUESTION #2
Is God really needed?

ALL THROUGHOUT MY LIFE, I remember hearing people say, "God willing, to-morrow I will . . ." I know it's a throwaway line for many religious people. Muslims use a similar phrase: "If Allah wills, then . . ." I think these phrases show a perceived underlying assumption that God is involved in everything we see around us. These phrases reveal that theists believe God can and does routinely intervene in our daily lives.

But, if you look carefully at the evidence, the opposite seems to be true. With all the prayers to God for his help throughout the ages and civilizations, there is a glaring lack of irrefutable evidence of divine involvement in the affairs of man. Personally, I have prayed countless hours over the course of my life, and I must admit that most prayers I've uttered have shown little to no effect on reality. Sometimes I have sensed a hint of divine reaction, but by and large, most prayers I've prayed have shown no results. The overwhelming majority of my prayers have yielded no observable evidence of God's participation or interest in showing himself actively responding. If you talk with ardent theists, they would immediately argue against this notion. They will declare meaningful and demonstrable answers to prayer, maybe not direct answers, but God's "obvious" manipulation of secondary causes. But, when you look at the evidence, it can be classified as either circumstantial or accidental serendipity at best. I still haven't found anyone who has talked about an answer to prayer that cannot be more rationally explained by natural phenomena.

I think if we're truly honest about the evidence of God within our daily lives, there is so little evidence that it would be next to impossible to measure with certainty. I think most of us do want to have a God in our lives who is interested and capable of responding when called upon. But isn't that simply wishful thinking? I've been so disappointed over the years with the constant pleading with God through prayer yet seeing nothing result. Maybe I'm just a poor prayer. It's possible. Even so, prayer appears more like the actions of a madman than of a thinking, sentient being.

The atheist argues that everything can be explained without God. We assign God a role in our world because we want him to be part of it, not because there's a preponderance of evidence that he is actually present. What if we simply took God out of our worldview? What would change? Anything? Nothing? As best we can tell, our world functions just as well whether or not God gets inserted into the explanation of phenomena or not. Even the Bible refers to this when it says, "For he [God] makes his sun rise on the evil and the good, and sends rain on the just and the unjust." How convenient! How can you prove it *or* refute it? It's just as the Bible states: that God might be involved in our daily lives, but we're not going to be able to see the effect.

The dirty little secret theists do not want to admit is this: there is a glaring lack of data to support the notion that God is needed to explain anything about our daily lives. As the psalmist recalls the words of the arrogant, "How can God know?" (Psalm 73:11). These people referred to by the psalmist may be arrogant, but they do have a point. From all the evidence around us, how can we say that God knows anything about what is happening on this planet? It's not possible to demonstrably prove he is involved at all. According to the atheists, we can go on with our lives without inserting God into the mix, and nothing will change. The sun will rise and then set. The seasons will change. People will be born, and people will die. And all this will happen whether we insert God into our worldview or not.

Therefore, it is more reasonable to say, "God does not exist."

QUESTION #3
Why is it that all theists' arguments can be refuted logically?

MANY OF THE THEISTS' ARGUMENTS include an ambiguous term, a false prem- ise, or a logical fallacy. A good example of this is St. Anselm's ontological argument where there is ambiguity present. St. Anselm's ontological argu- ment, concisely stated in Peter Kreeft's book, is thus:

1. If I am thinking of the "greatest Being thinkable," then I can think of no being greater.
2. Being is greater than not being.
3. If the being I am thinking of does not exist, then:
   a. it is false that I can think of no being greater or
   b. it is false that I am thinking of the "greatest Being thinkable."

Conclusion:

If I am thinking of the "greatest Being thinkable," then I am think- ing of a being that exists.

David Hume, in his *Dialogues Concerning Natural Religion*, attacks this argument on its inherent ambiguity of terms when he wrote: "[T]here is an evident absurdity in pretending to demonstrate a matter of fact, or to prove it by any arguments *a priori*. Nothing is demonstrable, unless the contrary implies a contradiction. Nothing, that is distinctly conceiv- able, implies a contradiction. Whatever we conceive as existent, we can also conceive as nonexistent. There is no being, therefore, whose non-existence implies a contradiction. Consequently there is no being, whose existence is demonstrable."

Bertrand Russell, in his *History of Western Philosophy*, simply threw up his hands with Anselm's argument and said, "The argument does not, to a modern mind, seem very convincing, but it is easier to feel convinced that it must be fallacious than it is to find out precisely where the fallacy lies."

I know Anselm's argument hurts my brain. David Hume seems to have identified the problem concretely; yet, I must admit, I feel like Bertrand Russell. It's just too darned twisted and overworked to agree with. Even the great medieval theologian, Thomas Aquinas, had trouble with this argument.

But, it is arguments like these among many others that trouble the atheist. It seems that the theist arguments are, as a whole, riddled with il-logic and forced assumptions. If pure reason is unleashed on the faith of the monotheists, the truth claims of the faith appear to crack and fall apart.

That's why so many highly intelligent people grow increasingly skepti-cal of the truth claims of any faith. "Why should faith insult reason?" they argue. Good point. But, yet, there are many believers in God who chal-lenge this notion by attacking man's ability to reason. Since man is inher-ently sinful and wicked, his reasoning is flawed. He can no longer trust how he thinks about anything. Other frustrated theists will furrow their brow, flush their cheeks in anger, wag their offended fingers in the face of doubters, and exclaim with spittle flying, "Sir, who do you think you are to question the Almighty?!"

How can you answer that?

Reason has no good answer to bombastic irrationality. But, even in the face of cold logic, the truth claims of faith appear highly suspect. To a rationalist, atheism seems like a more logical explanation of most things.

Maybe God is a psychological construct because tough-minded philosophy is having a hard time swallowing it.

Therefore, it is more reasonable to say, "God does not exist."

QUESTION #4
Why is it that atheism explains more than theism?

THE ATHEIST CAN EXPLAIN BELIEF better than the theist can explain atheism. If God exists, then why would anyone ever walk away from religion? It doesn't make sense. According to virtually every religion, the greatest meaning and happiness for man is to have a meaningful relationship with its personal God or with the Absolute. It seems only expected that the more a person explores these tropes of the divine, the more he or she would become convinced of the veracity of faith. Yet, in recent years, many of society's most intelligent people have walked away from religion and have chosen to become either agnostic or atheistic. These intelligent people are accepting other important truths about existence, so they aren't just crazy. It's just this notion of a God that seems to be troubling them most. Some notable atheists who have gone on to do other incredibly notable achievements are Charles Darwin, Carl Sagan, Thomas Edison, Ernest Hemingway, Warren Buffett, Percy Bysshe Shelley, Lance Armstrong, George Eliot, Woody Allen, Brad Pitt, E.M. Forster, Mikhail Gorbachev, David Hume, Billy Joel, Katherine Hepburn, Thomas Hobbes, John Malkovich, Stephen Jay Gould, Hector Berlioz, Lucius Annaeus Seneca, Jodie Foster, George Orwell, Epicurus, Ian McEwen, Francis Crick, Stieg Larsson, Ayn Rand, Stanley Kubrick, Robert Lewis Stephenson, Sigmund Freud, Kurt Vonnegut, Dave Matthews, Richard Rodgers, Mark Zuckerberg, and more.

If a significant number of humanity's best and brightest are in complete denial that there is a God, then it makes you wonder about the truth.

Atheists can explain theism easily as a psychological crutch. Religion is humanity's dubious attempt to create a protective, all-powerful father in a world of uncertainty. It's an explainable illusion. The theist has more of a problem in explaining atheism. Are atheists just stupid? Hardly. Why would they deny such an idea of a heavenly Father? As arbitrary and uncontrollable as life's circumstances are, it'd be an attractive thing to have someone capable of inserting destiny and meaning into existence. But yet, atheism survives. And the tough minded among us seem more likely to reason towards atheism than the lesser thinkers among us.

Therefore, it is more reasonable to say, "God does not exist."

QUESTION #5
Why can't God's existence be proved by the scientific method?

IT APPEARS THAT THE SCIENTIFIC method cannot verify religion or the existence of God. The scientific method has unlocked more knowledge and discovery over the past 400 or so years than anyone could ever imagine. It has, for all intents and purposes, sent the advancement of human thought into the stratosphere. Before, God's hand was credited for so many natural phenomena that it was quite easy to assume his presence in all natural events. It can be reasonably argued that crediting God for so much involvement in the natural world slowed the overall growth of knowledge. But when the scientific method entered our thinking, many things changed—for the better. Many hard-wired assumptions about divine intervention into the affairs of man became easily explainable as natural phenomena. It was just the way things worked around here, not the arbitrary will of a being external to this universe. And we came to those conclusions because of the scientific method.

So, God as a phenomenon became less needful for us to understand and navigate our world. The most reasonable conclusion was to exclude divine intervention in the affairs of the natural world. The scientific method was key to human understanding. And the scientific method had no need of a transcendent being to be part of the data to explain the natural pulsing of the universe fully. The scientific method is blind to the sacred and lacks the ability to prove its existence. But, that's not a knock on the scientific method. From all we have seen thus far, there's no other tool needed apart from the scientific method to help us understand our natural world to its fullest extent.

Therefore, it is more reasonable to say, "God does not exist."

QUESTION #6
Is God's existence simply meaningless?

WHAT WOULD CHANGE IF THEISM were true? Or not true? Anything?

Theists pray for God's intervention in the affairs of man. But God's actions, or even God himself, doesn't seem to be provable by the data. The natural data seems to explain itself quite thoroughly. The religious person, as a force of habit, explains the data in terms of God's intervention into the natural world. Yet, we cannot measure, or perceive, an effect that is not completely explainable through natural laws.

Throughout human history, science has proven phenomena as an effect from natural causes—those same causes that theists used to reverently attribute to God. Thunder is a good example. For most of man's existence, thunder has been attributable to God because it seemed so powerful and inexplicable. But now, we see that thunder is quite natural and works in accordance within a set of physical laws that can be understood and reasonably predicted. Explaining it as Zeus angrily throwing thunderbolts at the earth seems completely unreasonable to us today.

Many of our prayers and petitions of God can be understood apart from divine intervention. We pray for the health of Aunt Mabel and her spastic colon. Aunt Mabel gets better. Similarly, we pray for Cousin Ed and his enlarged prostate. Cousin Ed dies from prostate cancer. The ardent theist links both outcomes to God's will for these individuals. But what would have changed if prayers were not uttered? How do we see the fingerprints of God in the data? Beyond the emotional benefits of a positive attitude on the human psyche, there just doesn't seem to be any reason to attribute a "God effect" that arises from prayer, or any kind of religious intervention for that matter, within the laws of nature. Divine intervention just doesn't seem to change a thing. Nature keeps on chugging along with no regard to anything that has to do with God.

Therefore, it is more reasonable to say, "God does not exist."

QUESTION #7
Do miracles really happen?

DO MIRACLES HAPPEN? WE HEAR stories from time to time of people claiming they have witnessed or experienced some kind of supernatural event that can only be explained as miraculous. If miracles do happen, then it takes a supernatural power for them to occur—something or someone affecting events beyond natural laws. To see testimonies to miracles, all you have to do is use a search engine to look up "present-day miracles," and you can see account after account of people who believe that miracles not only are possible but that they are happening today. Some of the stories are quite remarkable and breathtaking. But, when you look at them closely, it could just be an outlier, a simple freak incident that can be caused quite naturally even though the odds of its happening might be low. To the unscientific mind, miracles may appear to happen, but most likely they are phenomena we don't have the ability to explain by physical laws at this time. Give science enough time and it will more than likely be able to decode the event and explain what happened quite handily. Throughout history, many miracles have been disproven once dispassionate scrutiny and science were able to step in and explain the data more fully.

Especially in the monotheistic religions, miracles are very significant to the truth claims of the faith. From Muhammad's night journey from Jerusalem, to Moses' parting the Red Sea with his staff, to Jesus' bodily resurrection from the dead, miracles are absolutely essential for these faiths to maintain their moral and truth-creating authority. By their own design, they rely on miracles in order to substantiate their authority. The Apostle Paul wrote in his first letter to the Corinthian church,

> And if Christ has not been raised, then your faith is useless and you are still guilty of your sins. In that case, all who have died believing in Christ are lost! And if our hope in Christ is only for this life, we are more to be pitied than anyone in the world. (1 Cor. 15:17–19 NLT)

What makes us think that the miraculous stories of the monotheistic faiths are any less loony than the tales of the Greek and Roman gods—or of the Norse and Indian gods, for that matter? Do we simply take the words of men thousands of years ago who obviously had an agenda to prove that their religious claims should be accepted as true and authoritative? We've seen many a charlatan (both religious zealots and snake oil sellers) rise up and get debunked over time. How can we really know these stories haven't taken an innocent fact from the life of one like Jesus of Nazareth and have it retold again and again only for that story to grow in myth as long as Pinocchio's nose? It's a reasonable question to ask. Why is it reasonable? Because there's so much evidence of people retelling stories and adding fantastical notions to these stories in the retelling. So, the miraculous stories told may be nothing more than the overactive imaginations of those engaged in cultic hearsay.

If no miracles happened, then Christianity, Judaism, and Islam have no basis to be the ultimate authors and arbiters of truth. They may be pleasant, feel-good myths, but as truth, they crumble under the weight of their own "miraculous" doctrine. We would then be forced to dismiss these faiths as make-believe with no claim on ultimate truth. Concerning the truth behind miracles, the defenders of the theistic religions can only say to the doubtful, "Just trust us on this." And it is only the monumentally gullible who appear willing to do so.

Therefore, it is more reasonable to say, "God does not exist."

QUESTION #8
What about the conflict between the Bible and the Big Bang?

FROM THE VERY BEGINNING OF the monotheistic faiths, the Genesis account of creation has been a staple of doctrine. God, through special means, directly intervened and created Adam and Eve as the very first humans—completely intact as human and moral agents. In the view of many biblical scholars, the Genesis account of creation is an important foundation of their faith. Some believe that, if the literal creation story of Genesis falls, so falls the faith. Why? Because the reliability of the faith's Scriptures has been called into question. Yet, recent discoveries in physics, biology, geology, chemistry, and astronomy seem to refute the creationists' account of the beginning of our universe as being a literal six days of creation that happened just a few thousand years ago, as some biblical literalists teach. Much scientific evidence seems to point to a Big Bang cosmology that happened some fourteen billion years ago as the best explanation of the data.

All understandable, measurable, and refutable data gathered from nature by proven scientific methodologies appear to contradict the creation story as taught by many young earth creationists and intelligent design theorists today. This becomes highly problematic for the theist. The only means of refutation are two-fold: (1) to attack the scientific methods employed by the scientific community (which some have tried—and are still trying, but to little effect) or (2) to reexamine whether the literal interpretation of Genesis as a historical record of the earth's and man's beginnings must be challenged. The problem is that the scientific method has proven to be an extremely reliable means of creating knowledge, whereas the theists' rote reading of sacred Scriptures as valid scientific evidence has proven to be unreliable from time to time.

As science reveals more and more discoveries in its continuing quest for understanding, there is reason to suspect that certain biblical texts will cease to be taken literally while holding true to verifiable, and quite reliable, scientific discovery. Are the sacred texts that hold the elemental teachings of faith that inform us of this transcendent God of Judaism, Christianity, and Islam even more vulnerable as we learn more about our existence through the sciences? Right now, it looks like it is headed that way. I don't see any signs of a reversal of fortune on the horizon. What other faith stories are next?

Therefore, it is more reasonable to say, "God does not exist."

QUESTION #9
Why does most of the physical evidence counter theist claims about nature?

THE THEIST ASCRIBES CREATION TO a metaphysical God who spoke all things into existence *ex nihilo*. And the nature of this creation is the filling of the earth and the heavens with substance and meaning. But, when we observe nature, we find that nature is more empty than it is full. The empty space between planets, solar systems, stars, and galaxies is so much greater than the space filled with matter and meaning. Vast emptiness better describes the macro universe. Even at the subatomic level, we find that matter itself is more vacuous than substantive. According to the best calculations by leading nuclear physicists, within the atom itself, if the nucleus were the size of a marble, the electrons (only the size of the width of a human hair) orbiting around it would be flying around it two miles away. There just appears to be so much wasted space in the material world. Then look at matter itself; much of what exists is cold, harsh, and life-rejecting as opposed to life-nourishing. If anything, life itself is an immeasurable, infinitesimal quantity within all of the material matter that exists. How can we look into this empty abyss we call the material world and see the signature of the transcendent, loving God at the helm? Seems quite unlikely.

And look at the excessiveness of the universe. If man and his relationship with his Creator is the central story of the material world, why all the wasted creation? Why do we need one hundred billion galaxies in the universe when one would suffice? And why does each galaxy need one hundred billion stars in it when all we can see with our naked eye is, at most, five thousand? And why so many stars when all we need for daylight and life is one rather unimpressive, undersized star we call the sun for our fairly insignificant planet to orbit around?

And even on this earth, why is it that there is only a small, thin ribbon of atmosphere that wraps around this third rock from the sun that is actually benign enough to sustain life when the rest of the planet is a seething, boiling, unstable mass of nuclear fusion?

Just makes you wonder, doesn't it?

As a species, man is quite selfish and self-centered. Throughout our history, we have claimed that we are the center of the universe and that all that has been created was created for our good and for our pleasure. Even in Leonardo da Vinci's famous "Vitruvius Man" drawing in 1487, we see evidences that our species has arrogantly assumed that man is the prime measure, or setter of proportions, of all things. We have proclaimed ourselves as the top of the food chain and have declared all other species our inferior and have a résumé of atrocities as long as time itself regarding the cruelty and exploitation of other life forms to prove it.

Yet, God created all this for his good pleasure and to have a relationship with us. We, though such a small and insignificant portion of all that exists, have chosen to believe this to be true. Sounds quite silly when you think about it, doesn't it? It sounds like we are quite full of hubris and self-delusion.

If you look at the entire material world, it is next to impossible to conclude rationally that man is God's supreme creation and that we are at its center. Astoundingly, that's what the theists claim. But if there were a benevolent God behind all this, it doesn't seem from the evidence at hand that he holds man in as much regard as man holds himself.

Then, look at the nature of Nature itself. Is there evidence of a loving, caring Creator? Alfred, Lord Tennyson once looked around at the world and concluded in his poem *In Memoriam*,

> Who trusted God was love indeed
>   And love Creation's final law—
>   Tho' Nature, red in tooth and claw
> With ravine, shriek'd against his creed—
>
> Who loved, who suffer'd countless ills,
>   Who battled for the True, the Just,
>   Be blown about the desert dust,
>   Or seal'd within the iron hills?

No more? A monster then, a dream,

  A discord. Dragons of the prime,

    That tare each other in their slime,

  Were mellow music match'd with him.

O life as futile, then, as frail!

  O for thy voice to soothe and bless!

    What hope of answer, or redress?

  Behind the veil, behind the veil.

How can we see God in all this cruelty and meaninglessness? With "Nature, red in tooth and claw," it's hard to see the benevolent Creator as part of this. For this atrocity of nature can be best seen in the cruelty of the ichneumon wasp that lays its eggs inside a live host so that its larvae can mercilessly feast on the live animal's organs until the larvae are fully formed and then emerge only to kill the host. It was these wasps that terrorized Charles Darwin's faith in Natural Theology, thereby pushing him away from God and toward unbelief.

Where is this great Creator God in the evidence of the material world? The portrait theists paint of him contradicts the overwhelming majority of evidence in the universe that it's a cold, empty, and nasty existence all around us. Even in the face of all this evidence, theists will say it's because two people, Adam and Eve, in a garden chose to disobey God. And through their original sin, all this pain and suffering ensued. Their sin led to the creation of cancers, violent storms, earthquakes, the behavior of ichneumon wasps, and lawyers. The evidence from the material world seems to countermand the theists' claims of a benevolent Creator God.

Therefore, it is more reasonable to say, "God does not exist."

QUESTION #10
What good is this obsession over an immortal soul?

GENERATIONS UPON GENERATIONS OF MANKIND'S greatest thinkers obsessed over the religious nature of man, from the ancient Hebrews and Chinese 3,500 years ago to the early days of the Renaissance just 500 years ago. And, all through that time, what has really changed for mankind? Except for a few technological changes such as the invention of the clock, the development of water aquifers, and the invention of a few minor advances in agriculture, the lives of ordinary people didn't change that much for 3,000 years. It wasn't until the mind of man turned away from the obsession of religion and began to focus on the natural world that science and technology truly began to flourish and substantively propel the improvement of the human experience.

All of our cares for theology and the afterlife seemed to sap the creative energies of man for 3,000 years. It could have been the effect of man's 24/7 obsession with God. It could have been that theologians had a quick, snappy response to any scientific inquiry. Anything strange was quickly attributed to the ineffable nature of a transcendent being, therefore completely unknowable by human reasoning. All we have to do is look at the myths of early civilizations to see how ill equipped and un-curious many of the ancients were concerning the mysteries of this world. They found the mysteries, on the whole, gateways into the elevated nature of existence and never seemed motivated enough to ask the fundamental question of all learning: "Why?" God (or the gods) caused these mysteries. And who were we to question them? In fact, questioning may stir the anger of the gods, and they may, in turn, punish us for our insolence.

It wasn't until man shook off the aura of the supernatural and looked at natural phenomena through the lens of natural means that real scientific understanding and knowledge advancement began to explode. As humanity released its grip on the supposition that God was causing all these strange phenomena (like lightning, meteors, identical twins, the tides, solar eclipses, etc.) and began to look for natural causes for these effects (like electricity, genetics, gravity, the vastness of space, etc.) that the wonders of nature were able to be understood and harnessed for man's good.

So, religion has, in effect, handcuffed man's potential and ability to rise up and master the natural world. The concept of God, then, has the effect of pushing humanity down as opposed to lifting it up—the opposite of what the theists try to convince us to believe. Then it could be reasoned that believing in God's existence can have an unhealthy effect on us. And that this God, whom we always understood to be loving and life-giving, may actually be more selfish and life-taking than our religious doctrines portray. The evidence for the theists' doctrines of God seems to be more at odds with true human experience than many of us are willing to acknowledge.

Therefore, it is more reasonable to say, "God does not exist."

QUESTION #11
What spiritual experience can be easily explained materially?

THERE ARE MANY DEEPLY SPIRITUAL people who walk among us. All you have to do is go down to Venice Beach, California, and encounter every possible shade of spirituality ever imagined by "a trousered ape." Spirituality simply fascinates most of us. I think it has to do with its ability to add meaning and purpose to a whole host of emotions we experience in our lives. I've had the odd pleasure of reading through many of the new books on spirituality and, if you really take a close look at them, they really are merely emotional junk food and contribute so little to the true understanding of life's meaning.

Yet, we humans are spiritual junkies. We look for the next "spiritual high" we can experience. If we read that it is healthy for the psyche for us to spend time sitting in a comfortable chair, sipping green tea, and contemplating a flower, guess where you can find us spending our Saturday afternoons.

I'm not saying that there isn't some truth to be mined out of these teachings on spirituality, because there is. But, the overwhelming bulk is simply empty calories that offer a very limited understanding of the world at large. I may pick up some good psychological tips on relationships, discover how to make more money, or learn that I need to hug my cat more, but I won't find transcendent meaning.

I don't know if I can speculate why spirituality is such a part of us, but it is. But the most amazing part of it all is the psychosomatic connections between spiritual experiences and the body—in particular, the physical human brain. With the advent of medical imaging techniques, there have been many studies showing that everything we sense in a spiritual encounter can be easily explained in the electro-chemical mechanisms in the brain. This means that the spirituality that we sense as being something apart from the physical world can be measured in very material terms within the confines of the brain. This is quite astonishing.

We've also learned that brain damage can either activate or nullify spiritual experiences too. So, many of our feelings of transcendence may be only misfirings of chemicals in the brain or, even more cynically, brain damage itself. This does throw a bucket of cold water on many spiritualists' claims that spiritual auras and energies emanate from without the body and are sensed and observed. They, and our knowledge of God, may actually be ghosts from an overly stimulated brain.

Therefore, it is more reasonable to say, "God does not exist."

QUESTION #12

Why are there so many logical contradictions in religion?

CALL THEM GREAT MYSTERIES. CALL them contradictory thoughts. But, whatever you call them, the inherent ambiguity found in many religions has both inspired and appalled. In general, there seems to be an unbuckling of religious dogma at times from the most elemental premise of all logic, and that is the law of noncontradiction. The law of noncontradiction is expressed in this way: "Argument A" cannot be both true and not true at the same time. It doesn't make sense. And it is the law of noncontradiction that serves as the underpinning of all other logical means we employ as rational beings.

Yet Christianity says Jesus is both mortal ("man") and immortal ("God") at the same time. Buddhism plainly states there is no self, but requires the self to know this. Orthodox Christianity claims that God is a Trinity, both three persons and one person at the same time. But science remains free from violating the law of noncontradiction. Religion plays fast and loose with it.

Many look to ambiguities and the apparent contradictions within religion as being a spark to a higher enlightenment. Rationalists just see all this as sloppy thinking and craziness. The rationalists may have a point. If there is a God who has created all this and has built within it rationality, why does he seem to completely ignore the core basis of reason when expressing himself in the guise of religion?

Therefore, it is more reasonable to say, "God does not exist."

QUESTION #13

Why are there so many contradictions among religions?

HAVE YOU EVER NOTICED THAT all religious systems claim to be the arbiters of absolute truth? Most make exclusive claims to be the one place to know truth with certainty. Yet, if we just open up a phone book in any major city, we can see the evidence that there are just far too many of these religious systems out there—the many thousands of varieties of Christianity, the major divisions of Judaism, the many schools of Islam, the countless manifestations of Hinduism, the differing systems of Buddhism, the many applications of Taoism, and more. Yet, if any one of these unique variations of religion is the absolute truth, which is what most claim, it means the thousands upon thousands of other religious traditions are, by default, false.

Yet if we look at it from the opposite direction, we still find ourselves with a major problem of defending the veracity of theism. If all these faiths have within them a degree of truth as Universalists claim, then each religious tradition must have a significant amount of falsity within its teachings in order to accommodate the sharp, incompatible differences between the faiths.

From the evidence of ordinary life, then, it seems more logical to think that, within the whole of religion, there is more falsity than truth present to explain all that we see. If this is so, it is only reasonable to look at the whole and say that religion is terribly unsuited to be the definitive place to look for absolute truth—and, hence, God. It's more logical to assume all religions are wrong.

Therefore, it is more reasonable to say, "God does not exist."

QUESTION #14

Isn't religion harmful because it produces so many crazy fanatics?

HERE YOU GO. HERE IS one of the most compelling arguments against religion and against anyone who claims to have the exclusive path to God: fanaticism. How many atrocities exist because someone claimed to have the inside scoop on God and sought to lash out against all those rancid infidels who had not accepted the truth? Hundreds? Thousands? More? Probably more.

All throughout the twisted history of man, we see people motivated by religious zealotry do the most horrific things to other humans in the name of a beneficent, merciful God. We've already alluded to the insane notions of suicide bombings by Muslims who believe that those who martyr themselves are guaranteed a wonderful afterlife surrounded by the carnal pleasures of seventy-two black-eyed, virginal beauties. (Call me twisted, but I can't help but think that this Muslim doctrine also curses those poor virgins to a miserable eternity. *Have you seen the pictures of some of those scrawny and homely suicide bombers?*)

But the Muslims don't have the corner on fanaticism. Christians have been equally appalling. So have Buddhists and Hindus. Even Jews have blood on their hands. None of the significant religions of the world can claim innocence here. Religions produce fanatics. And fanatics do really stupid things. So, what good is religion anyway? Seems like it divides more than it unites. It destroys more than it builds up. It suppresses more than it releases. Ultimately, it has the unrivaled ability to bring out the worst behavior in man. So, what good is it? What logical reason is there for encouraging people to become religious when it has a bad track record of creating really crazy behavior? Is there a loving God in all this chaos of human insanity? It's hard to find.

Therefore, it is more reasonable to say, "God does not exist."

QUESTION #15

Why does religion seem to produce more self-righteousness than real, substantive righteousness?

RELIGION CONDEMNS SELF-RIGHTEOUSNESS, BUT YET it invariably produces self-righteousness. If religion is supposed to make us better, why don't we see more good people who are religious? There are a few, but according to virtually all stated religious orthopraxy, there should be many. Religion is doing a very poor job of producing good people. Religion's product, producing saints, has a high failure rate. Most religious people are far from righteous, yet most are fully self-righteous, thinking they are better than they actually are.

Self-righteousness is best modeled when religious people point their fingers at non-believing sinners and condemn them while being completely unaware of the unattractiveness and unrighteousness they are exemplifying. It's quite the irony, actually. There are few religious people who the nonreligious really enjoy being around. And it's not because their righteousness is so blinding; it's because of the self-righteousness that seems so preachy, nit-picky, self-centered, and artificial.

Religion just doesn't seem to produce in enough quantity truly righteous people—people whom we admire for their moral courage and self-sacrificing love (which seems to be really righteous attributes valued by any devout person regardless of country, color, or creed). It is arguable that atheists are doing just as fine a job of producing real righteousness as any religious system is. If religion is really that true and that compelling of a reality as theists argue, then we should see more fruit. Mostly, all the world sees is either immature or rotten fruit. The world just doesn't see enough evidence of true righteousness among the religious to be convincing. So, if God is the manufacturer of religion, the faulty products coming off his assembly line far outnumber the rare good products that are shining examples of righteousness. So, why does humanity need religion, then?

Therefore, it is more reasonable to say, "God does not exist."

QUESTION #16
Why does religion produce the most wars?

RELIGION HAS THE MOST SIGNIFICANT grip on the hearts and minds of humans. And, because of that grip, it has created animosity between different people groups who hold to differing religious traditions. Most religions have baked into their codex of doctrines an "I'm right and you're wrong" sensibility. It doesn't take too much reading into the great writers of any of the faiths to see this sensibility bubble to the top. You simply have to applaud John Lennon's idealism when he penned the song, "Imagine":

> Imagine there's no countries
> It isn't hard to do
> Nothing to kill or die for
> And no religion too
> Imagine all the people
> Living life in peace
> You may say that I'm a dreamer
> But I'm not the only one
> I hope someday you'll join us
> And the world will be as one

Yes, I must say, John was a dreamer. And I must admit he's not the only one. I too would love to see the world as one. But, we've got this whole reality thing to contend with. And the reality is this: we humans are, by nature, highly wary of people who appear different from us. We greet differences as suspect and tend to distrust anyone who has a different outlook on reality. Naturally, the tribal nature of man is aggravated and poisoned when we see other people who strangely worship the Absolute from a different perspective.

Hence, the wars commence. All throughout our history, we humans have killed and we have died because of our religious beliefs. I cannot say that religion itself is the only root cause of war, but it is inarguable that it is a primary instigator and encourager of war. Just ask the jihadists, the Palestinians, the Croats, the Zionists, the Christian Crusaders, the Irish Protestants and Catholics, etc. There are plenty of horrific stories of wars being waged in the name of God and religion.

You'd think a God (or gods) who created all of us and who had the power over the material world would do more to calm and unite rather than stir and divide. Yet, all the evidence we see demonstrates a world of faith that is blood-soaked and crying in agony over lost sons, fathers, brothers, and friends. On the battlefields of history, you can see the senseless carnage of dead soldiers clutching crucifixes in lifeless, bloodstained fists or bloated, cold lips pursed in terrorizing agony as last prayers were hissed, exhaling their last, fleeting breaths to Allah, Yahweh, or some other name for God.

Religion incites wars. Religion authors untold agonies. Religion has proven to be more of a scourge of suffering for multitudes than a "balm of peace" that it has shamelessly promoted itself to be. In many cases, religion hurts more than it helps. And, therefore, the eradication of religion, and the thought of God, is something that mankind may benefit from more than from its propagation.

Therefore, it is more reasonable to say, "God does not exist."

QUESTION #17
What good is there in all the guilt religion produces?

RELIGION DOESN'T JUST GIVE US life-affirming ideals to live for. In most cases, religion gives us too high of ideals—ideals that are next to impossible to attain. "Be perfect, even as your Father in heaven is perfect," Jesus tells his disciples. Most theists slog through life, hoping to attain an unobtainable ideal of self-mastery but find themselves stumbling through their days, choking in a cloud of guilt and self-flagellation. Within the "tsk-tsk" of the theist, humans are simply not worthy of the presence and attention of this transcendent God. Theists are taught to cower under the weight of divine displeasure and to spend countless hours and energy warring against man's natural desires. Even Buddhists are taught to embark on a lifelong path to "snuff out" (the actual meaning of Nirvana) all cravings, which result in suffering. Christians are taught to mortify the flesh. Jews are taught to act as a "holy priesthood," worthy of the bearers of Jehovah's name. Muslims are taught to live a life worthy of Allah's beneficence. Ultimately, man enters into a no-win situation when encountering God. In essence, all this unworthiness taught by religion seriously damages the human psyche.

Religion insults us and then has the audacity to offer itself as the only cure to our problems. In effect, it tells us how damaged we are and that our only way to get fixed is to buy the only solution that works: their rendition of God. It's the best sales job ever concocted. It creates its own special need that only its product can ever satisfy. Oh, that Madison Avenue never learns this deceptive advertising trick!

Yet, here we find ourselves swimming in a slime of guilt and shame that has been dubiously imposed due to unscrupulous religious charlatans. Religion, then, destroys the only life we humans are able to enjoy with all its high ideals and unreachable moral codes. If this is God's plan for man's existence within his creation, it seems rather unjust, bordering on sadistic.

Therefore, it is more reasonable to say, "God does not exist."

QUESTION #18
Why does religion promote hypocrisy?

THE RELIGIOUS AMONG US PRETEND to be good. Religion makes us lie to ourselves—and to each other. Our religions require us to sport actions and attitudes out of step with man's natural inclinations. And most religious people do a horrible job of living up to the reality. The result? We live a lie. We try to convince ourselves we are better than we are. We try to convince others we are more devout to our faith than we truly are.

Religion does not necessarily promote truth; it suppresses it. It manufactures illusions and terrorizes its followers into acting out of step with reality. And from all this hypocrisy, we see the birth of intolerance guised as moral grit and diffidence parading as self-possession. The result is a very ugly, hypocritical spirit that tears at the very fabric of a civilized society. It is done in the name of religion because most religions create this reality by their own design.

Therefore, it is more reasonable to say, "God does not exist."

QUESTION #19
Why does religion focus so much attention on the afterlife?

IF THE CHRISTIAN AND THE Muslim picture of the afterlife is true—an eternal existence of unimaginable bliss—then who would want to live in this world filled with pain and disappointment? "In my house are many mansions," Jesus promises his followers concerning heaven. To one of the thieves being crucified alongside him, Jesus says, "Today, you will be with me in Paradise." "God will wipe away every tear," claims the Apostle John. And Allah, in the Qur'an, promises an afterlife of untold pleasures for martyrs and the faithful.

So, why even bother with this life? Why invest in this temporal world when you can invest in the afterlife where your wildest dreams come true and where you can reap the benefits for all eternity? For many religious people, that's the exact conclusion they come to. And throughout human history, this religious teaching has caused many people to become "so heavenly minded that they are no earthly good."

The obsession over the "life to come" has served more as a diversion and a distraction than it has served as a benefit. It reduces the value and beauty of this life and makes you think only of what is in the afterlife. And it wasn't until man got his head out of the heavenly clouds during the Renaissance that he was able to think about the material world and figure out how to make our collective existence better in the here and now. Thoughts of the afterlife robbed man of thinking about solving real problems in this life.

It's good for man to have hope. But having hope to the point of distorting reality and diminishing current existence doesn't make much sense. If God created this time for us on earth, did he really want us to be pining for the afterlife the whole time? For many religious people, that's what they do—focus solely on the afterlife, leaving everything here in reality unobserved and untended. It's because that's how their religions maintain their control over their believers—promising eternal joys that can never be proven or substantiated. But, according to theists, if we ignored the afterlife, it could be to our eternal peril. So, theists are able to dangle over mankind a threat we cannot disprove and cannot ignore. And, as a practical concern, this heavenly-minded behavior has proven to be quite useless to the rest of humanity.

Therefore, it is more reasonable to say, "God does not exist."

QUESTION #20
Why does God discourage temporal pleasures?

MOST OF OUR PLEASURES ARE bodily pleasures, yet God asks us to restrict them or totally give them up for the sake of religion. Why? After all, sex and partying feel really good. And if religion weren't a part of their lives, I believe many theists and other religionists would find ways of indulging in these temporal pleasures as much as possible. And yet, God and religion frowns on these very real pleasures.

Theism can be a downer. Atheism is more fun. No religious brow-beating. No arbitrary feelings of guilt. Just us, the world at large, and a healthy imagination. Billy Joel immortalized this sentiment in his song, "Only the Good Die Young":

> They say there's a heaven for those who will wait
>
> Some say it's better but I say it ain't
>
> I'd rather laugh with the sinners than cry with the saints
>
> The sinners are much more fun . . .
>
> You know that only the good die young.

You know, it may not be a terrific proof for the truth about atheism, but it is a compelling case against prudish religion and an overbearing metaphysical figure many call God.

Therefore, it is more reasonable to say, "God does not exist."

In this short discourse, I can see why there are many people who have rejected the concept of a God and simply assume that the material world is all there is. Taken individually, except the first question concerning the problem of evil, any of the questions above asked by atheists may not have enough convincing power. But, taken as a whole, the arguments add up to a compelling case against the existence of God. It seems that any mechanism used to bring God into the picture simply confuses our reality and ultimately messes things up.

As I contemplated the possibility of existence without God, there was a sense of a cool breeze blowing through my overheated mind. I wasn't sure if that breeze was meant to be refreshing or whether it might be the first icy breath of a warning. I didn't know how to relate to a life apart from the presence of a transcendent God—whether real or imaginary. But I had opened my heart and mind to the possibility. And now it was time to figure out what a life without faith actually looked like.

The eclipse of my faith had now become total. Doubt completely blocked any spiritual light from reaching my soul. All I had left was a memory.

Chapter Thirteen

ALONE

Did I keep my heart pure for nothing?
Did I keep myself innocent for no reason?

I SHOULDN'T ADMIT THAT I'M afraid of the dark, but I am. What I imagine and what is actually happening are completely out of sync when there's no light to help me make sense of the data I'm receiving from all my other senses. I recently read about a research study done at Walt Disney World of children's greatest fears. What surprised me is that the greatest fear wasn't the sight of vicious animals or gory pictures; it was unknown sounds in the dark. I can attest to that. Some of the best horror movies create more fear with sounds than with visual images. "Let the imagination do its thing," I heard a movie-emaker say. "The imagination can create a much better film than you can ever manufacture on celluloid." So true. It seems that, without light, our imaginations can cause the simplest things to become really creepy: a foot-step turns into an approaching axe murderer or the crack of a breaking twig turns into a bone-in-nose cannibal stalking you for dinner. Just the thought can cause your hair to stand on end. In the dark, the imagination runs to the most horrifying places.

I call this my eclipse of faith, which assumes that light comes from the supposition that there's a God at work in this world. And I equate the loss of that certainty as a darkening of the soul. I think it shows more about my upbringing than the facts that are before me.

Shouldn't I view truth as the light? And shouldn't I view ignorance or superstition as the darkness? If my faith has always been superstition, shouldn't I liken my current state as a flood of light as opposed to its cessation? Yet, emotionally, I must admit, it *feels* dark now. And it is a darkness that terrorizes. What if I'm wrong? What if God exists and I have pulled away from him, whether by clever means or maybe even dishonest means? Maybe I didn't want him to exist so that he can have no power over me. So that he could not claim me. And I wouldn't then have to admit that I'm dependent upon him for my existence. If God exists and I am wallowing in darkness, I think it is more to his pulling away from me than my pulling away from him. I've searched for him in Christianity. I've searched for him in Judaism. I've searched for him in Islam. I've searched for him in Hinduism and, in some twisted way, in Buddhism too. And yet, here I am, unconvinced he's concerned about me and unconvinced that's he's even there.

For years I had attended church. Countless hours I had prayed. I had paid thousands of dollars in tithes. I had studied the Bible intently and taught hours upon hours in Sunday school. I had preached sermon after sermon. I had told many other people about my faith and why they should give their heart to Christ. I had read so many books on theology and Christian living that I'm afraid to even count them.

What if I had simply been wasting my time?

Had I kept my heart pure for nothing? Had I simply perpetuated a tradition of behavior and belief that was based totally on a fabrication? Up to this point, had I been a fool with my life? Has it been a total waste?

As I now drive past churches in my hometown, I find myself wondering. How did all this come about? How did all this religious activity get started in the first place? What can explain all the efforts expended in the name of God? Now, you must understand, I find myself in the Bible Belt of America: the Deep South. Within the South, there are so many devout, religious people. Just this morning, I sat in an IHOP and could hear a mother and son across the way praying over their food. In the booth directly behind me, I could hear a group of ladies talking about a new praise chorus they had learned at a Bible study. I could hear them humming the tune—a tune I knew quite well and could sing along with them.

All my life I had been surrounded by religion and the religious. And now to break faith with these religious people was proving more difficult than I first thought. I must admit I started feeling quite nostalgic for the days when Jesus Christ meant more to me than life itself. I missed the days when I took such great comfort in reciting memorized Scriptures and the cadence of the sublime words would fill my chest with warmth and comfort. I missed the rapturous prayers of a deep desire to talk directly with my Creator. Then, I felt life had a deep meaning and transcendent purpose.

But those days were no more. Had I lost more than I have gained? To stave off my instinctual desire to retreat back to the known, I needed to chart my own path into the unknown and figure out what was next. If God didn't exist, I might find myself reaching the same conclusion Ivan Karamazov reached in Dostoevsky's grand novel *The Brothers Karamazov* when he said, "If God doesn't exist, then everything is permitted." If you think about it, if there is no God, then there's no Judgment Day— or afterlife. If no afterlife, then this is all there is. In reality, we are slaves only to cause and effect and the physical laws of the material world. Other than that, all bets are off. If I hold onto anything else, I am only obeying the hollow voices of ghosts that are calling me to fear the nonexistent. I was truly free to course my own destiny. Ethics and morality were now negotiable. Nietzsche's question, "Why then be good?" becomes a quite reasonable question. What was my life to look like from this point forward?

Atheism, then, is totally liberating. Machiavelli's contention that politics is the art of the possible makes total sense. What is there in virtue? It's what works, what's practical. It's what makes me happiest. Machiavelli must have come to the exact same conclusion I am just discovering.

I've always found it amusing that some atheists are so concerned about the ills of society and social injustice. I get a kick out of Bill Maher complaining about the Republicans' insensitivity toward people and their total lack of moral responsibility. If I understand atheism properly, morality really doesn't matter. If a person is a true atheist, he shouldn't give a flying flip about whether or not the poor are being fed, the citizens of Burma are getting a fair chance in life, or whether there is such a thing as global warming. These issues are none of his concern. Let others suffer and die. Let the world implode. I think the true atheist should say instead, "Why should I care? As long as I get my fair share of pleasure out of life, I don't care if anyone else does. And, why would I protest at the advancement of religion? I think I'd be happy with others' being religious." Why? Because people who get themselves all tangled up in religion have to deal with all this morality and God-nonsense, making it easier for me to manipulate them. They have to be nice. I don't. They have to treat others fairly. I don't. They have to look after the interests of others. Not me.

Yet, even with all this newfound moral freedom, I feel hollow inside. It is inexplicable. And, I must admit, a terrible downer. It's what Sheryl Crow crooned about, "If it makes you happy, it can't be all that bad. If it makes you happy, then why ★★★ ★★★★ are you so sad?"

I should be happy with this conclusion. But, strangely, I find myself not. I feel a crushing weight push against my chest, robbing me of air and radiating a deep and indescribable pain. Maybe it's just a sense of loss. Maybe it's just the fear of the unknown future. But the reality is that this life apart from a relationship with God doesn't feel as freeing as I thought it would be.

Maybe I'm just a weak-minded lemming.

I stumbled across a beautiful, profound poem I had known since high school but never fully understood nor appreciated. Now, it glowed with meaning. It echoed the angst and ache that had overtaken me. It was Matthew Arnold's poem, *Dover Beach*. And to read those words not as a theist, but as one overcome with doubt, the poem unfolded new textures and meaning:

> The sea is calm to-night.
>
> The tide is full, the moon lies fair
>
> Upon the straits; on the French coast the light
>
> Gleams and is gone; the cliffs of England stand;
>
> Glimmering and vast, out in the tranquil bay.
>
> Come to the window, sweet is the night-air!
>
> Only, from the long line of spray
>
> Where the sea meets the moon-blanched land,
>
> Listen! you hear the grating roar
>
> Of pebbles which the waves draw back, and fling,
>
> At their return, up the high strand,
>
> Begin, and cease, and then again begin,
>
> With tremulous cadence slow, and bring
>
> The eternal note of sadness in.
>
> Sophocles long ago
>
> Heard it on the Aegean, and it brought

Into his mind the turbid ebb and flow

Of human misery; we

Find also in the sound a thought,

Hearing it by this distant northern sea.

The Sea of Faith

Was once, too, at the full, and round earth's shore

Lay like the folds of a bright girdle furled.

But now I only hear

Its melancholy, long, withdrawing roar,

Retreating, to the breath

Of the night-wind, down the vast edges drear

And naked shingles of the world.

Ah, love, let us be true

To one another! for the world, which seems

To lie before us like a land of dreams,

So various, so beautiful, so new,

Hath really neither joy, nor love, nor light,

Nor certitude, nor peace, nor help for pain;

And we are here as on a darkling plain

Swept with confused alarms of struggle and flight,

Where ignorant armies clash by night.

As the tides of faith withdrew, so did the comfort I could always count on. I now saw myself standing on "a darkling plain," wondering what all this had been for. What had I accomplished? Had I improved anything or simply tore things down? The "ignorant armies" had left enough carnage in their wake. All along, I had been in search for truth. I started with the notion that truth and God were synonymous. As I explored what can be known, I no longer could embrace that notion with certainty. And, as I freed myself from the idea of God, I thought

I had found truth—at least as best I could tell. But, what did I actually have? Truth? Maybe. And what was truth, anyway? Was it what it seemed? Would it become my friend? Or would it be consumed with destroying me? And, if it proved to be a friend, what good would it do once obtained?

Presciently, I knew my search wasn't quite over. Deep within, I knew truth still eluded me. I must go deeper. There was much more to explore . . .

DAYTIME BECOMES NIGHT

In a total eclipse, what has made day different from night, the sun, now appears only as small as a small coin in the sky. Its smallness has been misunderstood because of its domination of the daytime sky. Only when it has been reduced in total eclipse do we see how much the sun has blocked from view. In total eclipse, its effect is removed from the daytime sky, and we see there is more in the sky than we ever knew—that only darkness illuminates.

Then we feel the temperature begin to fall.

Chapter Fourteen

REASON, BE TRUE

Come now, let us reason together.

AS OF THE WRITING OF this book, we are approaching seven billion people alive at the same time on this earth. That's quite a few. I was in China recently. It's easy to get overwhelmed by the number of people in that country. I am amazed every time I travel, whether in Los Angeles or London, Indianapolis or Istanbul, just how many people there are. And, quite naturally, all appear to be caught up in their own little worlds, fretting over their existence—their stresses, their loves, their insecurities, their appetites, their secret fantasies—with little to no thought about the nature of life and living. They just go about doing life, ticking items off their mental to-do list, and hoping somewhere in the deepest part of their being that in some way their life matters.

By simple observation, I recognize in most people an overwhelming self-centeredness. If we were truly honest with ourselves, each of us would have to confess to thinking that the universe revolves around us. We process the meaning of everything we see and experience based upon how it affects us. And this innate self-centeredness is not just a human trait. We see it in animals and even plants. My dog Snickers interprets every move I make in terms of how likely I am at that moment to either walk her, play with her, pet her, or feed her. She never wonders if I'm having a good day or a bad day. She never considers the stress I feel to provide for my family. She never considers whether the walk she wants me to take her on is a good time for me or not.

And even a plant is self-centered. It forces its way toward more light, more food, or more water with no concern over whether its growth is inconveniencing or getting in the way of others. So, if the entire material world is innately self-centered, I guess it is completely natural and probably explains best how we humans, as well as all other life forms, have survived all these millennia.

But there seems to be something about humans that is unique to all other life forms. And it is our ability to reason. And when I talk of reason, I'm not talking about patterns of thought a chimp might use to learn from effects and respond accordingly to causes. I'm talking about the human's ability to understand the essences of things, grapple with abstract principles, and imagine things that have not actually been experienced or may never before have existed. For it is in this realm of pure reason where truth, goodness, and beauty are fully manifested and appreciated. In effect, it is our ability to reason that makes a discussion like this possible. All seven billion of us have this power of reason in generous supply. Having said that, it's amazing how often we do not put this power to good use.

I was talking with a good friend at a dinner party not too long ago about the nature of faith and God. He posed the classic question, "How can a good God allow such evil? If he knows about suffering, has the power to fix it, yet does nothing, then what does that say about God's character?" (He sounds a lot like Epicurus, doesn't he?) But yet, on the tail of that comment, he mentions that he is only concerned about these things in the practical sense. How does it affect his life today—in the "here and now," so to speak?

What he's wondering is how the concept of God will improve his life. His comments are the classic conundrum of a soul caught between sentient existence and pure reason. Most of us find ourselves in this uncomfortable place. We want to think about the sublime, but the noise from our practical existence is a constant screaming in the ears. And that cacophony of madness is enough to keep reason governed-down to the "art of the possible" and restricted to the task of managing everyday matters.

But yet, the human brain is capable of so much more thought than we allow it to think about. The ability to reason like Socrates, St. Augustine, Nietzsche, and Bertrand Russell is available to all of us. In our recent past (say, over the past 3,000 years or so), the freedom to rationalize was limited to the idle rich, not to the average Joe holding a full-time job. Indulging in speculative reason has been the sport of princes (and somewhat available to a handful of monks and hoary-headed scholars). The exercise of pure reason has just recently entered the world of democratic thought, where dock-workers could intellectually indulge themselves and spar with philosophers and other thought leaders. Yet, that "indulgence" is still considered an indulgence. Most of us succumb to the pressures of ordinary, everyday-ness of life and feel alienated by "the Great Conversation" of reasoners. Most of us, when given the option of exercising our reason or watching TV would prefer to watch a voyeuristic episode of *Jerry Springer* or an old rerun of *Seinfeld*. TV demands so little of us. It anesthetizes our worried minds and breeds mental laziness. Like a thickening fog, a general malaise has overcome us and is stealing away our rational capacity. In the words of Neil Postman, "we are amusing ourselves to death." And we are content to suffocate our spectacular powers of reason with vapid entertainment. We give lip service to being interested in truly knowing, but in reality, we are simply content not to understand ourselves or our place in this world. Therefore, we have seven billion people spilling all around us, bouncing off each other, each living a life of meaningless routine, frequently interjected with pain, and occasionally graced with a few moments of fleeting pleasure.

But it is this wonder of pure reason that gives me pause. In the natural scheme of living, procreating, and dying, what utility—or better, purpose—does reason bring to the party? Isn't this constant churning of thought about life's meaning a terribly unproductive and unnecessary waste of mental energy? If this material world is all that exists—and all that will ever exist—what evolutionary benefit does the search for meaning bring us? Does it make us physically stronger? Hardly. If anything, the stress of intensive thought destroys the body more than builds it. Have you ever seen a philosopher of strapping physical prowess? I don't think so. Most are pasty and soft-muscled. Does it make us intellectually more capable? Most likely not. Some of the finest minds have dedicated their total faculty to the accumulation of wealth and social standing, not the accumulation of wisdom. So, it is not necessarily an empirically provable fact that the pursuit of purpose does anything to advance the state of the human animal.

So then, what good is this faculty of pure reason? How has it come to be in the ordinary course of human evolution? We can explain many aspects of our existence to natural selection, but I don't think the high art of reason helps the fittest to survive any better. We may argue that reason has assisted in the development of community with other humans – that it has civilized us and domesticated us. We may conclude that complex relationships that result in the division of labor are evidence of reason improving and stabilizing communal living. But these arguments cannot go as far as to include the pursuit of truth, goodness, and beauty for their own sake, an obvious passion of ours. What good does Beethoven's Sixth Symphony serve the survival of our species? What good is a poem by Elizabeth Barrett Browning or Emily Dickinson? What good is self-sacrificing love—the kind of noble love that creates heroes such as when one soldier throws his body on a grenade to save the lives of his fellow soldiers? And what good is there in understanding *samsara*, the circle of rebirth as taught by the Hindus and Buddhists? What does it really do for us?

There is something unexpected and special about our capacity for reason. With it, we are able to live beyond ourselves and think of a universe much bigger than the everyday world surrounding us. With it, we are able to plunge into our collective subconscious and find hidden treasures that enrich a part of us that has a larger connection than the obvious material world. With reason, we can suppose the numinous and explore a level of existence that surpasses the here and now.

With reason, we're able to divine truth and engage our imaginations to plumb the depths of meaning.

If reason is all that, then I'm not sure I can be satisfied with the explanation of a world that is limited to the material. Because it is with this gift of reason that many have tried to argue that the material world is all there is. If God exists (as theists assert), and this God has gifted us with one of his own divine attributes like reason (as many theists believe), then I would find it quite ironic to find the atheist using this divine empowerment of reason to argue against the very Divine Being that has granted such a gift. I'm not sure many atheists have considered this ironic possibility. I know I never had. But, it is quite unsettling to think of reason in any other terms. Natural selection has no need for the development of pure reason for the advancement of our species. In terms of a material world, pure reason is an utter superfluity and, therefore, not needed. Natural selection would never have selected it. Therefore, the presence of reason itself tears apart the use of reason to do away with the notion of an all-powerful Creator.

Yet, is reason a reliable faculty? There is an underlying assumption that must be explored. Can I, with assurance, use reason to assess meaning and prove the existence of God? There are some who say yes, and there are others who say no. Take, for example, Bertrand Russell's classic argument against the existence of God: "If everything must have a cause, then God must have a cause." Interesting notion, no doubt. But just look at the question and see what is happening here. Logic is limited to the use of specific words that have specific definitions. Russell assumes that the operative word "cause" has equal understanding within both parts of the argument because the English language itself is limited in the use of the word "cause." It can only be used in a specific way. The first rule of good logic is in ensuring the proper understanding of terms. Here, we find a natural disconnect between the expansiveness of reason and the confinements of language. The term "cause" has an embedded ambiguity that cannot be easily explained. But, when put into the context of our normal usage of words, the argument "feels" as though it is reasonable yet still troubles us in a deep place we cannot easily articulate. In reality, though, it's no more than a heady word-game. So, when I look back at many of the atheists' arguments in an earlier chapter, I find the presence of quite a few word-games used to discount God's existence. The problem of evil in particular falls prey to this problem.

There is a level of knowing that transcends the use of formal logic—and even particular language. Fundamentally, we sense there is a larger creative force apart from the universe itself out there, even though otherwise intelligent people confuse us (and themselves) with logical arguments based on specific language rules that may or may not apply to the evidence at hand. Because the arguments appear reasonable, they can be devilishly convincing. But Bertrand Russell's argument frustrates an innate sense that most of us have: that there is a first cause, uncaused from our point of view, but that caused what we define as everything—the material world. It's just as reasonable to debunk Russell's statement as it is reasonable to accept it. The only problem with our accepting Russell's statement is that it ignores what is so obvious—this material world had to come from something other than itself. Russell's clever word play leaves us short of a full understanding of the evidences surrounding us. As Ludwig Wittgenstein, one of the greatest minds of the twentieth century (and a colleague of Russell's), once admitted, "The sole remaining task for philosophy is the analysis of language." I sure hope he's dead wrong because that would lead to all "knowing" as milky and undefined. But we see a bit of evidence in our discussion, like a flashing of truth, in what Wittgenstein said. If that is all that's left for philosophers to do, then what a terrible deconstruction of human thought that would be!

There are others who discount reason because they believe we humans are terribly brain-damaged from "the fall" of man (that's when Adam and Eve disobeyed God in the Garden of Eden by eating forbidden fruit as recorded in the Hebrew Scriptures). John Calvin and the Puritans believed this to be so. They claim that we cannot rely on reason because our ability to reason has been wrecked. We are incapable of making sense out of what's around us. To their credit, there's plenty of evidence of bad reasoning all around us. Just look at what Michael Jackson chose to do with his face. For the ultimate in empiricism, all you have to do is hang out with teenagers for half a day, and you'll get a sense of reasoning gone catawampus.

But there are many others who are not so pessimistic. They believe that Aristotelian logic can and does lead us to truth if processed rightly. St. Thomas Aquinas and many of those who accepted and perpetuated his ideas (called "Thomists") are some of those optimists. Ironically, even the Christian Scriptures give a glimpse of this optimism in the Book of Romans. As I looked into the polarity of positions on whether man could reason toward truth or not, I came to the conclusion that reason, if practiced properly, is completely capable of getting us to truth. The big problem is whether we can legitimately get our collective neuroses out of the way so that reason can do its thing. That's where my pessimism rests. But it is not an inevitable pessimism. With good logic, I'm confident we can get at truth.

If this is so, then why are there so many brilliant minds still not coming to "God as truth" using reason? A number of very intelligent people are not only mildly dismissing God as possible; they are downright evangelistic about their belief in non-belief. Consider Sam Harris of Stanford University. What about Richard Dawkins of Oxford? How about the great intellectual force of Christopher Hitchens? Do not these people disprove the very point we are currently trying to make? At first, I thought so. We have two options here: (1) that reason itself is a flawed instrument and cannot accomplish the task of discovering truth as we had hoped or (2) that the people using the instrument are using it improperly. As I read their books, I sense that the latter option appears to be more at work than I first thought.

It has been said that most disbelief in God has to do with sexual appetite. I know this sounds absolutely absurd. It does to me too. But—and this is a big "but"—there may be more truth to that than we are willing to admit. I cannot speak for Messrs. Hitchens, Dawkins, and Harris to what their true motivation behind their disbelief is. I personally think it is hard for any one of us to be fully transparent with ourselves concerning our true motivations. We create this craven rationale to explain away the deeper forces raging within us that we never want a polite society to have access to. I believe we do this semi-consciously so that we don't even possess the ability to acknowledge it through self-analysis. We have to observe these forces spilling out through telltale behaviors and tone more than from consciously willed declarations.

Back to the "but"—I do think we as a race are inwardly rebelling constantly against constraints. From the day we're born to the day we die, we inwardly seethe at the thought of being beholden to another. God, if He is who the theists say he is, is that one being we are deeply beholden to for our existence. His morality dictates ours. And He has put constraints on a very appealing and pleasurable appetite: sex. So, I think those who have postulated that puritanical sexual moralities are a common cause for atheism may be speaking more truth than any of us are willing to admit. It is when we have these semi-conscious, irrational quarrels with an Absolute Being as God that it comes out as sharp, intellectual attacks framed as atheism. Sex really is that good. (As you read this, if you feel that hormonal rush that flushes your face, churns your insides, and quickens your breath, then, like me, you understand the power sex has just when we merely talk about it!) It's so attractive that it can mess up the thinking of even the brightest among us. But is it worth risking your entire eternal destiny for its fleeting pleasures? Theists press us on this. And, I think if any of us thought about it long enough, whether it is sex for us or not, I think our disbelief can be run back to a quarrel with God because of a feeling of restraint we might possess or a crushing disappointment, just as it was with Charles Darwin.

Severe suffering can also send any of us off the high bluffs of reason. When something or, worse, some*one* of extreme value is taken from us, reason can easily become unhinged. The death of Darwin's pre-teen daughter, Anna, unsettled Darwin's faith fundamentally. Darwin's doubt had already been on the rise at the time of Anna's death, but when Anna died, the light of faith in Darwin died too. But Darwin is not the only one. I can think of many people who, like a wounded animal, have lashed out and questioned God's existence aggressively after a tragedy. Howls of pain bounce between hall to hall throughout the house of the soul. The only exhausted response remains, "Faith in God? Please! Where was God when I needed him most?" In the midst of the turmoil and hurt, reason is shoved aside—not purposefully, but inevitably. At the very least, reason becomes horribly twisted to accommodate and ultimately assuage the ache. Reason itself may not be the true thing to blame if many of us have "reasoned" our way away from faith.

So, here we sit with a powerful tool we call reason that seems to point to more than we can ever fully understand. And yet, we find it can fail us terribly if we are not mindful of its limitations. So, what to make of truth? Is it even knowable, then? Are we simply too screwed up or inept at reasoning to ever discern it? By what means can we seek after it? Seven billion inquiring minds want to know. Again, I know deep within my being that I do not want to live a life based on a falsehood. I want to know the truth, whatever that is. So, I need to loosen my grip on the metaphysical for a bit and take a close look at the physical. Maybe physics can lend a hand.

Chapter Fifteen

PHYSICS CRACKS
A WINDOW

"How much choice did God have in constructing the Universe?"
– Albert Einstein

STEPHEN HAWKING, IN HIS MONUMENTAL work *A Brief History of Time*, concludes his discourse that longs for a theory that would explain everything when he writes:

> If we do discover a complete theory, it should in time be understandable in broad principle by everyone, not just a few scientists. Then we shall all, philosophers, scientists, and just ordinary people, be able to take part in the discussion of the question of why it is that we and the universe exist. If we find the answer to that, it would be the ultimate triumph of human reason – for then we would know the mind of God.

This search for meaning goes beyond the theologian, the ethicist, and the philosopher. It is rich and real and relevant in every discipline of thought.

And it is a pursuit that is worthy of our greatest minds. Even as I have undertaken such a deep and expansive task as this book has ended up becoming, I have come to realize how one-sided my approach has been. I have forced my search through the lens of the philosophical and the theological. And it was John C. Polkinghorne who called me out on it when he wrote,

> I characterize myself as a bottom-up thinker. It is a natural stance for a scientist to adopt. We have learned so often in our exploration of the physical world that "evident general principles" are often neither so evident nor so general as one might at first have supposed. Many theologians are instinctively top-down thinkers.

"Voilà!" I realized I had been relying on a top-down analysis of truth. I had not even considered looking from the bottom-up. When I came to this realization, I knew deep inside I could not rest my inquiry until I took on the mindset of a physicist and looked at the problem of meaning and God's existence from a "bottom-up" perspective.

I must make a confession. As a student, I absolutely *hated* Physics. I remember how painful it was for me to sit in on a physics class in high school, briefly. After only a couple of class periods, I begged for a change of schedule because there was nothing I could imagine as more painful than a full year of study of fulcrums, math, electromagnetic principles, subatomic particles, nuclear fission and fusion, and all the other mind-numbing physical forces that populated the textbooks of physics. Who in their right mind would want to sit there and think about this stuff for hours on end? Not me.

When I first began my business career, I remember receiving some wonderful advice about the importance of creativity for the advancement of my career. It was explained to me that the way business gets advanced in the future is about to undergo a tectonic shift. And it was this shift that was going to set the stage for greater innovation and expansion. It was this shift that would redefine who leads in business and who will fall behind.

Over the past seventy-five years or so, the entire business universe has been obsessively focusing on technology as the strategic competitive weapon to succeed in business. Stories were told about rags-to-riches business ventures that exploded on the scene because of new advances in technology. Books were written. Seminars were given. And the entire business world caught the wave of technology. Business was learning to become more efficient with technology. Science, efficiency, and streamlined processes were the rage.

But the next wave of business success would not be so dependent on the creation of new technology but in the creative applications of existing technology. And, with this new emphasis, we saw the personal computer deliver us the Internet and the reconfiguration of radio technology to give us cell phones. Creative application is the new wave of technological advancement.

As I dedicated my career to developing my creative skills, I stumbled upon a thought that was simple, yet radically important: expose yourself to things that are different—experiences that are outside your comfort zone. Humans have a bad tendency to hunker down and restrict their access to new ideas and experiences as they grow older. Over the course of a lifetime, important principles have been learned. Many times, we mistake those learned principles as timeless and unshakable truths. In actuality, those principles may simply have been a practical means to an end at a certain time. And as our circumstances change, those principles may no longer apply. Yet, in all our stubbornness, we choose to hold on to those principles in the face of evidence that they no longer have the same relevance as they did in the past.

To become creative, you must always look outside your known world for information and inspiration. And it was this advice that pushed me toward the dreaded discipline of physics. Luckily, I started by reading works by famed physicists like Leon Lederman and Richard Feynman. Both of these irreverent, kitschy, and insanely brilliant physicists made the subject not only approachable but also fun. And, reading Lisa Randall, Brian Greene, and Lawrence Krauss was very influential on my thinking too. They explained so much with such clarity. That's exactly the kind of mentoring I needed, to step into a complicated world filled with very smart theorems developed by highly intelligent scientists.

As I opened up my mind to the world of physics, quantum mechanics became a favorite topic. The knowledge of the basic building blocks of everything physical transfixed me. The world of the subatomic particles—the quarks, leptons, gluons, neutrinos, photons, gravitons, etc.—gave me a rush like that of Sir Edmund Hillary's quest to reach the summit of Mount Everest. I wanted to know all about this strange, subscopic world. I also wanted to know the minds that discovered all this wonder. I wanted to know how they went about finding out about these subatomic treasures. CERN, with its 60-mile long Large Hadron Collider, and the Fermilab, with its Tevatron collider, became favorite mythical wonderlands like Xanadu as these great minds of science shot particles at each other at near speeds of light through miles upon miles of pipes buried underground just to see what would happen. And, kaboom! These collisions poured out more and more mystifying and strange data that scientists never could have concluded using common sense alone. The subatomic world has, quite simply, confounded the scientific community. It is so rich and variable, yet so elegant and beautiful.

My fascination with physics even extended into the heavens as I learned about stars, galaxies, black holes, and nebula. Places far away with strange names like Betelgeuse, Andromeda, and the Pleiades captured my imagination. And I slowly mustered the courage to read the great physicists like Stephen Hawking, Albert Einstein, and Niels Bohr. Their ability to challenge all my assumptions with incredible theories, observations, and philosophical insights excited me. Through their powers of reason and observation, these men have been able to make sense out of some of the most confounding observable data. How much more can we learn and know? The wider we look into the heavens using sophisticated tools like the Hubble telescope, the more infinite and expansive the universe becomes. Scientists are now wondering if we have only accounted for a very small part of matter. The thought now is that the universe may consist more of dark matter, estimated at 80% of all matter, than of the matter we can identify. Mystifying! (Scientists call this matter "dark" because they are not sure what it is.) The narrower we look into the interstitial gaps within the building blocks of matter with powerful measuring devices, the deeper goes the rabbit hole. The one basic building block of which all matter is built from still eludes us, though some are hoping they've found it in the theoretical, yet recently discovered in July 2012, Higgs boson. But will the boson be the very rudimentary level of matter? If history has any say in the matter, I'm skeptical. Democritus' theory two thousand years ago about the indivisible element, the atom, has been dissected and sub-dissected many times over, still with no bottom in sight.

And yet, Stephen Hawking is still hopeful that physics will be able to construct a "theory of everything," where the laws dictating the behaviors of the smallest subatomic particles can be reconciled with the laws orchestrating the planets, solar system, galaxies, and even the entire universe. So far, as of the writing of this book, three of the four forces of nature have been at least theoretically reconciled: electromagnetism and the two nuclear forces, strong and weak. But gravity still seems to frustrate all the theories thus far.

According to physicists, when the expansion of the universe began, the dispersion of matter and heat into the universe did not occur uniformly. This non-uniform spray demonstrated something unknown was at work at the point of inception. This seeming "imperfection" in the behavior of matter has many a head being scratched right now. Cambridge University professor Michael Green, a colleague of Hawking's, posited a new theory of matter called Super Symmetrical String Theory that describes the base level of matter as being a series of vibrating strings. At least on paper, String Theory seems to explain some of the phenomena about gravity's odd behavior. But, String Theory requires scientists to go beyond the simple three-dimensional world we all know—up, down, and sideways—and imagine the universe as an eleven-dimensional world in order to get the math to work properly. Indeed, this is all theoretical at this point because String Theory is not, at least at this moment, observable. But it does make you wonder about the basis of this world we live in—and its beginnings.

I'm excited about what Hawking and his fellow scientists are trying to figure out. And I think it just goes to show you how far we've come in our understanding while, at the same time, realizing how little we really know about the universe we live in. These huge problems are amazing co-nundrums that will occupy our brightest minds for generations to come. It seems to give testimony to the verse in Proverbs that tells us that kings get glory from searching out a matter, but God gets the glory to conceal it. But, in this whole process of trying to get to a "theory of everything," there is one part of the process that is most intriguing: physic's means.

Oddly, the most amazing part of physics is in neither its vast insights into nature nor its astounding projections into worlds we cannot see. The real beauty of physics is in its means. Billions of years ago, according to the best data that astrophysicists can make the most sense of, some type of birthing of the universe occurred. From that seminal event, first postulated by Belgian priest and astronomer Georges Lemaître in 1927, the known universe expanded rapidly from a single, primeval atom of incredible density and energy. The way the universe took shape and the means whereby it began its expansion and formation brought certain absolute and unchangeable laws into effect—physical laws such as the speed of light, electromagnetism, and gravity that have proven to be highly consistent. So much so that these laws, based on the essences of pure mathematics, became remarkably predictive. If this original explosion occurred randomly, and if life itself is a random effect of that random cause, then why is it we have such an amazingly consistent set of physical realities? Why should light always travel in a vacuum at the same speed? Why couldn't it be as variable and seemingly random as the blowing of wind? Why doesn't light travel sometimes rather slowly and other times surprise us and travel extremely fast? Why do magnetic opposites always attract? And when they do attract, why are the forces of magnetism consistent? Why don't they get stronger and weaker in unpredictable waves?

Yet this "random" birthing event of the universe can only be understood using physical realities that are based on highly predictable and understandable measures. It is through these predictable means that scientists are able to establish the age of the universe. Ironically, it is through the predictability of these absolutes within the material world whereby we can rely on the conclusions drawn from the theory of relativity. That's why Albert Einstein thought a better name for his "Theory of Relativity" would have been "Invariant Theory" because of his interest in the parts of a physical system that were invariant no matter what relative position you are measuring within the system. Therefore, his theory was pointed at the consistent, predictable realities that are invariable so we can apply good scientific methodology to measuring and understanding them. So, we must conclude, along with Einstein, how can we know what relativity is without absolute mathematical principles and highly predictable physical behaviors to demonstrate the relative observations within matter?

There's another hidden assumption in the presumed randomness of the "beginning" that we need to explore as well. That hidden assumption is that we can rely on reason and man's randomly developed brain to make sense of all this randomness. We assume that reason is an absolute thing that can be applied consistently to any data and be able to discern reasonable conclusions from it. How is it we can know that with certainty? And why should we trust an organ like the human brain, which also came into existence through random chance, to figure out that all this randomness exists? Is it even possible? It seems that we are standing on shaky ground, no matter how we look at it.

But with all this postulation that seems we are chasing words and ideas around in circles, we simply must conclude that reason still makes sense. The elegance and constancy of mathematics make sense. And the physical laws of the universe make sense. There's a lot to our ability to understand the material world that makes sense. It's this ability to understand our world with certainty that fascinates me most. And it is these truths (dare I call them that) that give me reason to hope. Lemaître's primeval atom theory, if it ultimately proves to be the best explanation of our beginnings, must be much more than just a random event. If it were random, the physical laws that dictate its aftermath by definition should be equally as random as the material that spewed out of that singular cause. But yet, they are not. As Peter Kreeft said quite tersely, "The Big Bang requires a Big Banger." Well said.

Maybe the real "foil" of the Big Bang controversy, and why it is so offensive to many biblicists, is that of its name's unfortunate connotation that a "bang" is something chaotic, destructive, and undisciplined . . . something unintelligible, purposeless, and devoid of a Designer. No self-respecting, intelligent Creator would create such as world so "willy-nilly," one might argue. Maybe the name of the theory itself (which was first coined as a pejorative by steady-state cosmology champion and lifelong atheist Fred Hoyle) is to blame for all the fuss. Maybe the best way to solve this is: (1) to allow the trained practitioners of science to inform us that some first cause event occurred at what is believed to be billions of years ago and, even though it was massive (the "Big") and it was rapid and powerful (the "Bang"), it was a thing of unimaginable intelligence and order—creating immensity, harmony, and balance—yielding as much beauty as it yielded brawn and (2) to assign the naming of the event to the poets:

> In the beginning, God created the heavens and the earth. The earth was without form and void, and darkness was over the face of the deep. And the Spirit of God was hovering over the face of the waters. And God said, "Let there be light," and there was light. And God saw that the light was good.

God spoke. The universe came into being. Maybe the better name for how God willed this universe into existence is to call it "The Great Speaking." Or am I simply trying to bridge a divide that cannot be bridged? Possibly. But one thing is sure: any form of beginnings of the universe, whether thousands or billions of years ago, is best understood through the use of Occam's Razor by reasoning that a designed creation from an intelligent source belonging outside of nature itself is, by far, a simpler, more elegant explanation of reality than an undesigned, purposeless, determined, and random "ka-boom!" that represents the beginnings of existence (as most materialists make an effort to assume.)

So, I find myself, from the position of a bottom-up thinker, reasoning my way against atheism as a reasonable position toward the more likely position of theism. This has been the biggest surprise for me. It was completely unexpected. John Polkinghorne, who challenged me to think bottom-up, also added,

> Christians do not have to close their minds, nor are they faced with the dilemma of having to choose between ancient faith and modern knowledge. They can hold both together. Revelation is not the presentation of unchallengeable dogmas for reception by the unquestioning faithful. Rather, it is the record of those transparent events or persons in which the divine will and presence have been most clearly discernible.

If Polkinghorne is right in his analysis, then maybe I was too quick to jump to the conclusions I did. Maybe there is more to this story than I first thought. But, where does one go after jettisoning faith as I had? Well, I wasn't about to stop my search just yet and languish because of my past poor choices. There were more questions I needed to consider first.

THE CROWN OF THE SUN

The hottest and brightest part of the sun is its corona, or its outer atmosphere. In the corona the temperature of the sun rises to 1.8 million degrees Fahrenheit. And the solar flares and solar tornadoes whirling at 300,000 miles per hour arc and churn, creating some of the most fantastic, eruptive, and brilliant elements of the sun's personality.

But, because of the sun's overall presence in the sky, we are unable to see and experience the sun's corona. But, when a lunar eclipse comes into play, the sun's corona can be observed. During a lunar eclipse, the central light source of the sun is blocked momentarily to allow the finer edges of the sun's corona to take center stage in all their glory. It is this ring of fire, light, and fury that has transfixed man's imaginations since the beginning of time.

Yet, if it were not for these eclipses, we might not ever get to appreciate the finer details in the sun's corona. The eclipse helps to even more fully reveal what a remarkable specimen the sun truly is.

Chapter Sixteen

TRUTH RUSHES IN WHERE DOUBT FEARS TO TREAD

Faith is the substance of things hoped for.
the evidence of things not seen.

IF THERE WERE GOOD REASONS not to believe in God, are there equally good, or even better, reasons to believe in God? Just as I investigated twenty arguments against the existence of God, as is outlined in the twelfth chapter, I also considered twenty arguments for God's existence.

My journey through these arguments is also based on the great scholarship of Peter Kreeft who, just as he so skillfully did with the arguments against God, has collected these twenty arguments for the existence of God. And they have had a profound effect on me. They made me go deeper than the simply obvious. I want to share these arguments with you and give you my reactions to their truth claims. For a full description of these twenty arguments, I must send you to Peter Kreeft and Ronald Tacelli's exhaustive work, *Handbook of Christian Apologetics*. In that book, Kreeft and Tacelli handle the arguments you are about to read with the skill and precision of trained philosophers. As Kreeft and Tacelli give you a detailed description of these arguments, I merely give you an impression. If you are struggling with these questions, I cannot recommend a better place to continue your search for truth.

The first five of these arguments come directly from St. Thomas Aquinas. Some of these arguments from Aquinas are admittedly thin. They do not prove with certitude the existence of the Jewish, Christian, or Muslim portrait of God, but they do give us hints of the need for some kind of deity to help us best understand the world we live in. If any one of these arguments is true, then, as Peter Kreeft says, "it only takes one fingerprint or one piece of DNA to prove the presence of the suspect." So, as I went through these arguments, I realized there was more reason to consider theism than I originally thought. And, quite honestly, I didn't expect that to be true. I thought the only way to believe in God is to blindly accept the religious teachings of a faith at their face value and never probe any deeper. Thankfully, others before me, like Thomas Aquinas, St. Augustine, G.K. Chesterton, and C.S. Lewis, chose not to accept religious dogma at face value and decided it was worth going deep to get at truth. As William James would have classified them, these intellects were tough-minded philosophers not willing to settle for comforting conclusions. They were not satisfied until they got at truth, no matter how they felt about its resulting conclusions or how a newly discovered truth might upset their pre-existing views of the world. As St. Thomas stated, "The study of philosophy is not the study of what men have opined, but of what is the truth."

So, the following twenty arguments serve as a catalog of ideas that caused me to question the nature of my doubt about God's existence. And they are quite reasonable when you look at them with a tough-minded commitment to seeking after truth.

QUESTION #1
If everything is in motion, then how did it get in motion?

EVERYTHING AROUND US IS IN perpetual motion. Everything on earth is spinning on the earth's axis like a piece of chewing gum stuck to the side of a spinning top. Just to discombobulate us even more, everything on earth is also circling rather rapidly around the sun. No wonder most humans walk around as if in a semi-drunken stupor. The sun, as the center of our solar system, is in constant motion swirling, around the center of the Milky Way, our galaxy, along with billions of other stars. The Milky Way is in motion as it moves in relation to all the other billions of galaxies as they are hurling away from each other in response to the original triggering event of the formation of the universe. All astrophysicists know this. There is nothing within the universe that is sitting still. Everything is moving.

Even if we were to look deeply into the building blocks of our material world—the frenetic world of the atom and its subatomic particles—we see nothing short of continuous, energetic movement, like electrons dizzily spinning around their respective nuclei. Even in the most static-looking pieces of matter, such as rocks, the intra-atomic movement within them is swirling and churning with activity. Again, everything is moving.

If you take the quite reasonable position that every effect must have a cause, then all this moving going on in the universe must have been initially caused by something that is not in motion. (By the way, if the logical premise of cause and effect is not true, then that fact alone totally destroys all possible reasoning—which is terribly ironic because the statement that I just made is based on the premise of cause and effect!—cause and effect must be true for anything to be knowable. Science would no longer exist without the fundamental principle of cause and effect. It's the means by which we can apply the scientific method. It's the basis of pretty much everything we experience. Experience and reason both tell us that every effect must have a cause.)

Then, to restate, if everything in our universe is moving, an "unmoving mover" must be present outside our universe that caused all this movement. As St. Thomas Aquinas put it in his magnum opus *Summa Theologica*:

> Whatever is in motion must be put in motion by another. If that by which it is put in motion be itself put in motion, then this also must needs be put in motion by another, and that by another again. But this cannot go on to infinity, because then there would be no first mover, and consequently, no other mover; seeing that subsequent movers move only inasmuch as they are put in motion by the first mover; as the staff moves only because it is put in motion by the hand. Therefore it is necessary to arrive at a first mover, put in motion by no other; and this everyone understands to be God.

That's hard to argue against. If this "unmoving mover" is outside our world, then it would have to be something like God, something or someone that is supernatural (or outside of nature) to get it all started. This logical proof might not give us the complete picture of who God is, but it does give us a reasonable thought that some kind of being outside the universe is necessary to explain what's happening here. All this motion had to be put into motion. We simply cannot say that no God exists. If we did, we would have an irreconcilable conundrum that would inevitably cast doubt on the atheist's assumption about the absence of God—or any unmoved mover. This argument is simply hard to get around. You might not like what is going on with all this moving matter called the universe, but it's inescapable that all this movement must have been cranked up somehow, and by some external Will. What the ultimate nature, or personality, of what that "Will" is cannot be extracted from the argument, only that this "Unmoved Mover" exists, or existed. It's irrational to say that it does not exist.

Therefore, it is more reasonable to say, "God exists."

QUESTION #2
What about "cause and effect" itself? How did it all get started?

AS I DISCOVERED IN THE first question, all this motion had to have been started from something; so does the very nature of "cause and effect." Everything we observe in our world is based on cause and effect. I hear a noise outside my house. It's a fast-moving swishing noise. I look out the window, and I see a car rushing by. I have just identified the cause of the noise. I also feel my stomach growl. It's early in the morning, and I've just gotten out of bed. I realize I am hungry. I haven't eaten in almost twelve hours. Cause and effect again.

Everything we understand depends on cause and effect. Twinkling lights in the sky at night are the effect of stars being present in the universe. The burning heat and light of those stars are the effect of the cause of nuclear reactions within those stars. Those nuclear reactions within the stars themselves are the effect of the cause of matter colliding together at some point in time in the distant past. And that effect of matter colliding together at some point in time in the distant past was caused by... and the chain of cause and effect goes on.

Every effect has a cause. But, this chain of cause and effect cannot go on infinitely. It defies logic. There is no possibility of infinite regress. It had to have an original cause to get it all started. It's what Thomas Aquinas refers to as the "first efficient cause" or the "uncaused cause." Scientists' current understanding of first causes point to an event they have chosen to call "The Big Bang" that represents the beginning of the known universe and sets into motion all the resulting effects we experience today. But the expansion of the universe from a primeval atom must have been caused too. But from what? Ironically, science's current understanding of the beginnings of the universe may actually be one of the greatest proofs of God's existence out there. For within this primeval event, all space, time, and matter become the effect of an original efficient cause. God speaks. The universe is created.

When I first started thinking about this, it really surprised me. I assumed the Big Bang waged war against God's existence. I thought it not only supported but also championed an atheistic worldview. Actually, the Big Bang cripples the worldview of the atheist. How? By requiring a triggering effect for all to come into existence from an original first cause. That's why so many atheists are still trying "patch up" the holes in their theories of origins with even more elaborate constructs (like multiple parallel universes, called "multiverses") to help explain the one truth they still can't get their minds around: a Creator God with so much power that he can speak *ex nihilo*, and so much substance, beauty, order—and science!—broadcasts so elegantly into an ever-inflating womb of a brand-new universe. Materialists misapply science by treating the reality of a supernatural first cause as yet one more link in an infinite regress of natural causes bound by the physical laws of a natural world.

In no way am I trying to be a crusader for a certain age of the universe in this short discussion. The only point I want to make is that even the Big Bang itself gets us back to the principle that the first effect of matter expanding from an original creation event requires a first cause. And to think that the Big Bang itself refutes the need for a first cause, as some have poorly argued, modern-day cosmologists are not thinking about the basic premise of this original creation event clearly enough. I say this in all due respect to Stephen Hawking and Leonard Mlodinow, who strive to argue that the universe's beginning can violate this principle using superstring theory, and

Richard Feynman's postulations resulting in modal-dependent realism.[5] (This is a bit of a heady stretch, in my opinion, especially since their postulations about the "Grand Design" of nature are still based on cause and effect at its core—all of which require an original independent variable, an ultimate first cause. Existence cannot rely on an infinite, convoluted string of dependent variables, no matter how cleverly manipulated, as Hawking awkwardly tries to prove.)

The reality of cause and effect begs for an original cause that is not the effect of anything else—at least within the realm of this system. If there is such a cause, then that cause must be something outside of nature itself . . . something, or Someone, *super*-natural. Even though this argument does not give us the personality or intent of the will of such an Original Cause, it's irrational to think that such an Original Cause does not exist.

Therefore, it is more reasonable to say, "God exists."

QUESTION #3
Why do things exist when it's possible for them not to exist?

TAKE, FOR EXAMPLE, MY FAMILY dog, Snickers. She's a wonderful dog. She has this wonderful mane of hair on her neck that makes her look like a lion. She also has the stature and coloring of a fox. The combination of the two make her quite an exquisite animal—she looks almost like the mythical Sphinx when she lies on the ground in a similar pose. As I write this, Snickers is sprawled out on the floor, feigning sleep. She's not asleep. I know she is secretly hoping I will put my laptop down and pet her a while. She doesn't understand why I am not always compelled to pet her. She loves to be petted.

---

5   Read *The Grand Design* for more information on Stephen Hawking and Leonard Mlodinow's arguments.

I remember a time, and it was only six years ago, when Snickers did not exist. I had no thought or knowledge of Snickers. She had not been born yet. The universe was moving along quite well before Snickers graced us with her presence. And yet, now, here she is. And I know, because I have seen these things happen in the past, that there will be a time when Snickers will die and cease to exist. I do not like to think about that day, because it makes me sad to think on it, but it'd be rather naive of me to think that day will not happen.

Did the universe need Snickers to exist in order to remain the universe? Perhaps not. I don't see how it affects the atmospheric moons of Jupiter that Snickers is alive and pretending to be asleep on my rug right now. I think the moons of Jupiter would get along quite well without Snicker's existence here on Earth. But, yet, Snickers exists even though she's not a necessity in order for the universe to function.

In this simple analogy, I'm trying to explain a quite intensive argument made by Thomas Aquinas about the necessity of things as a proof of God's existence. He says that there is a probability for anything within nature ultimately "to be" and "not to be" as in the case of Snickers above. Within a single summer, a stalk of corn grows out of the ground, matures, bears fruit, and then dies and is no more. The corn plant comes into existence and then out of existence as simple as that.

So it is with everything in the universe. There was a time when it wasn't, there is a time when it is, and then there will be a time when it is not. It is as natural a thing as the blinking of an eye. If this is the case, and if the universe is essentially a random collection of events, according to the certainty of mathematics, there must have been one point in time during the infinite past when everything that either has or currently exists did not exist at the same time. At that point in time, there would have been absolute non-existence. Everything that exists came into being because of other matter that existed at the point of origin. And, if that moment of non-existence ever occurred, no matter how brief that moment, all future existence would then be impossible—nothing would be there to re-exist, so to speak—unless there was a "necessary" existence that is beyond this natural world. Therefore, without such a self-necessary presence apart from all other forms of existence, the universe could never have existed. Mathematics and the principle of cause and effect preclude it from happening. Existence requires something, or Someone, for it to exist. Existence cannot come about from non-existence. This self-necessary Being does not need for anything else to exist in order for it to exist. It is what many people have labeled as God. This notion of God is totally rational and necessary to explain existence. Without this self-necessary God, it is impossible to explain how we have existence today.

Therefore, it is more reasonable to say, "God exists."

QUESTION #4
How do we know what "best" is if there isn't a "best"?

IN THE UNITED STATES, THERE is an obsession over determining what is best. I realize it is not just an American phenomenon. It's a human phenomenon. I'm sure if we went into any culture in the world, we would find people sitting in cafés, arguing over what's best or who's best. In America, we see it very clearly in sports. Who is the best point guard in the National Basketball Association? Which college football team has the best defense? You can go to website after website where there are endless arguments over who's best. If you have rabid sports fans as friends, you've probably been in those arguments over who's better, Michael Jordan or LeBron James. It's so much a part of our lives that I bet none of us ever stopped to ponder why we are driven to the point of insanity when we find ourselves endlessly comparing one thing against others to determine which is good, which is better, and, ultimately, which is best.

This concept of gradation requires contrast for it to work. In order for me to see better from best, I must understand a difference between two things. And, in order for me to know the value of more, or better, I must have some sense of best in mind before I can adequately make a determination.

I've heard many people refer to the ultimate good in something, yet say there is no God. They know that, somewhere in the ether of our existence, there is a best out there—a point of perfection that is appreciated, even though it may not be fully understood or able to be articulated. A "best" exists. And because of its existence, I can make statements of gradation concerning anything's relation to other objects—and occasionally even to "best" itself—by labeling it as "better" or "wiser" or "more compassionate" or "stronger" than another.

This is Thomas Aquinas' fourth argument for God's existence. And, I must say, even though it sounds quite heady and conceptual, it's profound and gives me pause. I remember watching Bill Maher's movie, *Religulous*, which is a biting, hilarious, and thought-provoking look at religion, especially Christianity, and see him struggle with this same thought. He concedes several times that there is some "best" or "absolute good" ideal out there, but he doesn't see that obvious best or absolute good present in the religion he sees around him. And, I must admit, I struggle with the same observation he so cleverly makes from time to time. You look at the crazy people who practice religion and you have to just shake your head and wonder if they even have a clue. It's amazing how much religious data many of these religious zealots have crammed into their heads, but, sadly, they seem to possess a total lack of understanding of what they so ardently profess.

But, because of this argument, I'm finding myself ending up in a different place than Bill Maher does. I simply cannot shake the idea that there is an Ultimate Best that gives me the ability to discern between good, better, and best. There is a noblest. And that noblest is something more than I see in the natural world. There is a purest. And that purity goes beyond the purity that is observed naturally among men. There is a strongest. And that strength is stronger than any strength I've ever witnessed. These superlatives must be defined by something transcendentally "Super"—a being many label as God. It's God's "best-ness" that lends value to all good, better, and best.

But, isn't all this "better-ness" really only subjective comparisons between one thing and another? Does it really require a determinable "best" in order for it to work? Peter Kreeft answers this objection in this way: "The very asking of this question answers it. For the questioner would not have asked it unless he or she thought it really better to do so than not, and really better to find the true answer than not. You can speak of subjectivism, but you cannot live it."[6] What a fascinating insight—and quite true.

Therefore, it is more reasonable to say, "God exists."

QUESTION #5
Why is it that everything looks like it has been intelligently designed?

IT LOOKS LIKE THE ENTIRE universe has been "gamed" to create and sustain life. It doesn't take much faith to come to the conclusion that this world has been designed in such a way that life as we know it was its original intent. If you engage in conversation with any physicist who understands the delicate combination of necessary conditions for life to have resulted within nature—the likelihood of life existing as it is—the mathematical improbability alone is staggering. The exact temperatures needed at the birth of the universe, the infinitesimally narrow ranges of atmospheric pressures;

---

6   Peter Kreeft & Ronald K. Tacelli, *Handbook of Christian Apologetics*, pg. 55.

the precise mix of chemicals and electromagnetic, nuclear, and gravitational forces that must have been present; the required sequence of events needed . . . if just one of these probabilities were the only thing needed, then it would be improbable enough. But, to string each needed, and highly improbable, system together properly with the combination of variables that must be aligned just so makes life even more improbable.

And that's just the beginning of life at the formation of the universe. To sustain life is equally as improbable. The exact combination of elements, temperature, the presence of water, the 21.5 degree tilt of the Earth, its exact distance from the sun, the presence of the moon, and the list of needed conditions goes on and on . . . all of which screams of a Designer with power and intelligence way beyond our pay grade.

Just look into the silent eye of a tiger and try not to wonder at its design. Look at the quantum structure of matter at its most granular level and not be mesmerized at the intricacy. Look at the human body and not be blown away at its interlocking network of systems and functionality. Just think on the amazing capacity of your being able to read this sentence: the focusing of the eye, the communication of light information chemically from the eye to the brain, the ability of the brain to decode and reconstruct the visual information within its organic network of neurons and synapses, the ability to catalog information in the seemingly limitless soft tissues of the brain that allows you to precisely recall millions of ideas and concepts instantly, the reason to be able to articulate thought, the self-awareness of grasping such a concept as a transcendent God who could be behind all this, etc.

Quite truthfully, it takes more faith to believe that all this life around us happened by chance than by some kind of design from a higher intelligence. I think there are many people out there who are raging against the need for a God-figure to explain our existence, who believe it's quite naive. It seems that the reluctance to accept a supernatural intelligence as being is being triggered by some other motive than rational thought. It's as if the anti-theist evangelists have a hidden agenda that may even elude their own consciousness. Why do I say this? Because the evidence of some kind of super-intelligence putting this universe together better explains the data. Any other proposition on the genesis of being pales in comparison. How foolish it seems to say that there is no God. It really is an unreasonable thought.

Therefore, it is more reasonable to say, "God exists."

QUESTION #6
Doesn't everything that has a beginning need a reason for beginning?

THE FIRST PREMISE OF THIS argument is, "The universe has a beginning." But, does it? According to creationists, yes. And, according to modern-day cosmologists, yes. The only people who do not see the universe as having a beginning are some Hindus, some Buddhists, and a few tree huggers huddled here and there who hold fast to a belief that we are going to be reunited with our alien ancestors during the passing of some apocalyptic comet in the not-so-distant future. About every other person on the planet has come to peace with the fact that the universe has a beginning.

It's not enough, however, to accept as fact that the universe has a beginning just because a large percentage of the thinking population believes it to be. In human history, we've seen many dumb things believed by majorities that have limited semblance of rationality. A good example of this is the notion of "bleeding out" patients in the Middle Ages. Back then, the smartest people in the room were convinced that bloodletting was the best way to cure sick people from harmful "humours" collected in the blood stream. Many trusting souls went along with the majority opinion on this medical wisdom and have the headstones with premature expiration dates carved into them to prove it. What these medieval minds didn't know was that blood plays a strategic role in the healing process of any disease. Not only that, but blood plays a critical role in sustaining life altogether. That's why bleeding wounds must be stopped from bleeding. Exsanguination unstopped leads ultimately to death. Blood must be present in the body, not drained away into some decorative porcelain bowl. The truth about blood had always been there. Blood simply hadn't changed properties or functionalities in modern times from medieval times. The medievals just weren't aware of the truth about blood.

That being said, everything in our experience and rational thought leads us to the quite reasonable conclusion that the universe did have a beginning. Any other theory appears completely out of sync with all other experiences we have in life. If we flip the coin and say the earth had no beginning, then reasoning tells us that its existence must stretch infinitely into the past. If this is the case, then we face all kinds of irreconcilable problems. Mainly, if the universe has been going on infinitely, then there is an infinite amount of time between its past and now, meaning that "now" is not possible because there is still an infinite amount of time to pass before "now" can arrive. This impossibility discovered through elementary reasoning makes an infinite past quite unreasonable. It's not merely a problem created by logic; it's a problem created by the idea itself. An infinite past with no beginning makes absolutely no sense in a world dependent upon space and time to exist. Therefore, this first premise holds.

The second premise of this argument is, "All things that have a beginning must have a reason for beginning." This smacks of cause and effect. But I think it goes even deeper. There seems to be a reasonable force needed behind the creation of something for it to come into existence. We see this all throughout life. A Monet painting of haystacks exists because Claude Monet decided one day to paint it. A Beethoven sonata exists because Ludwig von Beethoven decided one day to sit down at his pianoforte and hammer out a new musical idea. A bird's nest appears in the branches of a poplar tree because a certain robin decided one day to make its nest there. Fire ants form an ant bed because of the collective will of the ant community. A tomato plant climbs its way up the side of a mesh fence because its seed germinated in the ground, and the sun, soil, and water surrounding this seed conspired together to create a sustainable environment for this tomato plant to grow. A human baby forms because the will of a husband's semen unites with the consent of a wife's egg. All beginnings have reasons for beginning without exception.

There is a branch of Muslim philosophical theology that classifies this argument as *kalam*, or "speech," argument. It basically states that the world must have had a beginning. It cannot be infinitely old. God must have created it at a certain point in time. This is an argument made by Muslims and Christians alike. And, when looked at carefully, it makes all the sense in the world. A reasonable God has brought this world into existence. Every other explanation contains a fatal flaw.

Therefore, it is more reasonable to say, "God exists."

QUESTION #7
How can I be, if I do not have the necessary ingredients to make me?

PHILOSOPHERS CALL THIS REASONING THE argument from contingency. And it is quite a straightforward argument. Let me start with a simple example from everyday life.

I love to cook. It's not just the act of cooking that excites me. It's the result of cooking that makes all the stresses and labors of preparing a hearty meal worthwhile. One of my favorite things to prepare is a dish we call brown rice. Now, I'm not talking about the nutty-flavored brown rice you find in the grocery store that you boil and serve. The "brown rice" recipe

I'm talking about transforms regular white rice into this delicious, mouth-watering, savory taste sensation that turns any meal into a feast. It requires simple ingredients. Nothing fancy. But let me warn you: this is not a dish for someone who is trying to stick with a low fat, low calorie diet. Every time I cook it for my family or for friends, I can never make too much of it. Most people cannot stop at one serving. Most have seconds—or thirds. For a party of eight, I have to cook enough servings for 16-20 people just to meet the demand for this dish. It really is that good.

Not too long ago, I wanted to make this heavenly brown rice for some friends who were coming by the house for a meal. As I was gathering ingredients for it out of the cabinet, my heart sank. I didn't have one of the key ingredients: the one ingredient, besides rice, that is critical to the flavor of the dish. I wanted so badly to make the dish that I quickly ran to the store to get the missing ingredient. When I got to the store, they were sold out of the ingredient. I bought a substitute ingredient, came back to the house, and made the dish.

It wasn't the same. The taste was off. It tasted like a cheap knock-off. And I was very disappointed. Thankfully, the friends who came had never had the original brown rice recipe I knew existed. They politely ate their rice but didn't ask for seconds or thirds. It wasn't the same brown rice. It was missing something.

The original brown rice is what it is because of all the necessary ingredients and cooking techniques employed. It cannot exist without having something from which it was created. Philosophers would say my brown rice recipe has a dependency, or that it's contingent upon other things, for its existence. And the existence of the ingredients that make up the brown rice is conditional, based on its need for other things that make its existence possible.

This truth of contingency can be seen in everything tangible around us. The trees, the snow, the song *Eleanor Rigby* by the Beatles, the FIFA World Cup, a television show, a cat, traffic laws, the wind, the blue in the sky, light, even you and me. I wouldn't exist were it not for my parents. Nor would you. Our existence depends on the presence of so many factors that are outside of ourselves: not only our parents, but also the air we breathe, the food we eat, the forces of gravity, etc. My brown rice is made up of stuff outside itself (ingredients) in order for "it" to come into being. If this argument from contingency works for the simple things we observe around us, wouldn't it also work for the entire universe?

If this argument from contingency is (excuse the poor play on words) "universal," then the universe itself also must be contingent for its existence. And what do we mean by the universe? Peter Kreeft describes the universe as "a collection of beings in space and time." It seems to define things adequately. It covers the primary, common attribute of all things we observe and know about the world in which we live. It's a reasonable and defensible definition of the universe. If the universe is indeed this collection of beings in space and time, the argument from contingency states that there must be ingredients and forces outside itself to make its existence possible. There must be something, or better, some*one*, outside of space and time to make this universe come into play. It only makes sense for this to be.

There are many pseudo-cosmologists and pseudo-philosophers who violate this principle of contingency in their thinking. They say the universe simply exists. The matter and laws of matter self-exist. Nothing made them. No contingency. They just are. And if you push them on their thinking hard enough, they will concede to the indefensibility of their thinking by throwing up another argument, "Well, then, how does God himself exist? Wouldn't this argument from contingency apply equally to Him?" On the surface, this objection sounds quite reasonable. But, if you really look into it, you see the problem. We define the universe as a collection of beings in time and space. The argument from contingency is based on the observable and knowable universe. All our thinking and rationality is contained within this knowable universe. Our rationality cannot, by definition, extend beyond the known universe. It's impossible to know the extent of argument from contingency, but one thing is for sure, we cannot export it out of our experience within the universe. We know it works here. We have no idea how things work outside the universe. All logic and observation is completely dependent on universal principles (those contained within this universe).

But, even with that being said, our universe is contingent upon things beyond time and space. If God is a being who transcends time and space, as most theologians and philosophers would define him, it seems as though the universe necessarily depends on God to exist.

Therefore, it is more reasonable to say, "God exists."

QUESTION #8
How could all these interdependent systems randomly evolve?

THERE ARE SO MANY THINGS going on around us all the time that, if we ever stopped long enough to think on them, we'd quickly become overwhelmed: gravity, electromagnetism, chemical reactions, light, sound, biorhythms, etc. Because these things are always happening, it's easy to forget they are there and just enjoy the effect of their presence. We are good at noticing the novel and the infrequent, but we're terribly deficient at recognizing the ubiquitous and the constant even though the things most common are quite often some of the most astonishing when you isolate them and draw your attention to them. As Ralph Waldo Emerson once said, "If the stars should appear but one night every thousand years, how man would marvel and stare." Isn't that such an indictment of the silliness of man! We become terribly amused in the novel, however meaningless it may be—like Janet Jackson exposing her breast during the halftime show of the Super Bowl—but can miss some of the most amazing happenings around us, like the intricate crystalline nature of a freshly fallen snowflake.

I have a picture of my wife. It's a wonderful little picture taken while we were both still in high school. It's small—a simple black and white picture. But, all the same, I have it burned into my memory. Whenever I am away from Beth and think of her, quite often I recall this particular picture in my mind's eye. She's wearing this dark skirt and this simple, plaid cotton shirt. Her body is turned away from the camera, but she's looking over her right shoulder towards the camera. It's not a staged pose. It's a candid snapshot of her simply being herself. Beth's long, shiny dark hair is pulled back from her face and spills attractively over her shoulder. She is sporting a toothy smile and a slight, angelic (or is it devilish?) twinkle in her eye. When I see the picture, I have this uncontrollable churn of attraction that rises in my chest. With that look, Beth owns me.

But, it's not the nature of her look that I want to focus on right now. It's the ability to appreciate the picture at all. There is so much at play that allows me to enjoy the picture. First of all, the ability to create the picture—all the chemistry involved, the principles of light refraction, optics, and physics, including gravity and electromagnetism. Each of these systems as well as many others must be present and working together for a picture even this simple to be taken. But the creation of the picture is only one small part of what we're talking about. This picture also depends on the environment that surrounds Beth that allows for the picture to be taken. There is another whole set of intermingled systems. They include Beth's physical presence and the biochemistry needed for her existence, the laws of weather that allow the sun to shine and reflect off her face and cause her hair to blow just so, and the underlying genetics that allow her smile to remind us of her mother's smile. They include her two-X sexual chromosomal genetics that creates her essential feminine essence, her skeletal muscular system that allows her to stand and smile in such a way, and her emotive responses that give her the ability to communicate through her facial muscles that certain spark of personality that is just so attractive. Yet, there's a third set of systems also at play. Add all the requisite systems that allow me, as the holder of that picture, to perceive and enjoy the picture, such as the systems needed to see the picture (optics, light, biochemistry, nerve and brain anatomy, musculoskeletal function, gravity, etc.), recognize it (brain function, memory systems, more biochemistry), perceive its essence (cognitive systems, more biochemistry), and respond to it emotionally (glandular systems, blood pressure systems, and even more biochemistry). Now, we can see how interdependent all these elegant, individual systems rely on the presence of the others for anything to occur.

What is electromagnetism without the reality of chemistry? And what is chemistry without the basic principles of physics? And what is physics without the reality of mathematics? And what is mathematics without the presence of logic? And what is logic without the principles of biochemistry? And what is biochemistry without the presence of electromagnetism? The interdependencies are many and varied. All are needed for even one elegant system to work purely (and I use the term "elegant" in the scientific sense, meaning that these systems are ingenious, simple, yet complete). It's improbable to think that even one of these elegant systems was able to evolve alone apart from the others by sheer random possibility. But it is quite another for all these elegant systems to evolve intertwined as they are by mere randomness. The probability of such a thing is impossible to imagine because the probability of such a thing is incalculable. It's quite unreasonable for all this to have occurred without intelligence behind it. Now we run back to the basic idea of intelligent design.

Throughout history, many religious people have committed the logical sin of arguing "the god of the gaps" when something is not completely understood. What we mean by this is that religious people have routinely inserted God as an explanation for phenomena that lacked any known scientific evidence to explain the phenomena. A good example is lightning. Before we really understood the nature and cause of lightning, many religious people ascribed this quite natural phenomenon to the direct action of gods, like the ancient Greeks' Zeus, who sat in the heavens and with untamed anger chucked lightning bolts he obtained from the Cyclopes down on earth to express his resentments and wrath. We moderns know how lightning occurs and the natural systems at work to create its effect. We've removed lightning from the realm of a god-instigated action to a quite normal (or natural) occurrence like the changing colorations of a leaf in the autumn. Now that we look back at the religious explanation given to the phenomenon of lightning from Greek mythology, we are easily amused at their doctrines. It borders on the comic. But, to the ancient Greek, it was the best explanation based on the understanding of the material world they had at the time.

I do not want to be guilty of using the argument of god in the gaps in this situation either. Simply because we cannot at this moment explain how all these interdependent and interrelated elegant systems came into being does not necessarily prove that the existence of God is necessary for such a thing. What I want to focus on is the high improbability of it not being so.

There are many scientists and philosophers who equally sin in their thinking when they assume that if something can be explained quite naturally, as opposed to supernaturally, then God is not a necessary variable in the equation. This can also be just as misguided as the ancient Greeks' rather irrational stories of Zeus and lightning bolts. There are many effects at play to create naturally occurring, scientifically explainable phenomena, or secondary causes, that need a primary cause for them to exist or interact. Even if we were to develop a grand unifying theory of all these systems, as some are working around the clock to do, all of the originating effects will need a primary cause for them to be.

The improbability is quite large for any single elegant system, like bio-chemistry, to actually exist. Add to that the other necessary systems of elec-tromagnetism, gravity, inorganic chemistry—all of which are improbable in and of themselves—to be working together in a delightfully balanced re-lationship with each other, multiplies the improbability of it all many times over. In mathematical terms, it amounts to improbability times improb-ability times improbability times improbability. Therefore, the argument of "god of the gaps" doesn't even come into consideration. The mathematical improbabilities confound the rationalist in all of us. We cannot help but look to an explanation that makes the most sense of the data. These systems must have been created and put into place on purpose by an original, intel-ligent source. And that source is best described as God.

The genesis of this argument came from Norris Clarke. It's referred to as the argument from the interacting whole, meaning that all the interac-tions of systems and subsystems in nature are dependent on each other in order for them to function. When deeply considered, it makes the necessity of God even more palpable.

Therefore, it is more reasonable to say, "God exists."

QUESTION #9
If the universe is all there is, why is it understandable?

WHEN I WAS A KID, I loved playing with Legos. Now that I'm somewhat older, I don't think I'm allowed to play with them even though sometimes I'm very tempted to do so. Is it allowable for someone over forty years of age to play with Legos? I suspect that society would frown on this. I think I've been relegated to the level of putting together age-appropriate, thousand-piece puzzles (much more dignified, I guess) to scratch my Legos itch. Deep down inside, I still enjoy the thrill of spilling a gazillion plastic building blocks on the living room floor and having a go at building something monumental. It must be the kid still within me who wants to come out and play from time to time. (Quite personally, I think societal mores about grown men playing with Legos needs to be done away with. If all ages can enjoy ice cream, I think all ages should be able to enjoy building things with Legos. But, that's just my opinion.)

Imagine you are visiting a toy store and see in the window an exact replica of the Golden Gate Bridge built out of Legos. You're inspired. You decide you want to build the Golden Gate Bridge too. You go into the store and purchase a large collection of Legos to start your project. The box of Legos you purchase has a picture of the Golden Gate Bridge right on the front. You're sure you have the right box. When you get home, you open your box and you take inventory: you have plenty of red blocks to build the support beams and plenty of flat gray blocks to lay across to represent the roads. You even have thin Lego pieces to represent the crossbeams. But, you notice something is missing: there's nothing in the box to make the cables that support the bridge. You look at the inventory list of the blocks that are to be in the box and you see all the blocks that are supposed to be in the box actually are there. Your Lego collection simply didn't include string—nor did it ever intend for it to be there. It's not part of the Lego building blocks package you have. You now have a dilemma and must go purchase string in order to simulate the cables of the bridge. Frustrating.

Materialists today believe the universe that we find ourselves in is all there is. There is nothing more. Any idea of something more is fantastical, wishful thinking. There is nothing outside of nature. Nothing *super*-natural, if you will. If there were, it has no bearing on our existence or on the functioning of matter. We are in this "closed" system. There is nothing more, nothing less.

So, what does this closed system we call the universe look like? Well, we know it is made up of matter. If you are holding this book, or you are viewing it on some electronic book reader, the fact that there is matter in this universe is self-evident enough. Just pinch yourself and you will empirically prove that matter exists in the universe. But, what is the state of this matter? What can we know about it? If the universe "randomly combusted" from a seminal atom as scientists best understand it, and if evolution spawned life by chance occurrences as the materialists argue, then our "box" we have dubbed as the "universe" is filled with random matter. Nothing more. And, if there is no intelligent force, or person, who has designed this inexplicable collection of matter, then this random matter's behavior must also be dictated by the same effects of randomness. By the very nature of their arguments, the materialists unwittingly pre-suppose that the universe can be consistently observed and understood even though randomness totally dominates this system.

But, is that even a reasonable position to hold? What I mean by reasonable is this: my ability to intelligently grasp and form reliable, non-random judgments and detect consistent, non-random patterns from the world as I experience it. As I look into the universe, I see many things that are quite intelligible: observations that are reliable and consistent. In fact, the scientific method (as applied by thinkers throughout history such as Roger Bacon, Galileo, and René Descartes) relies heavily on the ability to reliably and consistently infer from observable data truths about the world we live in. Therefore, if the scientific method has any merit, it must be free of randomness itself looking at something free of randomness in order to work properly. A system dictated by mere randomness would never allow us to experiment, observe, conclude, and verify as needed by the scientific method. Ironically, it's this same scientific method that materialists have used to postulate its idea of this closed system called the universe filled with random matter. The scientific method is obviously not a random grouping of randomness. There is intelligence, reliable and consistent knowledge, as part of it. And the ability for any of us to think intelligently about it defies the materialists' notion of the universe as being all there is. As C.S. Lewis recalls a quote from Professor Haldane: "If my mental processes are determined wholly by the motions of atoms in my brain, I have no reason to suppose that my beliefs are true . . . and hence I have no reason for supposing my brain to be composed of atoms."

Just as with the Lego model of the Golden Gate Bridge, we find string in the universe (intelligence) that isn't included in the materialists' box of materials: a random collection of matter that has evolved quite randomly. So, where did this string come from? It must have come from somewhere outside the box—from some source outside nature. Therefore, it must be *super*natural. Throughout history, intelligent, sentient beings called men have called this supernatural force "God." This force must possess some form of intelligence because we see it at work in the universe. The presence of intelligence is best explained as having its source come from outside the material world. To make the point even more remarkable, man, by some action instigated apart from the material world, has been given this sense of intelligence (reasoning ability) innately—almost as if he/she were created with the intent of bearing a remarkable semblance to this intelligent, *super*natural being. (Sounds eerily familiar, doesn't it?)[7]

I call this argument the, "I think, therefore God must exist" argument. If you want to know more, this argument is much better articulated by Peter

---

7   This could also explain cosmologists' fascination with the notion of the Anthropic Principle that suggests that a physical world capable of sustaining life must also be compatible with conscious life that observes it. It is merely a back-door argument to a more fundamental argument of a Creator creating the universe expressly for the creation of a conscious life. They both converge on the same reality rather nicely, don't you think?

Kreeft and Robert Tacelli in their *Handbook of Christian Apologetics*. Also, if you want to dive deep, spend some time with C.S. Lewis in the third chapter of his miraculous book, *Miracles*. If you want to know what Lewis had to say on the matter, my best advice is to read C.S. Lewis directly. I don't think I can adequately summarize his insight into this argument, which his is a far richer argument than the argument I just put before you. But I hope you get the point. Intelligence is a signature left in the universe that clues us in on what is really happening all around us. There are bigger things at work than we could ever explain from the bottom of our petri dishes.

Therefore, it is more reasonable to say, "God exists."

QUESTION #10
If our minds are temporal, why are there eternal truths?

"HOW DO WE KNOW WHAT we know? And how do we know that we know it?" For most people who are busy living life and scratching out an existence, these two questions border on the absurd. They are questions not worth thinking about. If you were to walk along the suburbs of Boston and pose these questions to people outside their favorite Dunkin' Donuts shop, they'd look at you as if you were loony at best, and at worst, they'd think you were itchin' for a fight. And they'd have good cause to think so. They'd probably respond (with a slight degree of irritation for the inconvenience), "I know something when I know it. What's the big deal? Now, leave me alone and go pester someone else!"

There are others who dedicate their lives to the study of how we gain knowledge. These wonderful yet sometimes strange people call this area of inquiry *epistemology*. It's the science of knowing. And it is a field of study that dedicates itself to the question, "How do we know stuff?" Even though most of us never need to get to that granular level of understanding, these people are doing us a whole lot of good. They are learning how it is that we learn, and, consequently, how to make us better at it.

There are certain things we all know that we know. These are the big, eternal truths that appear throughout human history and span all human cultures. This understanding of knowing can be traced all the way back to Plato and beyond. But, I think we all realize this, even if we are not trained philosophers. It's just a part of us. There are ideas and concepts that simply appear within each of us that can only be explained this way: they are those things we already know deep within ourselves without the need of societal input. One of these ideas is that of fair play. Every child knows it well. Observe children at play. Watch two toddler boys play with a toy truck together in a sandbox and, within a moment or two, you will suddenly hear the phrase, "That's not fair!" screamed in frustration by the one who wants the toy but doesn't have it. Where did that toddler get the notion of fair play?

And every adult, whether we practice it personally or not, knows the value of fair play too. We look at any person who does not practice fair play as deviant from a norm. It is a concept of human behavior we do not seem to have (or have demonstrated or modeled) in society. It's just there within us. It's not simply a behavioral quirk we carry within our DNA like breathing or the desire to stand on our own two feet and walk. "Fair play" has exceptional value that goes beyond the proper functioning of a proper human. Most of us would simply give credence to it, roughly classify it as an eternal truth of the nature of things, and leave it at that.

But the reality of this eternal truth, among the many other eternal truths that are present, has significant ramifications for the materialist. If we believe that what is in the universe is all there is, then we must also view the individual human as something temporary in this world, which all materialists necessarily conclude. We are here for a short time, and then we die and are no more. But this eternal truth is here. It keeps popping up. It's a truth that is not temporal even though our minds, which contain that truth, are temporal. We are born with a mind, we live, and then we die with a mind. And, according to the materialist, our minds die with our bodies. Our brains turn back into dust, and we are no more.

During our temporal existence, we have this knowledge of eternal truths. These truths are inconvenient to the materialist because they do not fit into their prescribed worldview. These eternal truths must then come from some mind that is not temporal, but eternal. And the only eternal, existing mind that can contain these eternal truths is best described as the supernatural God we keep ending up with.

Therefore, it is more reasonable to say, "God exists."

QUESTION #11
How did we end up with this notion of God anyway?

THIS IS A FASCINATING ARGUMENT. We have to credit René Descartes for his effort in putting this one together. It's a rather simple argument, but profound. When I first considered it, I rejected it out of hand as being wrong on some indeterminate level. It was too simple. And, because of its simplicity, it could not be relevant in dealing with such a weighty issue as the existence of God. But, the more I think on it, the more interesting an argument it becomes. Here's the basic gist of it:

The mind of man is full of ideas. These ideas, man has come by rather honestly. He sees something, thinks about it, sometimes even draws conclusions about it, and forms new ideas from it. Yet, all these ideas that man generates have some basis of experience attached to them. In other words, in the realm of ideas, there's really nothing new under the sun. For instance, say we are a product designer for a furniture manufacturer. We are tasked to come up with new ideas for furniture to take to market. We think about a new, funky design for a chair (a design no one else on the planet has ever come up with!), and we're convinced it is going to revolutionize the chair business. Everybody is going to want one of these fantastic chairs. But we got this idea from the experiences we already know. It's a new chair, but it's a chair nonetheless, based on an accumulation of ideas that have occurred to us as we have experienced life over time.

If we were to take all the newest breakthroughs in genetic engineering, cell phone technology, nuclear fusion, modern music, and even space travel, we could quite easily trace the knowledge we have in any of these areas back to simple experiences man has accumulated over the eons. We simply have to ask a series of questions like, "Where did Francis Collins get the ideas he had about mapping the human genome? And where did those ideas come from?" and so on. If we were to reverse-engineer all of Francis Collins' ideas, we would end up with a collection of experiences that he has had over the course of his life.

What's curious about the existence of God is that, if he does not exist, and we have no experience with such an otherworldly, *super*natural force like this to begin with, then where did we get this idea of God in the first place? If ideas come from experience, and if this material world is all we've ever experienced, how is it that, all throughout human history, we have had grand ideas of an all-powerful, all-good, and ever-present God? It's impossible, if we were to take the purely materialistic approach to man's understanding. There would never be an experience for us to conceive of such an idea. Yet, as is painfully obvious to all of us, the notion of the idea of God does exist. Even the atheists would admit to that. That's their biggest beef with the world—all these crazy religious zealots have this notion of a God that human experience doesn't ever tell us exists. Why would ancient man blame lightning on the god Zeus if the experience of a god had never given rise to such an idea? It's inconceivable from the worldview of the materialist. Therefore, using strict logic, God must exist.

Therefore, it is more reasonable to say, "God exists."

QUESTION #12
If the idea of God is that he's greater than anything we can think of, then doesn't God have to be real?

THIS IS ST. ANSELM'S FAMOUS "ontological argument" that is famous for both its philosophical acuity and its originality. In virtually every Christian apologetics textbook, homage is given to Anselm's argument as a basis for proving the existence of God. It's an interesting argument but is not without its weaknesses. Let's take a closer look at it. Peter Kreeft, in his book *Handbook of Christian Apologetics,* summarizes it in this way:

1. It is greater for a thing to exist in the mind *and* in reality than in the mind alone.
2. "God" means "that than which a greater cannot be thought."
3. Suppose that God exists in the mind but not in reality.
4. Then a greater than God *could* be thought (namely, a being that has all the qualities our thought of God has *plus* real existence).
5. But this is impossible, for God is "that than which a greater cannot be thought."
6. Therefore, God exists in the mind and in reality.

It's hard to find anyone who would deny that the idea of God does not exist. I think even the most strident atheist will have to admit that there is this idea of God out there and that the idea is fairly consistent in its general definition from language to language, culture to culture, and people to people. I think it would be difficult for any historical anthropologist who would reduce the idea of God to a small idea like a hamster or a ham sandwich. Even if the idea of God might be as multi-variant as the Greek polytheists and the Hindu deities, all would still say they have a general idea of God, or gods, in their minds. And it would be that their conception of God, or gods, would be that of a being that no greater can be thought.

There is a foundational assumption at the beginning of this argument that physically existing things are of a higher value than things that only exist in the mind. For the purely materialist argument, I think there would be no need to argue against this. I don't think any of us, no matter how we are bent philosophically, would feel compelled to make much of an argument against this. Reality is better than mere thoughts. Thoughts may be imaginative and fantastical, stimulating strong emotive responses from us, but a real thing ultimately possesses more value. For example, the idea of a unicorn would be eclipsed in value if we were to discover on some small Pacific island there actually existed unicorns. We would all naturally say that the imaginative value of a unicorn doesn't seem so attractive when we find out that a unicorn actually exists. Santa Claus, if actually delivering Christmas presents by sleigh on Christmas Eve night, is infinitely more valuable than a fable of a Santa Claus in a pop-up picture book. (Just ask any five-year-old if he or she would agree that a *real* Santa is better than the idea of a Santa!)

So, we combine the two thoughts above together: (1) God is that then which a greater cannot be thought and (2) that which exists in the mind and in reality is greater than that which is in the mind alone. From this combination, we end up with a God that exists in the mind only cannot be the greatest thought about God. A God that exists in the mind and in reality is greater. Therefore, God is greatest when he exists both in the mind and in reality. Therefore, God must exist.

For most of us, this is fairly obtuse. I must admit it seems to be more about chasing words around than actual truth, but it does have an interesting notion to it that is directional at least. God as a concept, then, is greatest when it is both in the mind and in reality, not just in the mind alone. Anselm's argument is less than convincing for me, but it is affirming when taken with other evidences like those that we have already discussed. I don't think I would be convinced by this argument if it were the only one directed toward the proof of God's existence. Fortunately for the theists, there are other good arguments. Unfortunately for the materialistic atheists and agnostics, there are other good arguments that must be honestly considered. I am finding the preponderances of proofs of God's existence beginning to pile up on the terribly compelling side. And I'm finding the arguments against the existence of God thinning. Anselm does give us something to think about here. And it's making it harder and harder for me to accept the materialist perspective that this material world is all that there is. There has to be more. And it's more than an imagined more. It's a real more—existing not only in our overactive imaginations, but also in the material reality that surrounds us and fills our realm of experience.

Therefore, it is more reasonable to say, "God exists."

QUESTION #13
Why do I feel compelled to act morally?

THERE IS A MORAL COMPULSION lodged within the consciousness of each one of us. Some say the moral obligation we feel is simply a matter of self-interested organisms (man) meting out a social contract with all other self-interested organisms for the purpose of improving the odds for a happier, more tolerable life. Those people believe that morality has no other function than for a community-dependent species like *homo sapiens* to best achieve its main aims: survival and happiness. I can see the underlying merit of their argument. Many of our moral acts can be comfortably categorized under this theory of human behavior.

We all feel compelled to act morally. And when we don't act according to our morals, or we experience others who do not comply with this rather vague and often unspoken notion of morality, we feel the prick of conscience. We either internally stew over it or lash out in outrage, "Unfair!" or "That's not right!" To see this phenomenon in full bloom, all you have to do is spend a bit of time listening to talk radio, watching a daytime soap opera, or watching reality television for just a few minutes. Or, even better, just gather around the coffee pot at your office. After a brief conversation about weather and traffic, most conversations quickly begin to sink into the muck of observed immoral behaviors of others. And when the moral failure is ours, we have a natural defense mechanism to deal with it: making excuses. C.S. Lewis in *Mere Christianity* observed,

> Heaven knows I do not pretend to be better than anyone else. I am only trying to call attention to a fact; the fact that this year, or this month, or, more likely, this very day, we have failed to practise ourselves the kind of behaviour we expect from other people. There may be all sorts of excuses for us . . . The point is that they [our excuses] are one more proof of how deeply, whether we like it or not, we believe in the Law of Nature. If we do not believe in decent behaviour, why should we be so anxious to make excuses for not having behaved decently? The truth is, we believe in decency so much—we feel the Rule of Law pressing on us so—that we cannot bear to face the fact that we are breaking it, and consequently we try to shift the responsibility.

Lewis nailed it. What Lewis dubs "the Law of Nature" is the same moral law we have been talking about. The tug of morality runs very deep within every human. It spreads across culture and time. And, even though there may be slight colorings of what constitutes moral behavior from community to community, the overwhelming weight of moral consistency is plain to see. Probably the best I've read on the subject, Lewis makes this point of moral consistency very convincingly in the opening chapters of *Mere Christianity*. Regardless of race, sex, religion, language, or location, moral expectations and laws will be much more similar in content than they will differ. We see it in humans from their earliest years all the way through to their dying days. It's inarguable that a hidden moral code is latent within all of us. The big question is, "Where does this idea of morality come from? And why is it so similar between varying people groups?"

Historically, the default answer to why we feel morally obligated has been because of religion. For most philosophers, scientists, and moral sophists who have observed human behavior from the beginning of recorded history, they have universally agreed that morality's origins lie in religion. Yet, recently, we are seeing philosophers, and even some theologians, begin to question this. As mentioned earlier, some are now concluding that morality is an idea necessitated by evolution that allows community living to be possible. Their conclusion is that morality is subject to the need for harmony in order for man to preserve his selfish need to exist and live well. Others say it is more elemental than that. That it is in the physiology and chemistry of the human brain that generates morality. Sam Harris, a noted philosopher, makes this case in his book, *The Moral Landscape*. Harris makes some pointed arguments in his book in defense of his premise, but I must say it appears he's more interested in wrenching morality away from religion than from any attempt to place it elsewhere. Harris chooses to soften the definition of science in order to accomplish his task by trying to bend scientific inquiry to accommodate the exploration of morality. He is successful in doing so to a limited degree, but his intent on blaming religion for all that's wrong with morality is his obvious blind spot. Sure, there have been, and continue to be, many moral problems within religion. But, there are many moral problems outside of religion too. Sure, many atheists seem to be quite decent folk who seem to behave in a more moral way than many we might call "religious nuts." But that's just confusing the issue. There are two ideas battling within Harris' line of reasoning: first off, the absolute moral claims of religion and secondly, the practice of that religion by imperfect people. Sam Harris depreciates the moral claims of religion by the observed abuses of religious teachings by its so-called followers. If we all were honest, we would have to admit to observing a huge difference between what a religion teaches and how that religion is practiced. Harris' two arguments must be analyzed independently. If not, we may make some false assumptions about truth and reality.

Both religious and nonreligious people behave quite immorally from time to time. I wish it were not so, but it is. In fact, the first time I saw how badly Christians around me behaved, I reacted by pulling away from the Christian faith of my youth. And, as is also common with humans, I'm sure I wasn't seeing my own bad behavior very clearly. I'm sure I viewed the situation from a slanted perspective. All of us do. But whether or not religion were present, we would be stuck with the exact same problem: humans will behave badly. So, I do not accept the wholesale diminution of religion just because man is an idiot. Man can be equally cruel and immoral without religion.

So that leaves us with the question of analyzing whether morality is a by-product of religion (regardless of man's meat-headed practicing of religion) or whether it is something that's simply hardwired into our biochemical makeup. We all can agree we all feel a sense of morality—and that idea of morality is rather consistent between humans. For example, we all possess a sense of fair play and place value on honesty, loyalty, and honor. We believe that intentionally killing another human is not good. We know we should be sensitive to the needs of weaker people, like children and the elderly.

And we believe that we should not do anything that harms another. These elemental concepts of right and wrong, among others, resonate within each of us, regardless of language, creed, geography, sex, century, or race.

In the same way, we also can agree that man will behave immorally, or against our moral nature, from time to time and in varying degrees. But, here is where I become stuck with the "morality is just a product of biological impulses" idea: we hold onto morality as a very high standard in our minds, and yet we do not actually live by that morality. I can't think of another situation where man acts in a similar fashion. For example, we all know we need to eat. That impulse is biological. But any normally functioning human doesn't go around refusing to eat for no apparent reason when given a reasonable access to food. If we did meet such a person who refused to eat, we would quickly peg him or her as having aberrant behavior and treat it as a sickness. Along the same line, we all know we need sleep. But most of us don't try to avoid sleep for no apparent reason, either. Yet, we have this thing called morality that some claim is biological. Yet, we don't really obey its moral impulses as consistently as we do with food and sleep. We act against our moral impulses—not just occasionally, but regularly. We lie. We act selfishly. We don't help someone who is in need when we can. We take advantage of other people. In summary, we regularly do not live according to our "moral nature." I'm not sure the idea of a biological impulse towards morality really holds water. It doesn't fit the preponderance of empirical evidence.

Religion states that God has implanted a moral code within each of us by his design. And because of original sin, that moral compass within us is broken, and we tend to act against our own moral nature. That thought is better explained in Christianity and Judaism than in any other major religion. Many of us quite routinely know we ought to behave in such a way, but we find ourselves quite incapable of reaching that high level of morality. The moral code within us is calling us to a moral responsibility that is so much higher than we observe or experience in ourselves and the people around us. It is a moral imperative that comes from without, not within. Even so, we still feel this itching within us whenever we see an act of immorality—and we know such an act to be immoral right there on the spot. Yet, we suppress this moral compunction within us and act against it repeatedly, leaving us feeling out of sorts with our true selves and the world we think should be, even though we realize that it is not. This internally implanted moral code leaves us conflicted unlike anything else we see around us. It is the cause for most of our anxieties and stress and, if we were truly honest with ourselves, it is the leading reason so many people feel the need for therapy and self-help groups. We do not live up to the very nature we call human. And it is slowly killing us. Those who say morality is just another biological phenomenon—as is hunger, sleep, breathing, and so on—are not opening their mind to all the evidence. From what we can observe, morality is best explained as coming from some place other—from some place outside this natural realm. It is best understood as something supernatural from an external source like God.

Therefore, it is more reasonable to say, "God exists."

QUESTION #14
Why do I have a conscience?

CONSCIENCE IS NOT JUST SOMETHING I choose to have. It is there. I feel its presence every day. And so do you. We know when we have violated our conscience because we are overtaken by a bitter stew of ugly emotions and self-belittlement that can paralyze us if we allow ourselves to dwell on it. For all the calls to moral subjectivism within our postmodern culture, the power of the individual conscience still holds strong within us. It's one part of a subjectivist's worldview that remains firmly absolute: no one should ever act in violation with his conscience, no matter how subjective morality becomes within a community. Regardless of your chosen moral code, it is universally understood that you should never act against your individual conscience. This doctrine of proper behavior can be seen in most popular novels, movies, self-help books, TV shows, and music. The conscience is a sacred diadem crowning the individuality within each of us.

But, what is this thing called conscience? And where does it get its power to upset us so? For the materialist, it should be viewed as enigmatic. As Peter Kreeft and Ronald Tacelli put it,

> If we are the products of a good and loving Creator, this explains why we have a nature that discovers a value that is really there. But how can atheists explain this? For if atheists are right, then no objective moral values can exist. Dostoyevsky said, "If God does not exist, everything is permissible." Atheists may know that some things are not permissible, but they do not know why.

Conscience is an absolute call to the absolute. Even though our call of conscience may be different from one person to the next, the call itself is an absolute principle that must be protected absolutely. No matter how morally relativistic any of us may be, we snap and sneer at anyone who would act against their own conscience as being untrue and untrustworthy. If my conscience told me to live deliberately on the shoreline of Walden Pond as Thoreau did and yet I chose to abrogate that call of conscience and pursue a soul-emptying corporate job instead, any moral relativist and absolutist would lash out at me with equal venom, proclaiming me to be a "sell-out" and a person of weak moral character. I did not act in accordance with my conscience. It is the plot line of most blockbuster movies probably showing now at your local cineplex.

We see the rare person acting in accordance with a moral code and personal conscience, and we readily acknowledge that person as ethical, right, and good. Who among us would not look at the life of Mother Teresa or Dorothy Day and not admire these women for acting in an honorable way in accordance with their personal consciences? Don't we celebrate heroes like this? Isn't that why we admire historical figures like Spartacus, St. Francis of Assisi, William Wallace, Abraham Lincoln, and Martin Luther King, Jr.? Are they not people who lived a life of personal sacrifice for the sake of an ideal that was firmly planted within the soil of their consciences? And isn't it their call of conscience that attracts us so?

But this call to conscience clashes with the relativistic worldview. It is a call each individual gets from without himself. It is a metaphysical "goodness" and a "rightness" our souls resonate with when we get even the briefest glimpse of it. It transcends the natural. It is bigger than the individual. It cannot be borrowed from the normal functioning of community. It is neither an inevitable nor an unexpected by-product of evolutionary forces. It is from some other place—something outside of us and our world. It is bigger than we are. It is built from ideals that are beyond us. They are ideals so big we use them to judge even the behavior of the gods by. Socrates pungently makes that point in Plato's *Euthyphro*. But, is there anything that big that is beyond this world? Nothing? Something? This call of conscience is a call from beyond. And there must be something beyond from which that call must come.

Therefore, it is more reasonable to say, "God exists."

QUESTION #15
Why does man have this desire for God?

WHETHER YOU ARE A SHRILL atheist or a dogmatic theist, it's hardly worth denying that in general man has an innate desire for God: to know him and live a life worthy of him as best we can. Some of us have concluded that we can no longer hold onto the concept of a transcendent God in our world-view, but we must acknowledge there is something about the idea of God that we desire to know. We may say that the idea of God is a mere figment of an uninformed yet highly imaginative mind. We may even conclude that this God idea may be a sinister mechanism to control and manipulate others to one's selfish will, as religion has been accused of. But one thing is sure. This idea of God is out there, and our desire to understand him is actual.

Human desire is a simple thing. We see or imagine something, and then we want it. Some of our desire is biological. Our bodies crave things. Our desire for food is there because we know food exists and it satisfies a craving that is real. Our desire for sex works in similar ways. We desire sex because we know that sexuality is real and it slakes urges for the "otherness" and "connectedness" we all feel as it relates to sexual activity. Our desire for wealth is because we know that money exists and that privileged lifestyles may result from the accumulation of wealth. Our desire for friendship is because we know that human relationships satisfy our desires to feel wanted and included in a community of other humans. In fact, we could list every possible desire humans have ever had, and can have, and we will be able to attach that desire to a real thing that can satisfy that desire. We are even able to attach fantastic dreams and imaginative desires to real things. We want to have the super powers of Superman because we know that flying is possible even though "flying through the air with the greatest of ease" is not possible for humans naturally.

But, can you think of even one example of a desire we have for something that we do not have any concrete connections with? I can't. This takes us back to the desire for God, which we've already established is present in massive quantities among humans of all times and cultures. If God does not exist, nor has he ever existed (which materialists emphatically argue), then why do we have this desire for him? Is he simply a fantasy of a bigger and bolder heavenly Father that we've dreamed of based on the reality of our own earthly fathers? Hardly so. Because we are desiring a person so wholly other from a merely imagined super-father. This God, by our own definition, is above and beyond the material world. And our desire for him is because he is exactly that. If we have no experience with anything outside of our material world, how is it that we created this one desire? It defies what we know about all other human desires.

Every time we look into the beauty of a sunset, or Monet's painting of a haystack, or the attractive face and figure of another human being, our souls sweetly ache for a beauty yet fully known. The glorious counterpoints of Bach, the grace notes of a Miles Davis trumpet solo, and the punctuated rhythms of Japanese war drums echo from a world that is more real than reality itself. And our spirits climb to a place we've never known but that possesses the comfort of our most intimate secrets and passions. It is these desires based on something we cannot point to in our current reality that defy the normal flow of human desire. They are the desire that springs from transcendency. They are the desire for the great otherness of another world. No matter what we call them—yearnings, inklings, or desires—they are no less real. And their reality is derived from an even greater realness. For they are the deflected desires of a created human to know his Creator God.

Therefore, it is more reasonable to say, "God exists."

QUESTION #16
Why are there so many who claim to have had a religious experience?

SOME WOULD SAY IT'S A simple collective of deluded, psychotic behaviors. So many people, whether they are from India, China, Tunisia, or the United States, claim to have "experienced the divine." What is this anyway? How can so many people have similar experiences that are based on an untruth? Why is it that you can dig back into the annals of history of every culture and find people speaking openly and glowingly about religious experiences? It's next to impossible to find a place and time where religious experiences have not been claimed by humans.

Are all these people simply crazy? If God is simply a figment of an overactive imagination, how can so many people be so terribly wrong? I know this argument can be split apart quite easily through logical analysis, but the obvious is still out there: if there is no God, then we as a human race are more mixed up and touched in the head than we could ever imagine. Religion and religious experience has been testified to over and over again. I'm thinking there is some weight to this collection of observable and verifiable data. It may not be a complete destruction of materialistic assumptions made by the atheist, but it's definitely something.

Therefore, it is more reasonable to say, "God exists."

QUESTION #17
Why do so many people believe in God?

YOU WILL RECOGNIZE THIS AS similar to the last argument, but with a slight recoloring. So many people have believed in God and currently believe in God. In fact, there are only a few throughout all of human history who have not believed in God. Because some are quite vocal about their atheism, it's easy to think there are more atheists out there than there actually are. If you slip into a typical coffee shop or bus station, you will find that most people you encounter have some belief that a God exists. In fact, some social pollsters in the United States estimate that 98.5% of all Americans believe in the existence of some kind of God. That means only 1.5% say there is no God. If you think about it, it's rather arrogant for some of these virulent atheists out there to denigrate the collective beliefs of so many over so many generations. But they do.

I know truth cannot be determined through the democratic process. There are countless times when majorities have been wrong. But never has there been such widespread wrongness on this mass scale. And how could such a terrible deception carry on for so long among so many people? The fact that there are so many who do believe in God—and have since the very beginning of recorded history—doesn't that have some kind of evidentiary value? I think it does. At least it should require us to be doubly diligent before making an over-generalization against the existence of a God. Coincidental value, yes, but value nonetheless. Even though it's not a full proof of God's existence, I think it lends strength to more formal and rational arguments.

Therefore, it is more reasonable to say, "God exists."

QUESTION #18
Why is there the music of Bach?

I WILL QUOTE PETER KREEFT directly on this argument: "There is the music of Johann Sebastian Bach. Therefore, there must be a God. Either you see this one [argument] or you don't."

Kreeft's point is rather simple. There are aesthetic realities that just simply have to be from another world. They are just too beautiful to be from this one. If music as glorious as Bach's music exists, there must be a God behind all this creative imagination. If you need further proof of this, listen to some Bach music. I think you will see how compelling of an argument this may actually be. But it's an argument that cannot be contained in books like this. It has to be experienced to be understood.

Therefore, it is more reasonable to say, "God exists."

QUESTION #19
Considering the alternative. why wouldn't I believe in God?

THIS IS ONE OF MY favorite arguments. It's called Pascal's Wager because it was first articulated by the great French mathematician Blaise Pascal. He first posited this argument in order to break the stalemate between rational arguments against the existence of God and rational arguments for the existence of God. If you are unconvinced one way or the other, Pascal presents you a thought that's less of an argument but is efficiently practical. According to Pascal, there are four conditions in which you can find yourself:

1. God doesn't exist and you believe that God exists.
2. God doesn't exist and you do not believe that God exists.
3. God exists and you believe that God exists.
4. God exists and you do not believe that God exists.

In conditions #2 and #3, you believe correctly with reality. In conditions #1 and #4, your belief is not correctly aligned with reality. Now, if we do not know with certainty whether God exists or doesn't exist, we must look at the potential outcomes of being in each of the four conditions. If we agree with Aristotle that man's ultimate good is *eudaimonia*, or happiness (which every one of us, if we were honest with ourselves, would agree that happiness is what we all strive for), let's see which of these four outcomes leads us to that ultimate good.

Condition #1: God doesn't exist and you believe that God exists. This would make you a person who sincerely believes in something that is not true. Many atheists look at religious people today and consider them to be in this condition. But what happens to a religious person when there is no existing God as the object of his perceived faith? If we take happiness as the aim of our lives, we find out the religious person ends up okay. One thing that has been proven by psychologists is that religious people tend to be happier with life than nonreligious people. Yes, as a religious person, you may sacrifice some opportunities to have "fun" by not feeling beholden to act religiously and righteously under the scrutiny of a make-believe deity, but, overall, you are happy. And your happiness is deeply felt and enjoyed.

Condition #2: God doesn't exist and you do not believe that God exists. This would make you an atheist who has concluded rightly that God does not exist. This is where most atheists see their condition. They are generally happy, even though many still feel the pangs of not knowing whether they are truly right or not. It feels like there is still some possibility they could be wrong. But, overall, the happiness and freedom many atheists enjoy bring them the happiness they are ultimately seeking, so no harm done with this condition. When you die, you die and no further reckoning in an afterlife is there to worry you. You achieve the happiness you seek in the here and now.

Condition #3: God exists and you believe that God exists. This would make you a religious person who sincerely believes in a very real God. In terms of Christianity, your belief in the very real Creator God as revealed through Jesus Christ in the Bible ushers you into not only a blessed life in this world, but also the promise of a glorious eternity in God's presence in heaven where there are streets paved with gold. Your happiness is available to you now and forever. You do not lose out in this condition.

Condition #4: God exists and you do not believe that God exists. This would make you an atheist who sincerely believes in something that is not true. In this condition, God does exist, however. In keeping with orthodox Christian teaching, you would find yourself at odds with the life God calls all people to live. Your happiness may be with you in this life because, as an atheist, you can still live your life on your terms. You can remain deluded that you have no higher Other to contend with, namely God. But, your day of reckoning comes when you die. Because the God of Christianity demands belief in him in order for you to enjoy heaven and not be sent to a terrorizing existence in hell, you find your happiness in the afterlife not attainable. You lose out. Instead of enjoying eternal life in heaven, you find yourself suffering in the fires of hell for eternity. It is only this condition that has a negative outcome. All other outcomes end in happiness in one form or another.

So, only one question remains: are you willing to take the risk and not believe? Or are you going with the sure bet: if you believe in God, you can only win. If you do not believe in God, you're rolling the proverbial dice. But you are not simply risking chump change at a Las Vegas casino; you are putting your eternal soul at risk. Pascal, the consummate mathematician, thinks it's a sucker bet. Go with the probability, he says. Go with the sure win. Believe in God. To not believe in God is downright stupid.

Now, some argue that this wager doesn't produce saving faith as is described in orthodox Christian doctrine. But, if the Christian God does exist, his personality as described in the Bible will work with even a feebly motivated faith based on the wager. He can work with even that little speck of faith, even if it is only the size of a mustard seed.

Therefore, it is more reasonable to say, "God exists."

QUESTION #20
Why are there miracles?

MIRACLES, BY DEFINITION, ARE EVENTS that fall outside of natural laws. They are *super*natural events. Most atheists and agnostics believe that miracles do not exist. Theists affirm that not only are miracles possible, but they have happened. There are even still a brave few who assert that miracles are still happening today, that they aren't merely an ancient collection of inexplicable happenings that ancient man recorded.

When we talk of miracles here, we are not talking about miracles in the common parlance like when we refer to the 1969 "Miracle Mets" or the 1980 hockey game between the USA and the USSR that was called the "Miracle on Ice." Even though these two sports stories were extraordinary indeed, I don't think anyone has referred to these events as being *super*natural, where physical laws of this universe were either bent or broken during the course of these events happening. They were amazing, even shocking, stories. They defied the odds. And they are now permanent members of sports folklore.

The miracles we are referring to in this discussion are those events that actually did bend or break physical laws. They are called miraculous because the universe split open for a brief moment and something outside this universe inserted extraordinary power, defying natural law to make a point. If God is who many theists believe he is, then the miraculous is as "natural" to him as nature itself. If God created the material world, and he exists beyond it, then it is only plausible that he can come inside of his creation and mess with it anytime he likes. As the painter Georges Seurat is to his painting, *A Sunday Afternoon on the Island of La Grande Jatte*, God is to his universe. Inside that Seurat painting, we see people enjoying a sunny day by the water. Those characters Seurat created are bound inside that painting with no ability to go outside of it or interact with anything outside of it. If Seurat would like to change the painting and add another boat to the water, he can do so. He can paint a character out of existence, or turn her into a tree, or he could even add another two characters as he saw fit. It's completely within his discretion as the creator of the painting. It'd be absurd for his characters in his painting to rise up and protest, "You can't do that! Those kinds of actions cannot be predicted by what's already here in this painting! It's impossible what you are doing!" Well, from the point of view of the Seurat characters, their outrage is completely understandable. They probably don't even know who Seurat is unless Seurat decides to reveal himself to them. His painted characters have no concept of what Seurat is capable of. Their "world" doesn't account for Seurat having the ability to paint in new things on the canvas or painting over things at his discretion. Their "natural world" cannot predict such supernatural capriciousness. Which leads us back to God . . .

According to theists, we are God's created characters. We know the painting we are in, like Seurat's characters, and can see how our natural world functions as it currently works. Our practical means of knowing God's painting techniques resides in mathematics, physics, chemistry, biology, psychology, and so on. If God decides to change things from outside his painting, the universe, to perform a task beyond our means of understanding what exists, who are we to tell him he cannot do such a thing?

Miracles serve as a deal-breaker for many agnostics and atheists. Miracles cannot be possible because the natural order of things cannot account for them. How can a man live in the belly of a great fish for three days? How can a snake talk? How can Jesus feed five thousand people with only five loaves and two fish? And how can Jesus bodily raise himself back to life from being a dead corpse in a tomb? These acts, or miracles, defy our understanding of the painting. "God, you can't do that—it's impossible!" they yell.

But do miracles actually happen? Or can all miracles be explained by natural means if given enough time to explore and understand the phenomena? Materialists say no to the first question and yes to the second. Materialists then conclude that all the miracles cataloged in the holy writings of religion are the result of overactive imaginations of people who just didn't have the tools to explain odd phenomena with ordinary natural means. If they had the scientific understanding we have now, they could have explained as "natural" all the events these ancient theists erroneously classified as supernatural—or miraculous.

Atheistic or agnostic materialists simply deny that miracles are possible. The laws of this universe are fixed. They cannot by manipulated from within. Nor can they be manipulated from without. What is, is what is. For the theist, who may choose to argue that God is capable of interjecting himself into his creation and defying his own natural laws, miracles are possible and, indeed, have occurred throughout the course of history. To God, bending light is as natural as not bending light. Stopping the normal rotation of the earth around the sun is as natural to God as designing nature in such a way that the earth quite naturally rotates around the sun. Miracles are nothing but fingerprints of a God involved in human history and interested in the affairs of his creation.

In the case of Christianity and Islam, faith depends on miracles to be true. Christianity is nothing if Jesus of Nazareth is not the Son of God, who miraculously arose bodily from the tomb by his own volition. And Islam is nothing if the Qur'an is not a miraculous revelation from Allah to Muhammad. Both faiths are bolted to the miraculous. In the case of Christianity, which seems to be the most defensible and believable faith of all that are out there, the miracle of Jesus Christ's resurrection is the ultimate dealmaker or deal-breaker. It's a dealmaker if Jesus actually did bodily raise from the dead. It's a deal-breaker if he didn't. All it takes is one miracle— one!—for God's existence to be inevitable. If one miracle has occurred in all of human history, the materialist has nothing to grasp. It proves there is something beyond creation. God must exist for a miracle to occur.

Yet, many hard-nosed materialists say, "Give any 'miracle' time and science will irrefutably disprove it." And they have a point. There are many proclaimed miracles throughout history that have been successfully disproved. Yet, some still remain and have not been disproven yet. The probability of ultimately disproving these unproven "miracles" is highly likely, though.

But, still, all it takes is just one true miracle for God to exist. When it comes to Christianity, I don't think there's a better miracle to hold onto than the miracle of the bodily resurrection of a very dead Jesus Christ from the tomb. If Jesus did arise from the dead and is alive today in bodily form as the Christians claim, then that's a showstopper. Christianity must be true. God must exist. All other religions that deny Jesus as God's Son are terribly wrong. And every soul on earth today ought to convert to Christianity because Christianity is the ultimate truth to the meaning of life. That's how significant this miracle claim of Christianity is to both the Christian faith in particular and the world as a whole.

There are many great books and inquiries into the validity of this resurrection claim in Christianity. I'm not going into all the evidence there is to this claim. Personally, what bothered me most about the resurrection of Jesus was how people responded to it right after the entire event occurred. Many thousands of bright minds have looked into this event over the past two thousand years. The validity of the resurrection story appears irrefutable. Even though there are some today who are using scant scientific evidence to make a claim that the resurrection of Jesus was, at best, a misunderstanding or, worse, a hoax, the preponderance of historical, scientific, and archaeological evidence stacks up to support the story and the trustworthiness of the storytellers. Why would men, namely Jesus' disciples, be willing to suffer terrifying deaths for a hoax? Why would so many people suffer so much persecution during the first few generations after the resurrection of Jesus if it were a simple misunderstanding of the facts? Just read the accounts of the early Christian martyrs. Their stories are both shocking and inspiring. The blood of the martyrs testifies to a surety of belief that is grounded in an idea much stronger than a nice bedtime story. There has never been a phenomenon like the bodily resurrection that has stirred up so much fidelity within its faithful, especially so soon after the event. These first Christians were willing to put themselves through unimaginable peril for their faith based on the truth of the resurrection of Jesus Christ. Human history has never seen that kind of devotion before or since. Admittedly, Islam did spread rapidly at first. But the cause of Islam's spread is most obviously attributed to the effect of persuading others by the tip of the sword than on its new adherents trusting in a certain faith-claim based upon the reality of a miracle.

But, let me clue you in on something. At this point, I must come clean. I've done a lot of exploration of this topic, and I've come to the conclusion that the Christians have it right—that God does exist and that God is best understood through the life and teaching of Jesus Christ. It is the point from which I first started and had subsequently abandoned. Now, I find myself heading back to the beginning, with a few psychological battle scars earned along the way. It is a true and trustworthy saying . . . there is a God, and the Jesus of Orthodox Christianity *is* God's deliberate act of painting himself into his own painting. He became one of us. And it has made all the difference.

As the early church fathers agreed upon in the first ecumenical council in 325 CE. in Nicea (and clarified during the First Council of Constantinople in 381 CE), *The Nicene Creed,* the first universal creed of the Christian faith, was ratified as follows:

> We believe in one God, the Father Almighty, Maker of heaven and earth, and of all things visible and invisible. And in one Lord Jesus Christ, the only-begotten Son of God, begotten of the Father before all worlds, Light of Light, very God of very God, begotten, not

made, being of one substance with the Father; by whom all things were made; who for us men, and for our salvation, came down from heaven, and was incarnate by the Holy Ghost of the Virgin Mary, and was made man; he was crucified for us under Pontius Pilate, and suffered, and was buried, and the third day he rose again, according to the Scriptures, and ascended into heaven, and sitteth on the right hand of the Father; from thence he shall come again, with glory, to judge the quick and the dead; whose kingdom shall have no end. And in the Holy Ghost, the Lord and Giver of life, who proceedeth from the Father, who with the Father and the Son together is worshiped and glorified, who spake by the prophets. In one holy catholic and apostolic Church; we acknowledge one baptism for the remission of sins; we look for the resurrection of the dead, and the life of the world to come. Amen.

Ever since, the various creeds of the Christian church, whether in the traditions of the Catholic, Orthodox, Anglican, Oriental Orthodox, or Protestant, have unflinchingly echoed these seminal dogmas throughout the millennia in response to that one stubborn fact of the miraculous: Jesus Christ's bodily resurrection. It's that one piece of evidence, that single divine fingerprint, regardless of all other evidences or the seeming lack thereof, that turns the case for Christianity from fantasy to certainty.

Therefore, it is definitely more reasonable to say, "God exists."

Chapter Seventeen

A SURPRISING PRAYER

Deep calls out to deep.

IT WOULD BE MISLEADING TO say that all the thoughts I've been discussing with you came in a linear fashion as you find in this book. I took the liberty of organizing these thoughts in a more topical fashion rather than a purely chronological fashion because it would make more sense to you. If I had tried to list them in chronological order, I'm not entirely sure if I could actually be accurate in recreating the ebb and flow of doubt and belief. The entire process was quite messy. The thoughts came in fits and spurts. Doubts would rise up within me and then would retreat when doubts even about my doubts would echo back. In some ways, the whole process of thought remains choppy even up to this day.

That being said, I must give you one concrete point in time where there was a dramatic plot shift in my story. Rarely do I have moments of clarity and epiphany, so the ones I do have come with great significance for me. I'm not sure why God, if he is as we see him in his creation and his revealed Word captured by his first followers, would not choose to give us more of these moments of unmistakable intervention because they mean so much when we have them. Maybe God knows that if he were to interject himself continuously into our lives, we would begin to treat him as common and diminish his involvement as being unneeded or insignificant. Ironically, maybe that is what God has been doing all along, and we have treated his interventions as natural and expected. That's Emerson's point about the glory of the stars. In that vein, maybe the miracle of childbirth really is miraculous. But because childbirth happens so often, we treat it as rather ordinary—an everyday matter. Maybe even more personally, we feel the pounding of our hearts in our chests and never stop to marvel at the inexplicability of this phenomenon; instead, we are dulled by its constancy. It's rather hard to know. The problem of our dullness to the presence of God may be so obvious we cannot even see it. God may be more present and active in our lives than our unimaginative senses could ever make sense of.

Which leads me back to my original thought . . .

God, when he does choose to make himself known in an extraordinary way, does so using some of the most amazingly simple devices. You'd think a God who has all power, wisdom, strength, and imagination at his disposal would like to flex his divine muscle from time to time (as if a star that is in supernova is not a form of this)!

I've been in conversations with people, especially those who have presupposed that God does not exist, who try to spark a theological discussion with the shock, "If I were God, I'd . . ." and then they give a corrective to the world and try to convince us that their particular brand of morality trumps God's obviously weaker brand of morality. I must confess that I have been one of those people. And, on really upsetting days, I have the exact same thought pop into my head. I remember having it on September 11, 2001. I remember having it when my son Bo was in the intensive care unit receiving blood transfusions after a bike accident. I remember having it when I first read about the terrible actions of Al-Shabab in the Sudan. God's actions, or more accurately, inactions, can sometimes frustrate and dismay. His ways remain mysterious.

I'm very thankful that God does not act as I do. I would make a terrible deity. And I'm reasonably sure you would too. If we are honest with ourselves, we really don't want God to act and think as we do. Our hearts are far too selfish and inconstant. That's why I was surprised by the outrageously hilarious film *Bruce Almighty* starring Jim Carrey and Morgan Freeman. The movie builds off the thought of "If I were God, I'd . . ." and speculates on some possible outcomes. And while some of the outcomes are hysterical, others are deeply unsettling. After you get over the uncomfortable portrayal of God by *any* human being (even though Morgan Freeman is probably one of the best choices you'd have if you had to cast an actor to begin with), you find yourself identifying with a God who can be "just plain hard to get" from time to time.

God, in all his glorious otherness, is still interested enough in each of us individually to insert himself into our lives in meaningful ways when he deems the time is right. He did that with me. If you look back through your life, you may see telltale signs of his intervention if you stop and muse deeply enough. It's not that God is trying to be sneaky with us when he does enter in these unassuming ways; he's actually acting with our best interests at heart. If he came into our lives with all bluster and heraldry, I think we'd end up more overtaken from the experience than if he nudged us gently. I suppose his fullness would scramble our brains and explode our hearts. Bombastic insertions of his presence into our world is not in keeping with his personality. Even so, he seems quite intent on staying involved with us. For a God who obviously needs nothing, he sure acts as if he needs us to be part of his creation, doesn't he? Yet he does so gracefully and kindly. When he inserted himself into our world as a God-child, he did so on the most humble of stages. And when he began to teach us the true meaning of life and the ways of his creation, he did so with ordinary, unschooled fishermen from backwater hick-towns surrounding the Sea of Galilee two thousand years ago. He didn't enter his world with unfurled flags, pomp, and circumstance. He came in through the womb of a Jewish peasant girl, unmarried and unknown, but a distant heiress to King David's throne with the blue blood of divine promise coursing through her veins.

It was August 2008. As I flew from Greenville, South Carolina, to Green Bay, Wisconsin, I finished reading the book *The God Delusion* by Richard Dawkins on the plane. At that point in my spiritual journey, I had embraced the possibility that atheism was the best explanation for everything I saw around me. Dawkins made some excellent arguments in that book about faith and reason. He portrayed people of faith as small-minded and irrational—even dangerous. As I probed into my past, I could see how his depiction of my previous worldview was more accurate than I wanted to admit. Many Christians are small-minded and irrational. And a few are quite dangerous. What's troubling about deeply religious people is that they can become so fanatical about small issues that they forget to consider the bigger ones. And, during this plane trip, I was becoming more and more convinced I wanted no part of it. Give me real and true, not imagined and false.

The purpose of this particular business trip was to help Northland Baptist Bible College, a rather small college, begin a multi-year strategic marketing planning process with their administrative team. Before this consulting engagement, I had only heard of Northland and had acquaintance with a few of the administrators there, but I didn't know them well. I knew that Northland was of the creed of Christianity I had known as a child, so I was comfortably certain that I could relate to them and ultimately help them with their marketing problems. I must admit that I did feel strange going up there because I was no longer convinced that their type of Christianity—or Christianity in general, for that matter—was true. I was a professional, however. I was confident I could hold these meetings and assist them with their business. Even though I didn't believe in their product, I was okay with the notion that they had every right to believe as they did. Why not? Earlier in my life, I had. And Northland, along with every other religious entity out there, may be serving people well simply by making them feel better about their lives and their place in this world. I saw their product as nothing more dangerous or helpful than a real estate developer selling luxury homes on a golf course. Some people like how they feel about themselves living in gated communities next to a championship golf course. It brings them happiness. Personally, it's not for me, but it sure seems like it means a lot to them. So, why couldn't other people "get their thrills" from a religion that allows them to feel equally as happy about their lives? As long as they didn't force it down my throat but behaved civilly about it, I think they have as much a right to live religiously and insert their brand of happiness into the marketplace of ideas. And so, with that internal justification, I began my hour and a half drive from the Green Bay airport to Dunbar, Wisconsin, in the middle of the night to make an 8:00 a.m. meeting on the Northland campus.

I got to the meeting room early that day. I remember the rich golden sunlight had painted glorious highlights on the stately evergreens surrounding a rather spartan building on the Northland campus. The air was fresh and sweetened with the smell of pine. I breathed in deeply to drink in lung-full after lung-full of the unpolluted, crisp morning air of Wisconsin's Northwoods. I went into the building and began my routine preparation for day one of a two-day planning session. The folding tables were organized in a horseshoe that would seat about twelve people. Members of the administrative team of Northland Baptist Bible College began streaming in. They were all very kind and took special care to come over and introduce themselves. They seemed to be close friends of each other, and their pleasant jibes and teases with each other signaled a special brand of playfulness that can only come from people who, from the start, take each other quite seriously.

Matt Olson, the then president of the college, came in, and the meeting began to organize immediately. All attendees found their places. Matt greeted me warmly but professionally. He opened his Bible and shared a thought from Scripture. After a minute of summary comment and reference to a theological book he had just been reading, he called the attendees to prayer. And the praying began.

Who prayed, what exactly was prayed for, and how long the prayer lasted, I cannot recall. All I can remember is what was happening to me. I heard, probably for the first time in my life, people communicating with God. They were not praying as I had always experienced in the past, prayers of theological exactitude, religious rhetoric, or preachiness of language that gives you a sense that those who are speaking are not actually praying to God but are instead trying to impress the mere mortals who are obliged to politely listen and endure. They were talking *with* God.

The sweetness of this moment weakened my knees. As everyone's eyes were closed around the table except mine, I found myself gasping for air. I couldn't breathe. My chest felt as if it had imploded within itself. I was involved in a moment I knew was not of this world. It was beyond a simple emotional feeling. It was visceral . . . and spiritual . . . and emotional all at once. I didn't hear a voice, or even an expressed thought, but a deep sense of communication directly from God.

He spoke to the deepest part of me without words. "Steve, it's time. It's time to come home."

Hot tears welled up in my eyes. I leaned forward with an incredible urge to throw up. I wanted to vomit out all the uncertainty, the fear, the disappointment, the hurt, the doubt, the tension, and the rage. I dry heaved. My head felt light, and I sensed a floating within me that terribly disoriented me. I felt as though I were floating outside of myself. I gulped a lung-full of air and slowly breathed out trying to right myself out of a free-fall. My heart's pounding, now loud and fast, began to calm. The vertigo lifted, and I settled back in my chair with little time to process as the last "amen" of the last prayer was offered by the Northland administrative team.

The meeting commenced. I was on. All eyes locked in on me, their guest facilitator. I didn't know if the effect of what had just happened to me was evident to these men, but inwardly I was shaken. Terribly shaken. I regained my composure as best I could and launched into my business-planning mode rather mechanically and out of sheer habit. I had run these meetings many times in the past. And my training and experience took over where my spirit and consciousness left off. I got through the day without missing a beat. My professionalism served me well, though I knew something much larger than this meeting had occurred in that brief moment of prayer.

That night, after a dinner with the administrative staff, I settled into the guest room on Northland's campus with only myself and a newly regained sense of God's presence. I knew my conversation with God was just beginning.

I must confess—I'm highly skeptical of people with personal religious experiences. I get really nervous and suspicious when people begin talking about having some kind of supernatural, out-of-body, vision-thing from God. Many times, I've heard people say the most bizarre things and hold to some rather unorthodox ideas that are based on some ecstatic religious event in their lives. I think a high degree of skepticism of these claims is called for by rational people because I cannot trust the imagination of man to be even reasonably accurate in areas of the supernatural. It is, largely, a world filled with kooks and charlatans. And for that reason alone, I have never wanted any part of it.

Naturally, that night, alone in that guest room, my mind went straight to that skeptical place as I began recounting the events of the day. Could I have just had an emotional rush based on the sincerity of the prayers of these good men? Like looking into the big eyes of a self-interested kitten and thinking that kitten is expressing affection for me the way I am feeling affection for it, had I just picked up a simple, honest vibe from some very likable guys and mistook it for something more potent? Was my reaction self-manufactured to satisfy some psychological need for a more meaningful bond with these men? Quite possibly.

But, it was the intense clarity of thought that began that day that convinced me that something from another world had entered into my rather insignificant consciousness. I saw a reality that eclipsed all thoughts of reality previous. It was as if a shroud of self-deception lifted. I began to understand and reason more clearly. And I could sense the deepness of God calling into the deepest recesses within my spirit.

God was not bringing me new knowledge previously unknown. Nor was he showing me new ways of thinking. He clarified instead of revealed. He began connecting the dots of my experience and even my long journeys of inquiry, showing me truths already present but now transported from known to understood. I began to "get it." He began with the loving process of transporting truth in head to truth in heart. And the path that I had been taking all along was intentional on his part. All that I explored began to settle into a better understanding of reality. All that I strove to disprove came back to me in re-proving what had always been. When I read this quote from G.K. Chesterton, I was glad to know that my path back into truth was shared with honorable company:

I did try to found a heresy of my own; and when I had put the last touches to it, I discovered that it was orthodoxy. It may be that somebody will be entertained by the account of this happy fiasco. It might amuse a friend or an enemy to read how I gradually learnt from the truth of some stray legend or from the falsehood of some dominant philosophy, things that I might have learnt from my catechism—if I had ever learnt it.

My seeking to pull away from God ended up giving me the fortitude to believe in his truth with greater certainty. God had been there all along, even when I refused to acknowledge him. He knew what it would take to break me. And he did. But as he did, he was patient and kind. And he allowed me to kick against the pricks for a while, knowing that those incidental scars would turn into comforts, not torments. And, with a surprising prayer on a sun-drenched morning in the Northwoods of Wisconsin, a renewed sense of reality brought forth its first bud. But, the journey wasn't concluding. It was just beginning. And the changes to come next in my life were more astonishing than I could ever have realized.

TURNING AROUND

"Here it comes!" someone shouted. "Where?" "Over there," pointing to the northwest. "Oh, yes! I see it!" "It's getting dark now . . . it's getting real dark now . . . it's getting really dark now . . . it's really getting . . . oh my [goodness]!" Cheers and gasps accompanied the beginning of totality. It took everything I had to keep my mind focused on the task at hand, and even that didn't work when the lady behind me broke down crying. Her husband wrapped his arms around her.

As totality ended, I shot a last few exposures, blinded by my own tears, gave up, and turned around and photographed the couple behind me."

–Excerpt from *"My Favorite Eclipse,"*
story told by *Ken Willcox from* Totality: Eclipses of the Sun
by Mark Littmann, Fred Espenak, and Ken Willcox

Chapter Eighteen

TRULY LOVING

Who do men say that I am?

I MUST SAY, IT WAS a whole lot less trouble reconnecting with my faith than I first thought. There was half of me that had always longed for the reconciliation to occur. But, there was another half of me that fought it. Both halves were still at war with each other. I realized neither could be trusted outright. The half that desired reconnection seemed happier with the comfortable and known. Christianity had been a part of me for most of my life, and the worldview it offered, I understood. I didn't have a lot of adjusting to do. I also didn't have to guilt myself any longer with thoughts of betrayal and family disharmony. I could run back to a safe place.

The other half that resisted the reconnection seemed interested in protecting my personal integrity and, more accurately, my reputation. I had been very vocal in my criticisms of Christianity from time to time. I took some kind of thrill from being a contrarian in an overly Christianized culture. I had felt smarter and more reasoned among the crowd. I had showed the world that I was willing to ask the hard questions and come to nontraditional conclusions. It felt good being different and edgy. I wanted to be the guy who changed people's attitudes and opinions with new, exciting insights into philosophy and religion. I wanted to be that "go-to guy" whose thoughts and opinions people sought out more than most. I knew I was losing that. And, at the outset, I didn't want to lose that feeling.

So, here I was . . . essentially conflicted and at war with my own thoughts and struggling with how to process everything I had been through.

My quest now circled back to where it originally began—asking the big questions:

Why am I here?

What is this life all about?

What kind of a story am I in—if it's even a story at all?

And now I found myself finally in a position to begin to answer those questions definitively. I had found the basis to begin constructing meaningful answers. Through all my searching, I found that there really is a God, that religion is more than a mere psychological tool to help us "freakish mutations of blind evolutionary chance" deal with an otherwise meaningless world, and that God is best understood through the life and teachings of Jesus Christ.

We really are part of a story. And it is a story of epic proportions. It is this story where we find the true meaning to our lives, not just collectively as a human race, but more importantly as individuals who are individually made by a truly loving Creator who wants to know and enjoy each of us, one soul at a time.

Throughout human history, individual men and women have sought after meaning or purpose to their lives in a variety of ways. Some have looked to the accumulation of wealth as the "be-all and end-all" of human existence: "The one who dies with the most toys, wins." In modern developed nations, through the help of the advertising community, this ultimate meaning is more prevalent than we'd care to admit. First of all, is it a good "end game" for humanity? Should we pursue wealth as our ultimate purpose? The Beatles sang of "Can't Buy Me Love," but money does enable us to buy things that lead to a sense of personal fulfillment: well-being, freedom, happiness, and even social standing. Yet, money in and of itself is quite a capricious thing. It does not fulfill our ultimate desires even though it claims to make those ultimate desires accessible. Therefore, it is a means to an end and cannot be the end game. Secondly, for those of us who pursue wealth as our life's purpose, we find it to be rather elusive. In fact, it is disturbing to note that the rich are more prone to commit suicide than the poor. And, no matter how much money one has, it's never quite enough. We always wish we could be richer. Seeking after wealth as our ultimate meaning to life proves to be an inferior prospect.

Others have desired fame and glory, thinking that celebrity and others' good will is where life is most meaningful. Since we are innately social creatures, our desire to be known and valued by our fellow man is quite appealing. But should it be our end game? If this is our end game, we have a dilemma similar to seeking after wealth. We are asking our lives to be based on an end game that is never quite within our possession. Fame and glory are states of reality that appear not in our lives, but in the hearts and minds of others. It is others who determine whether to value us enough to grace us with their admiration and affections. If we choose such an end result, we are, in effect, tying the meaning of our lives to a rather unstable mooring. All we have to do to see this ill effect on people is to walk along "The Boulevard of Broken Dreams" (to borrow a phrase from the band Green Day) among has-been celebrities and see the terrible dysfunction. If fame and glory are our end game, we would all live a rather sinister and pessimistic life because fame and glory are terribly inconstant and cold.

Some have sought after physical health as the most important pursuit of human endeavor. To live well is to live well. To protect one from pain, disease, and the effects of age is all our existence needs to garner enough meaning to occupy us through the years. Yet, we find that the fountain of youth does run dry in every life without exception—unless one's life is ended prematurely and unnaturally. And the final result of everything physical ends in predictable fashion—as Ernest Hemingway framed it, "All stories, if continued far enough, end in death." We are left, then, with the shallowness of this end game. It is not enough to explain our full existence. It only serves a minor role in a greater purpose that transcends physical health.

Yet others have looked to the accumulation of wisdom and experiences as being the main purpose for life. While this aim has a more noble bearing to it, even the writer of Ecclesiastes knew its ability to serve as a *summum bonum* to be nothing more "than a chasing after the wind." For what good is all this knowledge if I'm not seeking to do something greater with it? What does it do on its own? So, we pursue wisdom, understand, and are able to discern, but that alone is an empty quest if not serving a greater master than itself. Just as the accumulation of wealth serves best as a means to an end, the accumulation of understanding is not enough. It needs to anchor itself to a higher, ultimate meaning.

A rare few—including Socrates, Diogenes, and the Buddha—looked to virtue and goodness as our ultimate purpose in life. The pursuit of virtue feels like an ancient idea to us moderns. If we simply perfect ourselves to such a degree and avoid wasting our lives on vain passions and pursuits and, instead, seek after the more noble virtues, our lives will be lives well spent. No doubt, it is good to be good. Virtue is a pursuit that is necessary for all men. But for what? As Nietzsche once asked, "Why be good?" This question becomes even more relevant when we expect virtue to be our purpose. If not moored to a higher purpose, virtue for virtue's sake becomes instantly meaningless. There is no answer to Nietzsche's question that satisfies. There must be something beyond virtue that makes the pursuit of virtue attractive.

So, could I spend all my life pursuing virtue and never fulfill the ultimate meaning for my life? Again, we find that the pursuit of virtue leaves the picture incomplete. It is a means to something else. Virtue needs to hang also on a higher purpose.

Many less ascetic souls have concluded that pleasure is everything and there is nothing more to pursue. And so, most have run to the ultimate end game of personal happiness (in varying shades of understanding of what happiness truly means) as man's highest source of meaning. They would agree in a limited way with Sheryl Crow: "If it makes you happy, it can't be all that bad." Many pleasure seekers scour the world with travel and fill their otherwise empty lives with exotic experiences as if they were running scared of being overtaken by boredom. Aristotle was one of the first to clearly posit happiness as an end game with his idea of *eudaimonia*. Yet, by the way he talked about it, he was talking about something much greater than simply satisfaction and contentment as we would use the word "happiness," even though *eudaimonia* did include elements of these. But Aristotle was talking of more. He was expressing a deeper sense of happiness that went beyond feeling into a place of higher connection. St. Augustine and his philosopher friends called it the *beata vita*, or the perfectly happy life. C.S. Lewis framed the idea more as joy and wrote, "I sometimes wonder whether all pleasures are substitutes for joy."

If we are created and not self-manufactured, there's no better place to start our understanding of life's ultimate meaning than with what can be known about our Creator. He made us. He obviously had a reason and a plan. So, getting into his mind is a great place to start. But, how can one know this Creator God? Is it even possible for us to know him? Or is he as inconceivable to us as we are to a slug—or even more so? How can we expect a slug to understand why man falls in love, how man figured out calculus, or how we can send insipid jokes and statements of political conspiracies to hundreds of our friends all over the world via the Internet with the push of a button from our smart phone? A slug has no ability to process that kind of knowledge about us. Are we just as powerless in knowing the ways of God?

In the Book of Job in the Hebrew Bible, Job questions God repeatedly about why he is being forced to suffer without explanation. When God finally shows up and answers Job out of the tempest, God states rather forcibly:

> Who is this that darkeneth counsel
> By words without knowledge?
>
> Gird up now thy loins like a man;
> For I will demand of thee, and answer thou me.
>
> Where wast thou when I laid the foundations of the earth?
> Declare, if thou hast understanding. (Job 38:2-4)

At this point in Job's story, God launches into a scathing cross-examination of Job that is utterly devastating. This is the place where I do not envy Job in the least. Give me Job's suffering. Just don't give me an audience with an irate Creator. For all my self-aggrandizing attitude, where I have said I would welcome the opportunity to question God directly about the injustices of life, his intentions with this world, and why my life was filled with so much misery, I think I would have withered under such a naked examination by God Almighty as is recorded here.

If you really think about it, we are filled with all sorts of hubris to think we can teach God anything: about (1) how life in this world should be and (2) that all he has been doing is wholly inadequate since man's existence has been rather distressed in the process. Yet, when I get to the root of most agnostic and atheistic arguments, they say these things with unashamed swagger. They shake their pitiful fists in the face of an all-powerful God and try to tell him off for running his creation so terribly. Like we can intimidate God! As we look around us and see a world gone mad where children are being exploited, innocents being defiled, people starving, and evil dictators terrorizing the peace, all the while people who claim to represent God best turn a self-serving eye away from it all, leaving us to exclaim in exasperation, "Doesn't God know what's happening down here?" Then we reason, "If he does, then it's plainly obvious he either doesn't care or have any sense of justice and fair play!"

How silly we tend to be!

Most people who reject the idea of God do so not because the evidence of this material world demands such a conclusion but because they fundamentally disagree with the means with which God has chosen to rule over his creation. "Children should never suffer!" they exclaim. "Innocents should be protected. All people should have access to life-sustaining and nourishing food. Evil dictators must be removed from power. Swindling, charlatan 'God-peddlers' must be held accountable. And this all-good Creator God, the one who can change all this, can't exist because he's doing nothing about it!" This is the heart of the atheist's denial of God. And all the reapplication of scientific knowledge the atheist uses to prove he doesn't exist is merely a smokescreen to conceal the truth.

So, what do we do? Simply take life as we know it on the chin? Do we just grin and bear it? Is this the real lesson, or meaning, in life? Should we do no more than let God be God, and we simply need to get with the program?

So far, we've been dealing with emotional knee jerks to select data more than we've been dealing with the true essence of our reality. I went there first in this chapter because that's the rage that occludes our reason most of the time. I wanted to draw it out so we can know it exists and therefore place it to the side for a brief moment so we can look at the bedrock of our knowledge of God and see where it leads us. The way God chooses to reveal himself reveals a lot about his personality. We can determine if God is an honest God or if he is instead capricious and conniving like the gods of Mount Olympus. If considered honestly, there is ample evidence to lead to quite satisfying conclusions.

So . . . what can be known of God?

There is an entire debate raging among very smart people concerning how we can know anything about God. Some say that knowledge of God is known best from an evidentiary perspective. Others say, no. It's from a presuppositional standpoint. This is, I'm quite sure, an honorable and necessary discussion, but it's a discussion I am not willing to re-articulate in this book. There is plenty of ink spilled in many other books that dissect this issue to the most particular of nuance and detail. I will leave that discussion in their capable hands. What I hope to share with you is a broader notion of what we can know of God that gives a tinge of homage to this discussion but doesn't try to explain everything. The subject matter experts in epistemology and philosophical taxonomy may take issue with my breezy attitude about this topic, but I find that it's easy to get lost in the details and never see the golden thread that is guiding us from ignorance to wisdom.

If God is sole Creator, then he created everything. And his creation is based on his intelligence and his own personal motivations. Within this creation, we exist. And we apparently have a unique standing with his creation because of our capability to reason and to know him personally when nothing else in his creation appears to have that same capability. This is data. And it tells us something.

We also know he created many things in this world. The things that are in this world have an intriguing level of design and complexity that is impossible to comprehend. We see the intricacy of the human eye. We contemplate the exactness and predictability of physical laws and the abstract but ubiquitous logic of mathematics. We see the beauty and intrinsic value of created objects like a drop of water dangling precariously from a budding red rose or the intoxicating smell of freshly baked bread. This is also data and tells us even more about God.

We see incomprehensible variability throughout the cosmos. We see all kinds of stars, from red supergiants and blue giants to white and yellow dwarfs. There are brown stars, neutron stars, and even pulsars. There are even Cepheid variable stars like Polaris. And the list goes on. Is there a need for such variability in stars? If we think in terms of creation being anthropocentric, then no. And what about the hundreds of thousands of insect species that exist? They seem like utter superfluity and a waste of creative energy. When we get to the subatomic world of leptons, bosons, and quarks, where quarks can be charmed, top, down, up, bottom, or strange, or we consider leptons as tau, electrons, muons, muon neutrinos, tau neutrinos, and electron neutrinos, or even bosons classified as photons, gluons, and weak force, we can easily conclude that the basis of matter is quite variable and intricate. Or we look even at the different kinds of peoples and languages all over the globe, and we see a whole spectrum of creative variability. Seven billion people alive on this planet at the same time? Is this really called for? Why does there need to be so many of us? This is data too. And it informs us more about God's personality.

Why is it that God created us with the need to eat? As humans, if we do not eat, we will die. But we cannot just eat sand and rocks; we must eat vegetables, meats, and other life-filled substances. What's the point in that? Life must feed on life to survive. For us to stay alive, we must consume other life-filled material. This is part of God's creation, and it tells us something very important about his intentions. This is also important data to consider.

Conversely, we know that we, the favored part of his creation, are quite small in the overall scheme of things. From a cosmic perspective, we are only seven billion specs of life on a rather nondescript planet orbiting around a rather insignificant star within an ordinary galaxy among billions of other galaxies. This shows us that God is much larger, more powerful, and more expansive than we are. His essence is far beyond our essence. Again, this serves as data and helps us understand God more fully.

What we can know of God through his creation like that above is termed *general revelation* by most theologians and philosophers. General revelations are those pieces of knowledge common to all. It is a significant form of knowledge because, just as artwork tells us much about the inner life of the artist, God's artwork, his creation, also speaks volumes about his character. As the psalmist penned over three thousand years ago:

> The heavens declare the glory of God; and the firmament sheweth his handywork. Day unto day uttereth speech, and night unto night sheweth knowledge. There is no speech nor language, where their voice is not heard.

It is quite apparent that God wants to be known through his work of creation. Our studying of his creation through the sciences is simply a pathway into a deeper understanding of his mind, heart, and will. For man, God has made sure we have a pathway to him through everything he has created. As the Apostle Paul explained in the very first chapter of his letter to the Romans:

> Because that which may be known of God is manifest in them; for God hath shewed it unto them. For the invisible things of him from the creation of the world are clearly seen, being understood by the things that are made, even his eternal power and Godhead; so that they are without excuse.

Because we know God's creation is an expression—or, better, a communication—of his divine personality, we should look at science as a noble pursuit, not just a help in our understanding matter, but helping us understand its Creator as well. Christians ought to be the most interested and diligent in the pursuit of the material sciences among all people because of science's ability to inform our understanding of the God we profess to worship. Yet, ironically, we see so many Christians shirking away from the sciences as something we should not trust instead of being the noble pursuit of knowing our Maker better.

Yet, God has not limited his desire to be known through the means of his creation. God has given us also special revelation. And that special revelation has come most powerfully through his thirty-three-year stint here on earth as God-man, Jesus of Nazareth. This is the Christian doctrine of the incarnation of Jesus Christ that the Gospel of John speaks of:

> In the beginning was the Word, and the Word was with God, and the Word was God . . . And the Word was made flesh, and dwelt among us, (and we beheld his glory, the glory as of the only begotten of the Father,) full of grace and truth.

The doctrine of Jesus Christ as God Eternal is the cornerstone of the orthodox Christian faith. From the very beginning of the Christian faith, orthodox Christians believe that Jesus is more than a great moral teacher or spiritual leader; he was God entering his own creation. What we can know of Jesus, we can also know of the great Creator God. Jesus and God are one and the same. As the writer of Hebrews expressed it:

> God, who at sundry times and in divers manners spake in time past unto the fathers by the prophets, hath in these last days spoken unto us by his Son, whom he hath appointed heir of all things, by whom also he made the worlds; who being in brightness of his glory, and

the express image of his person, and upholding all things by the word of his power.

Jesus himself even said to his disciples, "He that hath seen me hath seen the Father." If this orthodox teaching of the Christian faith is true, it stands to be the most important truth, not just within the Christian faith itself, but the most important truth in the annals of time. However, if this belief is a myth, or a moralized tale as some assert, then Christianity is the biggest con game out there and should be cited as such. The Apostle Paul, the contributor of no less than thirteen books to the Christian Bible, wrote in his first letter to the church in Corinth:

> For I delivered unto you first of all that which I also received, how that Christ died for our sins according to the Scriptures; and that he was buried, and that he rose again the third day according to the Scriptures: and that he was seen of Cephas [Peter], then of the twelve: after that, he was seen of above five hundred brethren at once; of whom the greater part remain unto this present, but some are fallen asleep. After that, he was seen of James; then of all the apostles. And last of all he was seen of me also, as of one born out of due time . . . If Christ be not risen, then is our preaching vain, and your faith is also vain.

The story of Jesus' living as a man on earth, dying, then rising from the dead then becomes God's greatest revelation of who he is and how he wants us to understand him: the great Creator, Sustainer, Lover, Redeemer, and Restorer of fallen mankind. If Jesus is who the apostles and the Bible depicts him as, all other portraits of God apart from Jesus are incomplete. Indeed, concepts of God apart from Jesus can, and often do, contain elements of truth. However, if those who speak of God expunge this greatest revelation of God as Jesus, then they severely limit their understanding of God. The teachings from Muhammad to L. Ron Hubbard, or any other religious leader, still must contend with the knowledge of the truth of Jesus Christ in orthodox Christianity. And yes, I am going on the record and saying that, even as good-intentioned as many of these people who follow the teachings of these other religious leaders are, their religion cannot be complete but only contain partial knowledge. These religions do contain truth, just not a complete picture of truth.

However, I think it is dangerous for Christians to vilify these religions as complete shams. They are not. There is truth present in all these variant religions but, unfortunately, not full truth. The truths these non-Christian religions contain are the same truths that are manifest in Christianity, just not complete and rooted in ultimate truth, Jesus Christ. But to espouse an attitude of full renunciation of all truth claims of these faiths is unhelpful in establishing meaningful dialogue with other religions. I am convinced that Christians who choose to wholesale denounce these other religions tend to develop a warped sense of truth that inevitably causes their understanding of Christianity to become warped and reduced in truth. Why? Because if I deny a truth claim in Buddhism simply because its source is Buddhist even though it may be a restatement of a truth claim that is quite similar in Christianity, like the noble truth of *dukkha*, then I lose my ability to engage with Buddhists in understanding the greater reality of truth found in Jesus Christ.

Even so, I am convinced that what attracts followers to these other religions are the gleams of truth they contain. There is more in common with most religions than many of the adherents of these seemingly disparate religions would profess. I remember being surprised at the underlying doctrines of Buddhism being so similar to Christianity. But, the fact that there are a large number of similarities in religions should not give us the wrong impression. Some have postulated that differing religions may appear as islands in the sea of our experience. But, when you look underwater, you find each island is simply a mountain top jutting from a sprawling underwater continent. In actuality, they are not. Yes, there is a lot of agreement between religions, especially in the areas of morals and ethics, but the few distinctions they do possess can make a huge difference in our understanding of the meaning of life and our ability to grab hold of reality. As I went through my journey, Christianity won the battle of truth. There is more in Christianity that explains reality better than any other, including agnosticism and atheism. But, Christianity differs significantly from the other religions. So, the question remains, what key portions of the entire truth are those others missing?

The followers of religions other than Christianity need to understand they must reckon with the truth, no matter how foreign or countercultural Jesus Christ may be. Unlike any other, Jesus Christ becomes the key manifestation of truth for all religions to contend with. He is unavoidable. He is the one religious leader who claims not to simply state the truth, like the Buddha or Lao Tzu, but to actually *be* the truth. He, who created all things, must be included in the conversation about truth as either ultimate truth or ultimate deceiver. There doesn't appear to be middle ground here. Those who are promoting these other incomplete belief systems mentioned above are, unfortunately, peddling shards of truth, not the full-bodied, complete truth that God inserted himself into his own creation as Jesus Christ.

Anyone who responds, "Well, that may be true for you, but it may not be true for me" is simply not getting it. This kind of statement is common but irrational. The root of an assertion like this is based on the fantasy that I can choose my own reality—that reality is controlled by me, not me by it. So, is it reasonable to think that what I choose to believe will manufacture itself into reality? Hardly. And that kind of thinking is about as helpful as if I had just suffered a gunshot wound to the chest that resulted in my bleeding out terribly and I reacted by saying that I'm really not injured and don't believe in guns. The reality of guns is there whether I believe in guns or not. The gaping wound is real. The life-seeping flow of blood will not stop just because I refuse to believe. Our belief in anything does not affect the "realness" of anything. Belief, in order to be true belief, must be anchored to ultimate reality, not my personal fantasy about reality. So a person can believe in talking plants all she wants. She can also choose not to believe in gravity. Your belief system does not alter the hard-core, absolute truth that plants cannot talk and that gravity has consequences. Jump off a high cliff, and the realness of gravity becomes achingly clear.

Special revelation is any form of personal communication God makes apart from the general laws of nature. One of the most tangible forms of his special revelations before Jesus came to earth was in the teachings of the prophets and the collected Holy Scriptures classified as the Old Testament in the Christian faith. The Bible passage referred to earlier from Hebrews, "God, who at sundry times and in divers manners spake in time past unto the fathers by the prophets . . ." attests to this fact. God spoke in a special way that helped his people understand him and his intent for mankind. But, when God came into his creation as Jesus of Nazareth, everything changed.

Jesus' life is God's highest form of revelation. Even though Jesus did not leave any form of writing behind with us, he did inspire his early followers to record his life, his teachings, and the practical out-workings of his teaching in the form of the New Testament Scriptures. It was these writings that quickly recorded Jesus' teachings and actions within the first generation after his resurrection through first-person, eyewitness accounts combined with direct testimonies of those who walked with Jesus and knew him best. The scholarship that surrounds these twenty-seven books of the Christian holy canon has been uncommonly intense and rigorous. No other corpus of writings has withstood such exacting analysis and criticism as the Bible has. It has proven its veracity repeatedly. Thousands of the last two millennia's best and brightest dedicated their lives in the study of these sacred texts. Billions of ardent followers of Jesus Christ through these same years have witnessed these books' transformative powers. These writings have changed the course of human history in every conceivable way. The ultimate test of the New Testament's power is in what it can do in the individual life. Juxtapose the Christian Scriptures against any other sacred text from any other religion and it is easy to see the difference. The Bible is alive. It is not a dead book filled with dead stories. It breathes and actively works within the individual souls of man.

But to assign the power of the Christian faith exclusively to its holy writings as some today are in danger of doing is bordering on sacrilege. Because, even though God's Word is "quick, and powerful, and sharper than any two-edged sword," it is so not because of its own essence, but because of its divinely appointed purpose of speaking of Jesus Christ, the eternal and self-existing Logos, and delivering his words and his life with unthrottled authority. As C.S. Lewis once wrote:

> It is Christ Himself, not the Bible, who is the true word of God. The Bible, read in the right spirit and with the guidance of good teachers, will bring us to Him. We must not use the Bible as a sort of encyclopedia out of which texts can be taken for use as weapons.

Jesus Christ is the central truth of Christianity. The Bible is his portrait. When we focus solely on the portrait of Jesus alone and not on him, we are at risk of distorting the true, life-giving essence of the Christian faith.

When I look at my past, I realize how guilty I was of such a sin. My church experiences, filled with preachers and teachers ever diligent and jealous of the authority of the Scriptures, fell prey to limiting the Bible to some kind of legal contract between God and man that prescribed exacting behaviors in order to become holy. They became exacting literary technicians. They have carved up the Scriptures into systematized buckets of moral teachings, atomized descriptions of divine behavioral patterns, and cataloged moralized stories—all the while losing the heart, will, and personality of the Person being talked about. These determined and dedicated souls have dissected God in a chilling way similar to a forensic pathologist performing an autopsy on a beautiful young woman who met a premature death, describing her physical presence simply as one part spleen, one part liver, one part gallbladder, two parts kidneys, and one part epidermis. Such a record fails to convey the sweetness in her lips, the soft lilt in her laugh, and the sparkle in her eye when some random notion, like the purr of a kitten, delighted her. Unwittingly, I had been doing the same with my understanding of God. I had performed theological autopsy when I needed to spend time gazing into his ineffable beauty. In doing so, I did not realize the price I was paying with my faith. I had mistakenly viewed the Bible as a compendium of religious dogma instead of its highest purpose of speaking of Jesus Christ and serving him by revealing himself to us in all his truth, goodness, and beauty. All who seek to be theologians are at great risk of such a fate. Those of us who are most appreciative of the Scriptures are also the ones most at risk of turning them into an idol, promoting the Scriptures to the same Trinitarian level as Jesus Christ when the Bible never asks us to place it on such a lofty pedestal.

The risk of treating the Bible as the foundation of our faith instead of as a portrait and servant of Jesus Christ is this: we tend to stop at the words on the gilded page as the end. We do not see through the words of the Bible and see Jesus. We lose sight of the over-arching stories that make sense of the details. Details, when they take center stage, lose their context. Details become misapplied, even willfully twisted. Without a healthy, rightful approach to the Bible, I realized how easy it was to develop ideas and concepts about Christianity that contradict the character and work of Jesus Christ. In the fifth chapter of John's Gospel, we read a story of a group of highly devoted religious people, the Pharisees, who struggle with the same form of theological myopia. They had dissected the Scriptures with such precision and intensity that they were no longer able to see the true life it spoke of in the person and work of God himself—the Messiah they all longed to meet, Jesus Christ. It is a tragic story. The Author of the book that they were so highly devoted to stood in front of them, and they couldn't even recognize him. It is the same tragic story that is mine.

I realized that, in my early years of Christianity, I had lost sight of the real story of the Bible. The fact that I perceived the validity of the Christian faith to rise and fall based upon my ability to systematize, codify, and verify every word of the Bible with exactitude, showed that I had no clue as to what the Christian faith, or any faith for that matter, is about. By reading the higher criticisms of the theological writers in the nineteenth and twentieth centuries, along with modern-day scholars like Dr. Bart Ehrman, I see how equally as guilty they are in this matter as I have been.

The Christian story is not about a book, but a person. And that person is Jesus Christ. This story is not about a code of ethics or fast-quip moralisms; they are about God's revealing himself to us in the most loving way imaginable. He has done that for us. God has entered his own painting and has graced us with a portrait of himself in the form of the Holy Scriptures. We should study the Scriptures with the same passionate devotion of a lover who receives a letter from her beloved from afar.

Just as she cherishes her letter, we should cherish the Scriptures—our love letter from our heavenly Father—and press them tenderly to our breast with a deep sigh and a hot tear coursing down our cheek. But we should not limit our understanding of that letter to the mere words it contains, but of the life and love every word points to—to the lover himself and the love he has chosen to make known.

My faith hung in a balance because of my unbalanced view of the Christian Scriptures. I had treated them as something other than what they were. I allowed my mishandling of the Christian Scriptures to cannibalize my faith by veiling my view of God and, instead, presenting a picture of Christianity that had surprisingly little to do with the true author of faith, Jesus. To my own peril, I elevated "biblical ideas" divorced from Christ to the object of my prime devotion. Today, as I look around me, I see others falling into the same trap. These diligent but desperate souls have the same unfocused look in their eye and the same jittering cadence in their voice. They have lost the joy of their faith and have reduced their understanding of God to a lawyer/policeman of moral exactitude instead of the truly loving Creator God who is fully known as Jesus Christ. Ideas like these have consequences. And this may most fully explain why so many Christians are holding cold, theological blades to each other's throats while spitting in each other's faces. Those outside the faith see this and denounce the faith, not the ill behavior of the faithful. Many confessing Christians have lost sight of the supreme object of the Scriptures, the person of Jesus Christ, and have painted over his portrait with infinitesimal brushstrokes of religious systems and codifications to the point where Christ's face is no longer discernible. And then they fight over the details of their own making. The love of the truly loving God has been frustrated, and it has led to more heartache and disillusionment among followers of Christ than words can express.

Tragically, our misunderstandings do not end there. As of late, we have seen a great chasm forming between the material sciences such as astrophysics, biology, and geology and the theological disciplines of religion, meta-ethics, and biblical hermeneutics. This crack has formed mainly from the rapidly expanding use of the scientific method and science's ever-expanding corpus of knowledge. Science is now delving deeply into the far recesses of space and into the history of the universe. What scientists have been learning has clashed with certain theological positions on origins erected by panicked theologians in response to science's shocking findings.

If God is anything, he is without contradiction. St. Augustine, and virtually every respected theologian after him, sees a unity in truth. It has been the church's position throughout the centuries to see all truth as God's truth, wholly unified. There is no scientific truth that is opposed to revealed truth from Scripture. When there are conflicts, those conflicts should be resolved. The fact that our knowledge of God's creation is perceived by some at odds with church teaching begs the question of how we reconcile the two. Or, as some might wonder, are they even reconcilable? There are many loud and passionate voices today who see science and biblical teaching as utterly irreconcilable and, therefore, either see truth to be squarely in the lap of science while others see truth in the lap of current church dogma. The conclusion both of these groups reach is that the opposing view is a dangerous enticement away from truth and must be refuted at all costs. That is why we hear such shrill arguments being launched between scientists and theologians. Punch-drunk with new discoveries, scientists are abandoning the faith because science seems to refute established church doctrine. Ardent biblicists are abandoning science because their understanding of Scripture seems to refute scientific discovery. We are at loggerheads.

The truth-loving Christian, therefore, must be ever dutiful in how he treats knowledge—both natural and revealed. Many outspoken Christians who think they are doing the Kingdom of God a huge favor by defying scientific knowledge in light of unstudied interpretations of revealed Scripture have shipwrecked many a thinking person's faith. Even as far back as the fifth century, St. Augustine warned us of this kind of religious disgrace:

> Often a non-Christian knows something about the earth, the heavens, and the other parts of the world, about the motions and orbits of the stars and even their sizes and distances, and this knowledge he holds with certainty from reason and experience. It is thus offensive and disgraceful for an unbeliever to hear a Christian talk nonsense about such things, claiming that what he is saying is based on Scripture. We should do all that we can to avoid such an embarrassing situation, lest the unbeliever see only ignorance in the Christian and laugh to scorn.

It's all too easy to hear the laughter from the skilled scientist and throughout our better-educated popular culture. Could it be that some of the most branded and bellicose Christian voices today, especially in the United States, seem to be talking the very form of "nonsense" St. Augustine warned us of so many generations ago?

No matter. In the face of these seemingly irreconcilable positions, however, I am an optimist—as was Pope John Paul II when he published his 1998 encyclical *Fides et Ratio*. I believe true science and true Christian doctrine will always come together in the end because both are revelations from a very unified and consistent God. Could it be that many of these seemingly irreconcilable differences we perceive in God's methods of making himself known to us (in the forms of general and special revelation) are more of a statement of how unskillfully we have handled the evidence at hand instead of their proving that these two divine revelations are competing with each other? I predict that, when the dust settles and we understand more about our world and figure out how we can better interpret the Scriptures, we will find both the scientist and the theologian completely embarrassed.

One thing is sure, when the fog of uncertainty and misapplied enquiry is lifted, the embarrassment will not be on the face of God but on ours. For he will prove to be all that our wildest desires have always hoped he would be, a truly loving heavenly Father who is best known as Jesus of Nazareth, the Christ of God. Drink in his story deeply. The Scriptures, rightly divided, are there to usher us into his presence with great joy. His creation, accurately understood, reveals his glorious, divine nature. To know him is eternal life. To know him is the essence of our being. As St. Augustine stated so well and is worth restating, "Thou hast made us for thyself, O Lord, and our hearts are restless until they find their rest in thee."

**

God is infinite. God is spirit. God is holy. God is all-powerful. God is all-knowing. God is good. God is just. God is compassionate. God is truth. God is all-sufficient. God is all-wise. God is pure. God is eternal. God is light. God is life. God is glorious. God is merciful. God is gracious. God is long-suffering. God is so many marvelous things. But, when it comes to understanding the ultimate meaning for our lives, there is one dimension of God's character that unlocks it best . . .

God is love.

It is a statement that is not just a pleasant sentiment or nice catchphrase from the Bible. In light of meaning, it is the most important understanding of who God is. Love is that quality of being that ties together the reason behind existence to the means of our existence. Love is why we were created in the first place. Accordingly, love serves as our gravity, the thing that gives us weight, or substance. Love also empowers us and serves as our trajectory. Love and love alone pushes our lives toward achieving our ultimate happiness and fulfillment as God's created image bearers.

Love informs God's "other-ness" or holiness better than one might first imagine. Because God's love is at its core a word of action, not just a statement of quality, it serves as the primary motivation behind all other divine attributes. Just as gravity defines the longing between the stars and planets to be united as one, God's love is his eternal longing for all to be united with him. Through his revelation of himself as Christ, God calls all things, whether on earth or in heaven, to be fully reconciled—or brought together—in complete unity. This is his loving intent. And the universal force of gravity testifies of his divine plan.

I did not understand the importance of love in my early years. I had wrongly assumed, as I know many others have also wrongly assumed, that God's holiness was his most defining characteristic and that it differed in kind from love. Love, to me, appeared too soft an attribute—not noble enough of an attribute for an all-powerful Creator God. Love spoke of tea and cucumber sandwiches. It spoke of sympathy and tenderness. It did not speak of blazing power and glory. To me, holiness spoke of brandished swords, piercing brilliance, and unstoppable force. What did love have to do with these kingly attributes of God? But, as I went through this journey, I realized how off-center my ideas were. Love is much more than warm affection. It encompasses will and knowledge. To truly love is to understand, to commit to, and to engage emotionally, physically. It takes the entire soul to truly love.

To pair love against holiness as competing attributes of God—as I used to do, and I realize some unfortunately still do—is not to understand either that well. God's love and holiness are inseparable. God's holiness is best understood as everything that makes him different from his creation, which includes, among many other attributes, his infinite power, goodness, and, most of all, his pure, self-existent, and eternal love. To limit God's holiness to his implacable purity and withering presence is far too limiting. It is that, yes, and more. God's love is just as uncompromising and just as pure.

From God's vantage point, love is not that wispy, self-indulgent emotion we most associate with love as humans. Our experience with the term *love* is usually a want or desire, as in "I love pizza" or "I love my dog, Snickers." Yet, those uses of the word *love* describe more what benefit I hope to gain from the relationship (pizza tasting good and my pet fulfilling my need for companionship). God's divine love, however, is much deeper than that. It is an all-absorbing, self-forgetful energy that looks away from one's core needs and outside one's self. God's love is truly holy: transcendentally other. When God graced us with his presence as Jesus, we saw his holiness fully evident as love, even though God's all-powerful nature was not completely revealed to us in Jesus until his resurrection. His holiness as love is not diminished, but, as love, his holiness continuously overwhelms our ability to grasp its significance.

Throughout the Scriptures, God calls his people to worship him and to give him glory. When I was a younger believer first struggling with the idea of God, this biblical teaching of God's demanding our fidelity upset me. Why would God require this of man? Is God egomaniacal? How loving is it that? It makes God sound desperate and insecure in who he is.

As I matured in the faith and began to understand God more, I realized that he was not being jealous for our affection. Quite the opposite. He knows more about us than we can ever know. He knows our affections are easily diverted yet very strong in drawing our souls toward whatever object we affix them to. Our ontological health depends on being connected to him, not to other, lesser things. Our being can never fully flourish and reach its created potential without being connected to him. So, God's calling us to worship him and to bring him glory is not for his benefit, but for ours. This is in keeping with the nature of his holy love. So, when we hear the clarion calls to worship God, we must realize that God does not need our worship to enrich him—nor does he need it to bring him pleasure. God needs nothing. He is self-sufficient. Yet, we need to worship and glorify God in order to reach our truest aim and happiness as his created beings. Worship is for us. It is for our protection. It is the outworking of the "otherness" of God's love. It is a true love built on the reality of everything that is within us and that surrounds us. God is a truly loving heavenly Father.

Therefore, it is God's love that is most evident and, quite arguably, most relevant to our discussion. Our desire for meaning is our desire to know him. To know him is to understand him and know what makes him do what he does. If we have a glimpse of that, then we can make more sense out of our existence and our divine purpose so that we can climb out of our own heads and get along with the business of life.

Love is the motivating force behind God and his actions. It is in love he hung the stars and created the universe. It is in love God created man and woman to be the living, breathing souls that we are. And, it is in love that God entered his own creation to rectify the mess we created in his world because of our choice to disobey him and go our own way. The entire story of God, the universe, and our individual existence is a result of God's love.

God's blinding purity does not adequately explain it. Why would purity seek to create a world where impurity among his image bearers was not just possible, but inevitable? God's sense of justice does not explain it. Why would absolute justice seek opportunity to create an environment capable of injustice? God's goodness does not explain it. What does goodness gain from man's free will to do evil? God's infinite power does not explain it.

What does all power gain from setting limits that are so prevalent in his finite and much weaker created beings?

So then, what does explain all that we know and experience? His love. His desire for connection, to know and be known, explains more than anything why he created us. And the centrality of his love makes sense of why Jesus told us that the two greatest commandments are love-based: (1) love God with all our being and (2) love others as we love ourselves. Jesus made it clear that on these two hang all the law and the prophets. It is why the great Christian apologist William Lane Craig draws attention to these two commandments as "the ultimate apologetic." It is the best argument for the Christian faith. Every demonstration, inner urge, and call to love is a signpost pointing to the highest, most glorious doctrine of the Christian faith. Love is the best explanation of all reality—all imaginings, all reasoning, all desires, and all struggles—that populate the human experience. Why? Because love is at the heart of why we were created in the first place: to be loved and to love.

So, what does this mean? That intense longing we feel inside that never seems to be satisfied is our soul calling out to God for love. All our amusements, addictions, and obsessions are tinged with the core desire for love, only misdirected. It's what explains why the loftiest expressions of the human condition usually center on love and belonging. Poetry, art, music, dance, the performing arts, and many other expressions of human creativity most often use love (even when denuded to the burlesque of mere sexual gratification) as its central theme and that which anchors the motivations of its lead characters. The pursuit of love explains best our reality and the reason why we grow easily discontent in our reality when we are starved of love. This relentless pursuit we feel toward love is a faint echo of the love God shows throughout his story and creation. It's what best explains the force of gravity—love between the heavenly bodies. It's what best explains human biology and psychology—love between human bodies and souls. And it's what best explains religion—love for a connection to the transcendent, a truly loving heavenly Father.

Our individual purposes in life then are centered on love because our Maker has made it so. It is his expression of his being through mankind. Therefore, it only makes sense to see how a life of meaning in this context is to play out. And that's the subject of the next chapter.

Chapter Nineteen

LOVING TRULY

This is love: that we walk in Jesus' commandments.

And what are his commandments? That we walk in love.

LET ME BE BLUNT: WE think too much on ourselves. Not that we think too much *of* ourselves. That's another problem altogether. It's that we think too much *on* ourselves. This is the greatest disease of our time. Not cancer. Not heart disease. Not global warming. But self-absorption. We malignantly obsess over knowing ourselves and striving to find ourselves. We turn our search inward, thinking that to understand our inner self will be the surest way to get the ultimate answers to our lives. Ironically, the answers are not to be found within. The answers are too big to be stored there. By gazing within, we block the light of meaning by our own shadow. We focus so narrowly inward that nothing as expansive as the meaning of life can be discerned. We look through the fixed pinhole of our belly buttons while trying to grasp the magnitude of the galaxies. We look inward when we should be looking outward and upward.

I think this reality alone explains most neuroses and aberrant behavior we see all around us. Our existence was never intended to be sphinctered within. We are meant to soar, to broaden our sights to the far horizons of existence, to bind together what has been ripped apart, and to connect what has yet to be connected. Even this sweet thought resonates within us like the rich sounding of a well-tuned piano note. And this discovery is the sole purpose of this chapter.

Before we go too deep, let's step back for a moment and put everything into perspective. I have some friends who are very practical. I'm sure you do too. You may even be one of those fine, upstanding people. These are the sincere folks who tend to get restless with all this philosophical gum-flapping. They want to know what it means to their existence of waking up, brushing teeth, checking e-mails, doing laundry, paying bills, and squeezing in some exercise before the day is done. That's the stuff of life, and, in their opinion, this discussion on meaning is a ruse to avoid the daily-ness of life where teeth don't get brushed, e-mails don't get checked, dirty laundry piles up in the corner, bills go unpaid, and we sit around thinking as opposed to getting on our stationary bikes to burn off the extra calories from the doughnut we shouldn't have eaten this morning.

"So, what does all this discussion have to do with my life—I mean the real life I lived yesterday, am living today, and plan to live tomorrow?" Fair question. And that's exactly the place where I came to at the end of all this inquiry. What do I have to show for it?

Why should we even bother with the meaning of life?

A very active conversation has been going on about this topic for a long, long time. I began cataloging all the reading and researching I had been doing. Within the past two hundred years alone, quite a few very smart people have asked the "meaning of life" question and tried to answer it. Thinkers like David Hume, Arthur Schopenhauer, Bertrand Russell, Martin Heidegger, and Ludwig Wittgenstein all came to a motley collection of answers that ranged from the basic *Wille zum Leben* (or, a simple biological urge to live and reproduce) to a more problematic position that meaning is simply a matter of linguistic puzzles and gamesmanship. From these answers came the life philosophies (or, if I dare say, the lack thereof) as championed by Friedrich Nietzche, Sigmund Freud, Karl Marx, Jean-Paul Sartre, Jacques Derrida, and the like. And from these philosophies, we've seen towering humanitarian achievements to the cruelest worldviews evidenced in the political wills of Adolf Hitler, Josef Stalin, Pol Pot, and Chairman Mao.

What has mystified me about some of our more noted modern and postmodern philosophers is how their worldviews have taken all human knowing and understanding and changed it completely. It is as if human thought is now seeking to swallow itself like the Ouroboros snake, not to establish unity but to achieve ontological self-extinction. At the end of the day, all their postulating leaves us with is a sense of crippling anxiety and utter hopelessness. Where's the meaning in that?

To decry "meaning is meaningless" is shocking, for sure, but not very helpful. The postmodern philosophers of relativism, subjectivism, and de-constructionism make some fresh, thought-provoking points (ideas that intrigue us by narrowing the light of reason into unexplored, interstitial crevices, all the while darkening the whole cloth of reality), but their points may end up being altogether pointless. Some conclude there's really no meaning at all. There's nothing to hold onto in this life. We are free-float-ing and formless with nothing of substance to anchor us. They reason that any form of absolutism, or true knowledge, is wishful thinking and narrow-minded. Reason, therefore, can only lead us to unreasonable conclusions. But isn't that thought itself self-defeating and meaningless? So why should we trust it?

Most of us, when entangled in this mire of philosophical speculation hawked by some of these modern and postmodern philosophers, know something of fundamental importance is terribly amiss. Our deepest and truest selves, our rational selves, sense the utter disconnection their ideas have with reality. Our empirical selves see that we are surrounded by meaning in the material world, meaning so obvious that its denial is nothing short of madness. Sure, we cannot prove with absolute certainty that our understanding of reality is nothing more than a collection of particular sense perceptions created by chemical and electrical impulses within an individual's nervous system. Even so, we can use that same line of reasoning and say that our understanding of those perceptions is merely perception created by chemical and electrical impulses within an individual's nervous system. And the infinite regress begins, leading nowhere and crushing reason and reality through the agencies of absurdity and unreasonable doubt. Their ideas need to be unmasked for what they are: a spray of over-inflated words and thoughts disconnected from reality. Yet, because they sound so exotic and heady, we sheepishly question our own ability to analyze them. We feel overwhelmed by their verbal assault to call them out for what they are. They will then posit, "So what, then, is reality?" and they try to keep us from self-discovery by chasing shadows that prove not even to have enough substance to be categorized as shadows at all. They convince us that reality is something we can never empirically prove because what we think reality is can be nothing more than electrical misfirings in the human brain, leading to unreliable mental projections occluded by illusory language.

When we hear this from those thinkers, we feel bludgeoned by their verbal barrage of strange and nonsensical accusations of the banality of common sense. We become paralyzed, unable to ask anything more of reality. Their ideas have no mooring into reality that is really known, nor do they have any connection to the human soul. They are the emperor's new clothes. They feel empty to us because they *are* empty. Absolutely empty. Everything we know and experience in reality convicts their ideas of being a sham. They inform us of nothing, point to nothing, stand for nothing, and, when objectively scrutinized, persuade us of nothing.

Life has meaning. In fact, it is full of meaning. Every human in the deepest recesses of his heart knows this.

Only God's presence and his essence explain what is before us. Only he can make sense of the details of our existence. Only he can give us the true meaning of the life he and he alone imagined. God has made us for himself. And our hearts cannot rest until they rest in him.

Meaning best answers the question, "Why?" When it comes to our life, we can more easily explain the who, what, how, and when with direct evidences. The *why* is a bit more mysterious and deep. But, that being said, the why is the single most important question of all. The what and how can only follow the why.

"What?" and "How?" apart from "Why?" can become anything and lead us anywhere—which is terribly unhelpful.

Is the meaning of our life (the "Why?") the same as our duty and our chief end? We know that the Hebrew Scriptures tell us that our duty as God's created image bearers is to "fear God, and keep his commandments," but does that directly address the *why*, the meaning to our lives? Or, does it just explain the means (the *how*) with which our lives best achieve their meaning?

It's like the old story of the three bricklayers. On one bright morning, a stranger walked down the street of his town and saw three bricklayers building a wall. All three were doing the exact same work: buttering their bricks with fresh mortar, placing them carefully along the wall, and precisely tapping the bricks to line up perfectly in pattern, using a level and trowel. To the first bricklayer, the stranger asked, "Sir, what are you doing?" Without looking up, the bricklayer mumbled irritably, "I'm laying bricks." Then, to the second bricklayer, the stranger asked, "Sir, and what are you doing?" The second bricklayer glanced up and said, "I'm building a wall." Then, to the third bricklayer, the stranger asked, "And, you, sir, what are you doing?" The third bricklayer straightened up, looked the stranger in the eye, and declared, "Gentle sir, I'm building a cathedral so that the good families of this village may worship their Maker together."

In this tale, all three are involved quite intentionally with duty. They are doing what is required of them. Yet only one has grasped the true meaning of the duty. Yes, we are to fear God. And yes, we are to keep his commandments. But to what purpose?

The followers of Jesus Christ have wrestled with this question ever since the beginning. One of the most celebrated, concise statements of orthodox Christian doctrine is the Westminster Confession of Faith of 1643 CE. According to the first question of the larger catechism of the Westminster Confession, "What is the chief and highest end of man?" its writers answer, "Man's chief and highest end is to glorify God, and fully to enjoy him forever." This answer to this first catechism question has been a staple of teaching for the past 350 years. Concerning the first part of the answer, "to glorify God," the Westminster divines used as their source texts for this important question the following:

> For of him, and through him, and to him, are all things: to whom be glory forever. Amen. (Rom. 11:36)

> Whether therefore ye eat, or drink, or whatsoever ye do, do all to the glory of God. (1 Cor. 10:31)

And for the second part of the answer, "and fully to enjoy him forever," the divines leaned on the following texts from the Scriptures:

Whom have I in heaven but thee? and there is none upon earth that I desire beside thee. My flesh and my heart faileth: but God is the strength of my heart, and my portion forever. (Psalm 73:25–26)

That they all may be one; as thou, Father, art in me, and I in thee, that they also may be one in us: that the world may believe that thou hast sent me. And the glory which thou gavest me I have given them; that they may be one, even as we are one: I in them, and thou in me, that they may be made perfect in one; and that the world may know that thou hast sent me, and hast loved them, as thou hast loved me. (John 17:21–23)

But did the Westminster divines give us the *why* or another manifestation of the *what* and the *how*? To use the phrase *chief end of man*, as the Westminster Confession does, can give us the illusion that it is answering the why. In actuality, it is not, nor do I think it is actually trying to. Our why cannot be limited to providing God with glory, for there is no reason for us to exist if that is all our existence does. God's glory is already fully manifest in himself either with or without us. And the second part of the catechism's answer to our chief end being "fully to enjoy him forever" may be more closely linked to the meaning of our lives because of what it is pointed to—love.

I find it puzzling to survey the *Westminster Confession and Catechisms* to see how sparsely referenced God's love is in the entire document. God's love—which gushes like a swollen waterfall from the writings of the Apostles John, Peter, and Paul—is only lightly mentioned with glancing blows in passing comments. The centrality of God's love as is demonstrated in the Scriptures is muted and reduced in the Confession. But, its indirect signature rings in the certain portions of the Larger Catechism, especially in Question 90:

Q. 90. What shall be done to the righteous at the day of judgment?

A. At the day of judgment, the righteous, being caught up to Christ in the clouds, shall be set on his right hand, and there openly acknowledged and acquitted, shall join with him in the judging of reprobate angels and men, and shall be received into heaven, where they shall be fully and forever freed from all sin and misery; filled with inconceivable joys, made perfectly holy and happy both in body and soul, in the company of innumerable saints and holy angels, but especially in the immediate vision and fruition of God the Father, of our Lord Jesus Christ, and of the Holy Spirit, to all eternity. And this is the perfect and full communion, which the members of the invisible church shall enjoy with Christ in glory, at the resurrection and day of judgment.

Yes, even though unstated, you can sense the elevated purpose of love in our existence in the way the catechism answer describes our "perfect and full communion" with each other and with God himself. Even though the Westminster divines did not use the term love, it is obviously the effect of divine love they are describing: God's intentional drawing of all things unto himself in perfect and full communion, which was his purpose at the creation of all things and continues to be his will for his creation until all things are consummated. I find this fault of underestimating the love of God in the Westminster Confession important to note because if you read the Gospel of John, Romans, both books to the Corinthians, Galatians, Ephesians, Colossians, all three of John's letters, both of Peter's letters, among others, love is overwhelmingly emphasized. A summary of Christian doctrine like the Westminster Confession should not only be accurate in what it says, it must also be complete and properly balanced, meaning all thoughts are weighted as they are weighted in its source document, the Holy Scriptures. In no way am I assuming that the doctrine of love was not implicit, or understood, within the doctrinal statements maintained within the Westminster Confession—nor that the Westminster divines would have argued against the doctrine of love as being paramount within a full statement of Christian doctrine. I just find it strange it was not more explicitly stated within the document itself.

Once we know God and understand his purposes for his creation, we can then begin to understand our purpose in life. If you were to take the time to talk with a thousand different people and ask them, "What is God like?" you'd get a thousand different answers. Even those who are most religious and believe pretty much the same body of religious doctrine, we find their understanding of God is strikingly varied. Why is this? You'd think a basic understanding of God would be universal. But, it's not. I do have a theory about all this. And it has everything to do with how we view ourselves and the role of God in our lives.

Most people walk through each day with little to no thought of God in their lives. I know I do. And, I suspect it is also true with you. There are very few of us who maintain "the presence of God" in our minds and consciousness day in and day out. We go through our lives quite unaware of God even being part of our worlds. For us, God is like electricity. We know it exists, but we pay so little attention to it. We flip a switch, and lights come on. We check our cell phone, and the phone responds by lighting up its screen to display the latest text message. If we stopped to think about it, we would know that electricity has to be part of these systems, but we just don't pay much attention to it, though electricity has a profound effect on our lives. We just expect electricity to be there, and we are content not to worry about it.

The same goes for the awareness of God. Like electricity, most of us don't have much understanding of the God we have been created to be so much like. We are functionally unaware of the true nature of God.

When it comes to meaning, "God is love" serves as the fundamental dimension to understanding God's intentions. Why? Because the presence of divine love best explains the largest amounts of data about our universe, our existence, and our experience as human beings. Love animates us and gives us weight, just as gravity plays such a fundamental role in the physical universe. Life's meaning cannot be understood by mere perceptions, but life must be understood for what it truly is before meaning can be extracted. When we keep pressing our understanding of reality with the question *why*, we find that life is more than willing to share the answer. And this noble inquiry will run us back to God and the meaning he has attached to life, both from his point of view and ours: and it is love.

But even the term *love* itself is impossibly variegated. Talk of love to a doting great-grandmother and she will regale you with stories about her new great-granddaughter's first steps and how much she looks like her side of the family. Talk of love to a teenage boy with raging hormones and he will think of an attractive starlet and how much he would like to see her naked. Talk of love to a twelve-year-old girl and she will associate love to that swirly, flirty feeling of being thought of as pretty and the attention that comes with prettiness. Talk of love to a tortured poet and he will lament over a stew of unrequited yearnings for another.

Love, then, cannot be assumed as universally understood. It must be defined in its purest, denotive form: a form that best articulates God's definition of love. Our life's purpose and, as a result, our meaning must be based on something more than mere perception or subjective feeling; it must be bolted to its absolute. God is our Creator. He has declared himself as being love. And we must understand love on his terms.

But, how does God define love? How can this be known? We see love being defined for us in three areas of human knowing: God's observable universe, God's special revelations, and the conscience of man. Even more so, God best defines love in what he did when he came into the world as Jesus, the most special of his special revelations. He showed something wholly other about love that is remarkably different from the love we know on our own. In the Bible, God explains love in this way, "By this we know love, because He laid down His life for us. And we also ought to lay down our lives for the brethren" (1 John 3:16 NKJV).

C.S. Lewis, in his book *The Four Loves*, describes the difference in kind between most loves we commonly know from our human experience (friendship, affection, and erotic loves) and the charitable love described in Christianity. Lewis calls the loves we are most familiar with as "need-loves" and other loves that best reflect God's definition of love as "gift-loves." This is a fascinating distinction and explains a lot about the confusion some people have about the very nature of love, even among Christians who at times grow ambivalent about the doctrine of love, even though the Scriptures are overrun with commands, stories, and allusions concerning love from start to finish. We see one kind of love and assume all love (because the same word is being used) is to be understood in the light of that lesser form of love. We see need-loves at work in our world and, since we call need-loves by the same name as gift-loves, we assume that gift-loves are inferior to other Christian doctrines.

In the original Greek New Testament writings, God's gift-love is distinguished by a unique word not commonly used by normal Greek-speaking people of the time: *agape*. There has been much written about this word in Christian theology, and I will not replicate the effort. But from the fact that the writers of the New Testament used an uncommon word for God's kind of love, we can surmise that they saw this word as referencing something special. It seems they wanted us to view *agape* as a special sort of love that needed to be differentiated from the more commonly used words for love like *storge* (affection), *philio* (friendship), and *eros* (romance). The Bible's use of *agape* in critical passages of the Scriptures that describe God's sort of love seems to make the case for this view quite nicely.

God's love is purely a gift-love. It is a love that is not dependent on the object of its love for its strength, value, or reason for being. By looking into the story of humanity in general and God's plan of redemption in particular, we see how the God of the Universe, who needs nothing from us, still graces us with many proofs of his love and good favor. Need-loves, on the other hand, require good to flow back to the giver in order for it to sustain. My love of pizza is a pure need-love. Pizza provides me a reward for my love for it. Even some of the most glorious romantic loves between a man and a woman are more of a need-love than a gift-love. Why? Because our love for a life-partner offers us more back in the form of companionship, sexual gratification, and the heart-rush experience with the "otherness" of the opposite sex than the willing self-sacrifice of our needs for the object of our love.

Gift-love only requires the full commitment of the lover to love, regardless if there is any returned value from the object of the love. We see gift-love less frequently in our lives, but it is present. It is most apparent, but not entirely so, in the love a young mother has for her child. It's one of the great gifts God has given women: the opportunity to experience gift-love with more power and meaning than any need-love could ever provide. In our lives, there will always be need-love. Need-love is a many splendored thing indeed. But gift-love is the love that is rarest and most beautiful of all loves. Gift-love is the love that God is calling us to. Gift-love is heroic. Gift-love is loving truly.

God's fullest definition of love comes not in the form of a dictionary definition, but in bodily form when he visited mankind on earth as God-man: Jesus Christ. He came in love and as Love in order to redeem a people bent on eternal separation from him. Christians call this separation from God's love *sin*. He showed his love in every action he undertook as Jesus. Jesus came to remove all things that separate him from each human soul and called it "taking away all sins of the world." He sacrificed himself, becoming both the just and the justifier, in order to lift the burden of separating sin that was sucking the life-blood from mankind's psyche. In gift-love, he has prepared an eternal home for his creation in heaven for all who believe in his unrelenting love. God desires to remove all barriers between himself and man, as well as the barriers between men, in order to unite all into one big family. This is the explanation of his love. And he has communicated all these great truths to us in the form of the holy writings found in the Old and New Testaments of the Bible.

And God speaks of his love to us through our own consciences. When we read a grand novel of self-sacrifice, we feel the magnetic pull of absolute gift-love within us. When we watch a movie that shows people willing to sacrifice their own futures for the benefit of others, we see God's gift-love being demonstrated, maybe not in purest form, but the gleams of celestial beauty radiate nonetheless. When we hear of lovers—estranged by pride and selfishness—recant and reunite, we know we are in the presence of a transcendental love. When we are touched by pure goodness and beauty as they point us toward truth, we sense the only definition of love that is capable of affecting us so deeply. It is deep calling out to deep. And it is the truest definition of love—a fully self-sacrificing, self-forgetful love that reminds us of the type of love that spills without limit from the overflowing heart of our loving heavenly Father.

We will never understand our lives nor the world in which we live in, until we fully grasp how high, wide, long, and deep is the love that Christ has for us—and the unique role Christ has called us to in living a life of love as his image bearers. For God did create us in his image, not just as a physical specimen, but also as an image, albeit limited, of his soul. As he loves, we are to love truly: living our lives purposed by the divine love that is the truest of all loves.

As I surveyed my discontent with church in my early years of faith, I realized how selfish I had been. I had no knowledge of the why of the Christian faith. I only saw the surface and the superficial and came to rather uninformed, prejudicial positions on the nature of Jesus Christ and his teachings. Even though I could quote Scripture passage after Scripture passage, and even though I had read thousands upon thousands of pages of theological speculations and commentaries, I still had missed the point, or meaning, of the Christian life.

I don't think I have been alone in my blindness. I still talk with people daily who, just like I was, are still entangled in a web of loveless Christian doctrine and dogma (which, in reality, is no Christian doctrine at all, for 1 John chapter 3 reminds us that it's a sure sign we have passed from death to life when the evidence of love appears in our lives). These people have never stopped to get a picture of all that's happening around us and view life as God views life. They don't know the why, even though it is plainly obvious once it is seen. I was there too. We sense a dryness to our spiritual lives and are not sure why the tongues of our souls feel so parched. We wrongly assume (because this is what many of us are taught in our churches) that it is our own lack of spiritual discipline that makes us feel so alienated from God and the abundant life he promised.

To this day, I still hear it all around me. I hear preacher after preacher raging from their pulpits about the Christian life in the same lifeless, loveless form: that holy living is about duty solely with little to no mention of the reason behind all of it—to love. By no means do I believe it to be malicious on any preacher's part. Rather, I think he has lost sight of the why along the way, as have many of us. It's easy for this to happen. A love-filled Christian worldview re-clarifies everything and brings all back into unity and balance. We no longer see everything outside the church as suspect and wrought with danger. We see the world as God does, in love: "For God so loved the world, that he gave his only begotten Son." We see the peoples outside the Christian faith not as the enemies but as the supreme prize: God's image bearers whom God wants in his family. We discount culture, nations, and civilizations, in their own right, as ephemeral. We see people, even the strident atheist, as eternal and loved by God. We now judge every action not by a morality of prescribed religious duty but by the highest moral code of love that encompasses not only our actions but also our motivations and the circumstances that surround them. Love is both the animator and the animated.

This perspective on love comes straight from Scripture. The Bible pointedly tells us that any form of religious duty or moral action is meaningless unless it is motivated by love. The first three verses of the thirteenth chapter of 1 Corinthians remind us of that:

> Though I speak with the tongues of men and of angels, but have not love, I have become sounding brass or a clanging cymbal. And though I have the gift of prophecy, and understand all mysteries and all knowledge, and though I have all faith, so that I could remove mountains, but have not love, I am nothing. And though I bestow all my goods to feed the poor, and though I give my body to be burned, but have not love, it profits me nothing.

Here the Bible reminds us that acting out the what and the how of the Christian life is a waste of time and energy if it is not anchored to the why, and that why is love. Love is what explains everything about the commands Jesus gave us, the total story of God's redemptive plan for man, why God created everything in the first place, and why we are so moved deep within our souls whenever we see someone do some loving act that whispers of the gift-love of God.

God has created us in love in order to love. This is loving truly. But it's not a love that most people define (inaccurately) as "affections and desires." These are not loves, but cravings. Instead, this true love is the love of God that is about forgetting one's self and focusing on the benefit of another, no matter what happens. Some think love is about pleasing another. Quite often God's gift-love will ultimately please. But gift-love's truest aim is not on dispensing pleasure, but instead doing what's in the best interest of that person. If love takes aim at pleasure, it ceases to be true love. If love takes aim at the higher mark of acting in the best interest of the object, not only will it achieve this aim, but pleasure will be the ultimate result. If love is aimed at anything other than the good of others, it no longer takes on the quality of gift-love, but can, and often does, turn into a devilish desire that can destroy the soul of man by attaching our affections to ideas and items that will separate us from God and others, not unite and create connection.

God has designed his world to depend on love as the human body depends on oxygen to survive. Starve the body of oxygen and the body will die. Starve the human soul of love and the soul dies. Anything that stands in the way of love, separates. And that which separates us from God or causes needless separation from others is anti-love and should be known as such. For anything that has the power to tear apart what God is trying to bring together is best labeled as sin. And our call to separate from sin is, in its purest form, a double negative, an ironic call to loving unification of all things under the headship of Jesus Christ—his ultimate desire for his creation and the ultimate meaning to our lives. It's what the first chapter of Colossians is talking about.

What is sin? It is anything that destroys connection and unification of people to other people and people to God. It is everything that is unloving. What is adultery? It is an unloving act that separates by driving a terrible wedge between a husband and wife. What is lying? It is an unloving act that separates by destroying trust in relationships between people. What is selfishness? It is an unloving act or intention that separates by discounting the value of other people and pushing them away in order to please myself. What is idolatry? It is an unloving act or intention that separates us from God's direct love. What is hatred? It is an unloving act or intention that separates us from others. What is dissension? It is an unloving act or intention that separates people from each other and puts ideas ahead of relationships. What is envy? It is an unloving act or intention that separates people by valuing possessions or position more than we value the welfare and good of others. What is murder? It is an unloving act that assumes another's value, or existence, is worth less than my desires. What is drunkenness? It is an unloving act that separates people because it puts my own bodily and psychological desires ahead of others' well-being. And we could go on and on with a whole variety of sins and show how all sin is a lack of love that causes separation. Jesus said it often. Paul states it plainly in the thirteenth chapter of his letter to the Romans. The Apostle John writes about it in his first letter. God's law is love. Sin is the breaking of God's law. Therefore, sin is the lack of love. And that's why sin is so insidious.

But even actions done that appear to be good and honorable, if they are not motivated by love, can be just as sinful as some of the more obvious sinful actions. That's the lesson of 1 Corinthians 13: "Though I speak with the tongues of men and of angels, but have not love . . ." It's also the reason Jesus made it clear to us that the entire law is summed up in two commands: love God and love others. Maybe it also explains why many people will come to God at the Day of Judgment and declare:

> "Lord, Lord, have we not prophesied in Your name, cast out demons in Your name, and done many wonders in Your name?" And then I [Jesus] will declare to them, "I never knew you; depart from Me, you who practice lawlessness!"

To love is our meaning. It explains everything that God has created and has been doing through his creation. It explains why we were created in the first place. And it explains all the commands in Scripture concerning why God asked us to do some things and avoid others. We are called to be lovers. We are called to act against our natural, sin-soaked desires to separate and destroy unity so that we can show a love that shines light, or glory, on God's grand intention for his creation.

I don't think the world sees the glorious love of God through the current manifestation of his church in our generation early in the twenty-first century. I speak as an American who has been most heavily influenced by the state of the Christian faith in the United States. It is with a great heaviness I say this. As I returned back to faith, I inserted myself back into the church. I think it is necessary for all people who are following Christ's teachings to be actively connected to the church in some form—but not necessarily to a church organization, or a church building, but to a collection of believers who are working out their faith together in their everyday lives. Jesus, when he was here on earth, routinely sought out opportunities to engage people of faith in their public gatherings. And I think there is plenty of evidence that Jesus Christ wants us to be engaged with others of like faith. We were not meant to be islands, but connected parts within the

Body of Christ as living stones forming a living, breathing temple built to house the glory of God.

As I came to terms with the meaning of my life as a lover who loves truly, I realized how much work there is to do. The world is in desperate need of love. Yet, it will never be fully aware of the love it needs. Sometimes our artists have done a better job of drawing attention to our need for love. In Vincent Van Gogh's famous painting *Starry Night* that now hangs in the Modern Museum of Art in New York City, we see Van Gogh's use of the color yellow to depict love. We see explosive swirls of yellow in the sky showing God's love among the stars. We see bright yellow windows glowing from the houses of the town below representing the love found among family and friends. Ironically, there is only one building that lacks the glow of love in the town. And it is the church where the windows are a deep, cold black. It's the reason why, every time I turn on my cell phone, a picture of Van Gogh's *Starry Night* appears. It is to remind me of what Van Gogh saw over a hundred years ago. Love is everywhere, except in the place that claims to champion Jesus' life and his will the most. Van Gogh was, and still is, right. And I never want to forget.

We also hear John Lennon of the Beatles sing, "All you need is love. Love is all you need." And we mistake this simple tune to be a silly, frivolous pop song. But we know Lennon's song has more depth of truth than even he may have realized, especially if we understand the term *love* as something more than sexual appetite—a real possibility based on the overall theme of the song. Similarly and throughout the ages, art's most dominant theme has been that of love: that bigger form of love that draws from a similar, if not identical, wellspring as God's self-sacrificing, self-forgetful, gift-love. It is for good reason. Because artists in every generation have mutually concluded that all we need is, well, love. Love is all we need.

But, there seems to be so little gift-love out there. Deep down, all of creation groans and people lament because of the terrible tax that separating sin has levied on our collective consciences. This lack of gift-love in the form of communal greed, selfishness, and pride explains most atrocities. This lack of gift-love in the form of individual greed, selfishness, and pride explains most relational problems between people, whether they be family members, co-workers, neighbors, or romantic lovers. And it is the lack of gift-love, both communal and individual, that explains why most local churches are a muddled mess of infighting, bitterness, and suspicion. All are only interested in their own interests. No one is looking after the interests of others.

I can sympathize with those who would want to pull away from the church, at least the church as it is most commonly seen today. There is so little love there. Our hearts can discern the disconnect. But, pulling away from the church only makes the problem worse. What God is trying to do is unify and draw together, not break apart. When we disengage from the church in order to live a more truth-filled spiritual life, we are destroying what we think we are protecting. We are fighting against God's design for his people and his creation. Most likely, the temptations to pull away from the church are not actions motivated by love, but more so motivated by our own selfishness. So, who are we to point fingers?

Loving truly is a complicated journey, road blocked with frustrations and diversions. But it is the only path that puts all things right in our lives. Our reason for existing is not of our doing, but God's. He has designed this world in this way and for his own good reasons. After all, he is Creator God. The meaning for our lives is bound up in his intentions, not ours. His intention for our lives is most fully explained in his desire for us to love truly, not just him, but each other as well.

***

Yeah, but how does love look on an ordinary Tuesday morning?

Francis Schaeffer more eloquently stated it in the book by the same title, *How Should We Then Live?* I am choosing to ask the same highly practical question. In his book, Schaeffer chose to explore the great story of human achievement and thought and how it affected belief, from the Roman Empire to the twentieth century. I ask the question from a slightly differing point of view. As needed as the historical understanding is, I'm not so much interested in how life has been lived from a historical perspective as I am interesting in putting meaning into daily practice.

Our everyday lives are filled with all kinds of activities. Most are so ordinary we do not even think much on them. The processes of eating, breathing, having conversations, sleeping, brushing our teeth, taking out the trash, reading a good book, purchasing a new sweater on the Internet, balancing our checkbooks, listening to music, smelling freshly baked bread, going to a Green Bay Packers football game, cuddling with our spouses on the couch while watching a sitcom on TV, petting the dog, painting our living rooms a warmer shade of tan, updating our statuses on Facebook, and even daydreaming all have meaning. These are quite normal human activities. God has created us to be human; therefore, these very practical and very common activities are part of his purpose flowing through our lives. But, in the immortal words of singer/songwriter Tina Turner, "What's love got to do with it?" Good question.

I think there's great risk in over-spiritualizing our lives, especially for many of us who take our faith seriously. It's easy to come to the reactive conclusion that the spiritual life trumps the material life. I think there may be great risk here. I have held that position in the past, and I see it creeping into my worldview quite unexpectedly time and again. I think it is easy to begin to see the material world as at war with the spiritual world because we perceive so many aspects of the material world as being enticements away from God—those material things that incite lust, coveting, envy, and pride—when, from God's point of view, the material world is quite important and has been created to reveal his divine character to us and to draw us to him. How do we know this? Because he told us so in the Bible. He also created everything as both spiritual and material. It is quite conceivable that God could have created everything to be spiritual only. God is not material. He is spirit. So why should there even be a material existence? Why not create only that which is according to his essence? If God wanted to, he could have created us with no sense of materiality at all. Material existence is not a requirement. We are material and living in a material world because God wanted it to be so. It's his idea of what humanity should be. And it's an essential part of how we live according to our life's purpose of living a life of love.

If our love doesn't manifest itself both in the spiritual and the everyday material world, we are not thinking on love in its entirety. As I walk through my life, I now see the Buddhist teaching of mindfulness becoming even more important, though I do not consider myself a Buddhist but a Christian. Mindfulness is not an exclusive teaching to Buddhism, even though Buddhist doctrine does champion it best. It is also understood in the Judeo-Christian doctrines of "Be still and know that I am God," and "Whether therefore you eat, or drink, or whatsoever you do, do all to the glory of God." These are teachings of mindfulness. These are teachings that bring love into a "mindful" awareness both in the spiritual and material realms. We need to be aware of what is happening around us. We need to be aware that our reason for being is to love. Love is and should be active and present in all aspects of our lives. When we make breakfast in the morning for our family, or when we choose to forgo watching a favorite TV show in order to help a not-so-well-known neighbor find her lost dog, we are being mindful of our purpose as "lover." We become self-forgetful and full of the love we should have for one another.

The idea of the need for self-forgetfulness in the Christian life has never been better articulated outside the Scriptures than in C.S. Lewis' closing paragraph of his monumentally important book, *Mere Christianity*:

> But there must be a real giving up of the self. You must throw it away "blindly" so to speak. Christ will indeed give you a real personality: but you must not go to Him for the sake of that. As long as your own personality is what you are bothering about you are not going to Him at all. The very first step is to try to forget about the self altogether. Your real, new self (which is Christ's and also yours, and yours just because it is His) will not come as long as you are looking for it. It will come when you are looking for Him. Does that sound strange? The same principle holds, you know, for more everyday matters. Even in social life, you will never make a good impression on other people until you stop thinking about what sort of impression you are making. Even in literature and art, no man who bothers about originality will ever be original: whereas if you simply try to tell the truth (without caring twopence how often it has been told before) you will, nine times out of ten, become original without ever having noticed it. The principle runs through life from top to bottom. Give up yourself, and you will find your real self. Lose your life and you will save it. Submit to death, death of your ambitions and favourite wishes every day and death of your whole body in the end: submit with every fibre of your being, and you will find eternal life. Keep back nothing. Nothing that you have not given away will really be yours. Nothing in you that has not died will ever be raised from the dead. Look for yourself, and you will find in the long run only

hatred, loneliness, despair, rage, ruin, and decay. But look for Christ
and you will find Him, and with Him everything else thrown in.

Lewis' idea of "keep nothing back" is that self-forgetfulness can only
lead to real selfhood and happiness. It's that idea that our true meaning can
never be found within, but found outside through our relationship with
God and our relationships with our fellow image bearers. True gift-loving
is keeping nothing back.

Don't our hearts soar when we see truly loving acts in the world? And
those acts don't necessarily have to be pointed toward a spiritual end to
create such a response, either. Most of the time, it isn't purely spiritual
but quite material. It can be a soldier who, in the heat of battle, willingly
throws his body on a grenade to save the lives of three of his buddies in the
foxhole. It can be the mom who sacrifices all her hopes, dreams, beauty,
fortune, and self-importance in order to help her child grow up to live a
better life, like Victor Hugo's character Fantine in *Les Miserables*. It can be
a husband who sacrifices all his dreams in order to care for a wife who suf-
fers for twenty years from dementia, fits of depression, and incontinence. It
can be a teenager giving away all his birthday money to a hungry stranger
who comes to him in need on the street. It can be found in the actions of
a hip-hop artist (who would shock us with his personal life's lack of good,
Christian family values) who donates hundreds of thousands of dollars to
form a football league for needy kids like Snoop Dogg has done in Los
Angeles and Chicago. It can be found in those uncelebrated helpers at soup
kitchens in our urban centers. It can be found at the neighborhood play-
ground where a retired vet voluntarily picks up trash as he takes his daily
afternoon stroll. It can be found at the grocery store where a young co-ed
offers her place in the checkout line to an elderly stranger. It can be found
virtually everywhere. It's more than a simple idea of social justice. It is raw,
self-forgetful love. And our hearts resonate because these direct acts of love

point to something our hearts yearn for most. They are the jewels of heaven glistening with the refracted, radiant love of God. They add sparkle and wonder to our lives.

In the spirit of full disclosure, there is a dark side as well. The harsh part of this story is that we see these graces showing up more often outside the Christian church. Many times the acts of love best seen are not from those we would readily label as devoted Christians. We confessing Christians ought to sparkle brightest with God's love. But, as Van Gogh pointed out— and as our hearts are keen to remind us—we rarely see these graces radiating from within our churches. What we see most is a dry, loveless, moral grandstanding mislabeled as a "defense of Christian values" that is filled with a hissing "tsk, tsk!" accompanied with an accusatory finger-wag. So many in the church act not as God's ambassadors of the good news of Jesus, but, instead, as God's district attorneys hell-bent on locking up the whole lot of these amoral, fornicating, unwashed sinners when our own moral "center" is seven degrees removed from love. We have the beam in our eye. They have the speck. Ironically, our self-styled morality may be the most amoral. Love does cover a multitude of sins. Lack of love piles on a multitude more.

It is accurate to say that the modern-day Christian church, as a whole, is starved of God's love. The most strident moralists are those who profess to be the most fully committed biblicists, some of whom appear to even hate the sound of the word "love" and refuse to use it because it's just too mealy-mouthed and prone to abuse. Of course love is going to be abused. Everything God created that is good has been, is being, and will continue to be abused long after we have come and gone. Why should we expect love to be an exception?

Before I give you the wrong impression, I'm not a pessimist who enjoys pointing out the obvious flaws just to be sensational. I believe there is hope for the Christian church. That's why I'm back in it. Phillip Yancey, in his simply argued book, *Church: Why Bother?* reminded me that church is the means God has established for us to function as his followers while here on earth. Also, even with all our faults as believers, there is something glorious going on through the church even though we may not see it. In Paul's letter to the Ephesian church, Paul wants those believers to know "that now the manifold wisdom of God might be made known by the church to the principalities and powers in the heavenly places, according to the eternal purpose which He accomplished in Christ Jesus our Lord." In essence, we who are believers and who are working out our faith together in love are on this cosmic stage. And the theme of the play is God's wisdom and character. God has chosen to make himself known to all his creation through the work he is doing among us as we function as his church. The business of the church is indeed no small matter.

My only message to the church at this point is this: "Where is the love?" We have been so busy with the concern of living the Christian life that we may have missed the most important thing of all—the why, which can only be answered with a full understanding of God's purposes for his creation. His purposes are our meaning. And, the evidence is telling us that it is to love.

Could it be that we as members of the church have fallen victim to paralysis by analysis? Are we so caught up with mastering the Scriptures and learning new Christian techniques that we never get on with the business of living out our faith in the world? According to a 2006 Gordon-Conwell Theological Seminary study, there were approximately six million books about Christianity in print with up to two hundred thousand new books being published each year. That is not even factoring in Podcasts, radio programs, television shows, and the like. What's disheartening is that I'm adding to this bloating of our shelves. The sad part is that most of this explosion of Christian literature has happened since the mid-1990s, when the growth of Christian influence in the world has been diminishing precipitously. I think the two phenomena are eerily related. Could it be we are spending all our time in a religious huddle, staring at our own religious belly buttons and not living the gift-love purpose God has called us to? Most Christians today don't even know very many non-Christians needing to be loved on and introduced to Jesus. We are so busy learning how to *do* Christianity that we're not actually doing *any* Christianity.

So, how does love look on a Tuesday morning? It starts with taking our focus away from our own interests and focusing instead on loving others. What's really strange is this: only when we stop thinking about ourselves and begin thinking about others and their needs do we ever get the satisfaction out of life we all want so badly. It feels counterintuitive, yet it is so true. Do an experiment: put this book down and consciously stop thinking about what you want out of life and instead think on some other person who is in your sphere of influence and what they need. Begin thinking of ways you can make that person's life better. Don't simply aim to please that individual, but truly look at ways of making that life better. And then do something about it. Don't contemplate what you are getting out of the deal. Do this not once today, but twice. Maybe even do it three times with three different people. And make sure, as you go along the way, that you share with them how they can have a personal relationship with Jesus Christ. Why do that? Because a relationship with Jesus Christ is the most needed thing for every human heart. Introducing them to their Creator satisfies God's loving intent to "unite all things in him, things in heaven and things on earth," as the Apostle Paul explains in the book he wrote to the Ephesians.

After the day is done, take a quick inventory of your state of mind. I am confident you will find yourself in a better place. Why is that so? It's because when you act lovingly like this, you are acting according to your purpose—the purpose God has had planned for your life from the very beginning. You are, in effect, acting like him. You are living your life according to your Manufacturer's specifications; therefore, you are optimizing the way you were designed. And it is a glorious way to go.

Philosopher Terry Eagleton said it best in his brilliant little book, *The Meaning of Life: a Very Short Introduction*, when he concluded:

> The meaning of life is not a solution to a problem, but a matter of living in a certain way. It is not metaphysical, but ethical . . . It's just this kind of bathos that Matthew sets up in his Gospel, where he presents the Son of Man returning in glory surrounded by angels for the Last Judgment. Despite this off-the-peg cosmic imagery, salvation turns out to be an embarrassingly prosaic affair—a matter of feeding the hungry, giving drink to the thirsty, welcoming the stranger, and visiting the imprisoned. It has no "religious" glamour or aura whatsoever. Anybody can do it. The key to the universe turns out to be not some shattering revelation, but something that a lot of decent people do anyway, with scarcely a thought. Eternity lies not in a grain of sand but in a glass of water. The cosmos revolves on comforting the sick. When you act in this way, you are sharing the love that built the stars. To live in this way is not just to have life, but to have it in abundance.

Could the meaning of life really be that simple . . . that disarming? It must, because this kind of life-meaning explains more than any other philosophical statement or theological dogmatic I've ever stumbled across. At this moment, I sit in the Montreal airport on a Monday afternoon, waiting for a co-worker's plane to arrive. I see people swirling all around me, waving "Welcome home" signs outside of customs—reuniting with friends, family members, and lovers with squeals of delight. I hear their bursts of laughter and animated stories of grand adventures from other parts of the world. I see a couple giving each other a final, tender kiss and embrace before an obviously painful separation. I see a man sweeping up a piece of trash along the well-polished corridor that a young boy accidentally dropped as he playfully skipped behind his father. I see a young woman cheerfully mopping the granite marble of a bar after a customer spilled his drink. She laughs with him, not annoyed, but enjoying the shared moment with him.

Maybe I've been surrounded by more meaning than I gave myself a chance to see. Maybe I trapped myself in a stale, windowless room of abstract thought and thereby missing the spectacle of meaning on full display among the material. Maybe there truly are a lot of decent people who are scarcely thinking about meaning, but, even so, living a life chock full of meaning besides. Maybe I've been the wrong-headed one who has, in a fevered death-struggle to subdue meaning, allowed it to slip through my grasping fingers. If these souls I see around me are missing anything, maybe it's the mere knowledge that all the love they show day-in, day-out has a fountainhead: the Creator of meaning, a heavenly Father who wants nothing more than for us to enjoy a life of abundance if we only slow down long enough to open up our hearts to what Emmanuel Lévinas termed as "the Other." Maybe my struggle to define meaning actually extracted my soul from meaning altogether. Meaning, when we subject it to abstract dissection like a medical student does to an embalmed cadaver on a cold examination table, loses its animating force to show us all that it is. Sure, that medical student can discern from dissection each muscle, ligament, and internal organ of the body, but she cannot explain the joy that person's eviscerated body received when eating a piece of key lime pie.

Most people, including you and me, sense meaning even though we never stop to analyze it. It's there. We know it's there. And it is an irreducible truth impervious of any attempt at further deconstruction. We know it best as love. We know love best as God. And we know God best as Jesus Christ, God "in flesh." Our love, then, animates in the fleshy parts of our existence—in the material here and now. We don't label it as meaning, but we know that every act of love we experience in the everydayness of our material existence stirs us in the deepest part of our truest selves.

Our love is best when it is active and true and not just abstract expressions and disembodied sentiments. It is a tender kiss. An appreciative hug. A cup of cold water. A visit when we are sick. An extra hand lifting a grocery bag into the trunk of our car. It is love in motion. It is loving truly. It is God incarnate.

Chapter Twenty

BEFORE I GO

The Spirit and the bride say, "Come!"

THE CRACK IN MY FAITH has healed, but it has left a telltale scar. I can feel it. It leaves me with a bit of sadness and regret at times, yet it also reminds me of all that has happened to me and that my faith has also been healed. I am whole again. I am a bit wiser and more knowing than I once was, yet not fully so. I also find myself more prone to being reduced to tears when I encounter hurting souls and doubting hearts. I know their pains. And I even look at religious skeptics differently. I now look at their ideas, thoughts, and opinions with much more sympathy. I see these very smart thinkers wrestling as I did, some coming to the same conclusions I came to, yet others concluding that God and/or religion is not for them. I can relate to that. John C. Polkinghorne once wrote:

> It seems to me that many educated people in the Western world view religious belief with a certain wistful wariness. They would like some sort of faith, but feel that it is only to be had on terms that amount to intellectual suicide. They can neither accept the idea of God nor quite leave it alone.

The brightest among us are faced with a terrible conundrum. They are being told that they are betraying their mental acuity if they open their hearts and minds to explore faith as a possible explanation of the meaning of life when so much human knowledge *appears* to be warring against it as a reasonable answer. In many ways, they are being betrayed by the very mental acuity that has created the angst in the first place. How tragically ironic.

There is a stress put upon the more thoughtful among us when we encounter certain Christians who are promoting themselves as arbiters of the truth but are doing so in ways that seemingly affront everything that the truth espouses: love as meaning. They are arrogant even though ignorant. They are bulls in china shops wrecking the truth, goodness, and beauty of the faith by their own thoughtless actions and reactions. It is hard for us who have struggled so hard to get to truth to find people already there who have arrived by casual happenstance. It seems unfair. But, no matter how others have arrived at truth or how rudely they have come to faith, to live a life based on truth is still better than living a life based on something other than truth just to avoid awkward associations. I will enter God's family that also welcomes "the crazy Christians" as long as I have a relationship with Jesus Christ.

For those of us who are embroiled in doubt, know this: doubt is not necessarily the enemy of faith. I once thought it was. There can be honest doubt and dishonest doubt. An honest doubt is seeking after truth when there is no confidence that one has arrived at the truth. A dishonest doubt is seeking to distance one's self from an idea that one doesn't like regardless of whether it is true or not. If pursued honestly, doubt is actually faith trying to grab hold of reality. There is a foundation to honest doubt that is also very important for faith. Doubt is making the point that anything I believe must be based on substance. Faith shares a similar aim. Even the Bible states that "faith is the substance of things hoped for, the evidence of things not seen." There is a skeptical quality to faith we must embrace: substance and evidence that defines faith. Honest doubt is that skeptical faith at work. We must place our faith in the ground that is most sure. Alfred, Lord Tennyson, the great Victorian poet, once clarified this thought in his *Memoriam A.H.H. Obiit MDCCCXXXIII: 96* for Arthur Henry Hallam, a man who died unexpectedly of a stroke at the young age of twenty-two while engaged to Tennyson's sister Emily:

> You say, but with no touch of scorn,
>
> Sweet-hearted, you, whose light-blue eyes
>
> Are tender over drowning flies,
>
> You tell me, doubt is Devil-born.
>
> I know not: one indeed I knew
>
> In many a subtle question versed,
>
> Who touch'd a jarring lyre at first,
>
> But ever strove to make it true:
>
> Perplext in faith, but pure in deed,
>
> At last he beat his music out.
>
> There lives more faith in honest doubt,
>
> Believe me, than in half the creeds.

In a subsequent writing, Tennyson tried to make it clear that his work above is "a poem, not a biography . . . The different moods of sorrow, as in a drama, are dramatically given, and my conviction that fear, doubts, and suffering will find answer and relief only through Faith in a God of Love." Well put.

To simply accept faith without wrestling to make it your own . . . is that really making faith yours? Or are you purloining a faith that was never— and may never be— yours? Doubt is that harrowing process with which we strive to make sense of what is and make sure that what we believe is based on truth. This is a noble quest and one that should not be taken lightly.

God reminds us in the book of Proverbs, "I love those who love me, and those who seek me diligently will find me." God desires to be known. Contrary to our feelings sometimes, God is not trying to play hide-and-seek with us. Nor has he asked us to swallow a theological pill, expecting us to turn off our brains and get in step with the program.

Bertrand Russell, the author of the landmark book *Why I Am Not a Christian*, once responded to a question, "What would you say if God asked you on Judgment Day, 'Why didn't you believe in Me?'" Russell replied, "Not enough evidence, God! Not enough evidence!" There are many out there who are holding onto Russell's response and telling themselves that there is simply not enough evidence to conclude with certainty that God exists. Yet, there is more than enough evidence scattered around us to reach the exact opposite conclusion. Many simply do not wish to acknowledge it. Thinkers like Russell possess dishonest doubt. They *choose* not to look at all the evidence. They see an idea, a Creator God, and dislike the notion of being beholden to him. Then they pick a single strain of evidence and misapply it in order to prove that God doesn't exist so they don't have to deal with him.

Many look for God in a test tube and think that the act of boiling chemicals over a Bunsen burner is ample means of determining the full essence of the absolute. It's as if we're trying to record the color purple only using a microphone. We are trying to catch the wind in our butterfly nets. And we are trying to take in the magnitude of the Empire State Building by plastering our faces against a single, first story window. We have chosen not to take in all that can be known through human experience and reasoning to reach our conclusions. We, in all our methods of inquiry, are limiting our knowledge more than expanding it. We must reason with all our being, and that transcends the sensory and the empirical. It also transcends the metaphysical. God is wholly other, yet he has left us with plenty of light to know him well. It is his desire to be known.

If you are seeking after God, do so diligently. He will be found. He must be found. I have been through a process of doubt I do not wish on anyone because of the level of angst that accompanies it. But it is a needed journey for all of us. Through all my questioning and all the answers that I was able to gather, I found myself returning to the very beginning of my faith, which I stated at the beginning of this book: Jesus Christ is God's Son—the perfect representation of Creator God. Jesus, fully God, lived as a man on earth, shed his blood on a cross for our sins, and rose from the grave bodily and now lives in heaven at God's right hand. And all of us who believe will enter heaven to live with him forever. Those who do not believe will die eternally separated from God's love.

It is a straightforward story. And I, again, am totally okay with it. Why? Because it proves to be true. And it is true not because I wish it to be true. It is true because it is true. And, because of doubt, I believe it now with a belief that is more closely aligned with certainty, but not fully. And I pray you will come to belief too. It is the only way your life will make sense and have meaning. You have been created by God on purpose. He has big plans for you. And the yearning you feel in your heart is there for a reason. Don't try to suppress that yearning. Chase after it. Throw you entire life's energy into seeking it out. Truth will be found. Jesus Christ will be found. He is worth the journey. An examined life is worth living. And St. Augustine was correct when he penned this prayer:

> Thou hast made us for thyself, O Lord, and our hearts are restless
> until they find their rest in thee.

If you are concerned that coming to Jesus will rubber-stamp you into another dull-looking evangelical drone such as those you see around you, don't be. It is not necessary to drive a certain kind of car, join a certain type of church, wear a certain style of clothing, listen to a particular genre of music, vote a certain way in presidential elections, or speak with a pre-scribed vocabulary. All that changes is this: your life will now be animated by love and you will now have a relationship with your heavenly Father to enjoy fully. All the details will take care of themselves as you simply walk in love with God and with others around you. God's Spirit takes care of the rest. Knowing God's love for variety (like why are there hundreds of thousands of types of insects in the world?) will allow your uniqueness to remain. So, don't sweat it. It's all good, I promise.

Now that I have traveled way beyond my little world of faith and family, I have seen my journey come full circle. The richness of the Christian story has proven to be more than a calming salve to the heart of a freakish accident of natural selection. It has proven to be the bedrock of existence for a created image bearer of the glorious King of Heaven.

I took the road less traveled. And it truly has made all the difference. I hope my journey will help you along your path toward meaning and pur-pose. And, rest assured, the God who created you does want you to live a life of meaning and joy. So, run to him and ask honestly of him what you will. In love, he will reveal everything to you. And what he reveals will be a grander vision than you can ever imagine. Both the journey and your ultimate destination are worth the effort.

These prophetic words of T.S. Eliot in his poem "Little Gidding" now make all the sense in the world to me:

We shall not cease from exploration

And the end of all our exploring

Will be to arrive where we started

And know the place for the first time.

True. Very true.

BIBLIOGRAPHY

Many of the ideas contained in this book are based on countless hours of digesting the great thinking of others. I cannot tell you how wonderful it was to have such ready access to a collection of thought and insight to help these thoughts come to life. Although it is next to impossible to chronicle all influences, these are the works that affected my study most tangibly.

Ambrosio, Francis J. *Philosophy, Religion, and the Meaning of Life*. Chantilly, Virginia: The Teaching Company, 2008.

Adams, Jeremy, et al. *Great Minds of the Western Intellectual Tradition*. Chantilly, Virginia: The Teaching Company, 2000.

Aquinas, Thomas. *Summa Theologica*, translated by Fathers of the English Dominican Province. MobileReference, 2008.

Aristotle. *Ethics*, produced by Ted Garvin, David Widger and the DP Team. MobileReference, 2008.

Armstrong, Karen. *Buddha*. New York: Penguin Books, 2001.

Armstrong, Karen. *A History of God*. New York: Ballantine Books, 1994.

Armstrong, Karen. *Islam: A Short History*. New York: Modern Library, 2002.

Armstrong, Karen. *Muhammad: A Prophet for Our Time*. New York: HarperOne, 2007.

Augustine of Hippo. *The City of God*, translated by Edward Bouverie Pusey. MobileReference, 2008.

Augustine of Hippo. *The Confessions of St. Augustine*, translated by Marcus Dods. MobileReference, 2008.

Bartlett, Robert C. *Masters of Greek Thought: Plato, Socrates, and Aristotle*. Chantilly, Virginia: The Teaching Company, 2006.

Barzun, Jacques. *From Dawn to Decadence*. New York: Harper Collins, 2000.

Bloom, Harold. *Genius*. New York: Warner Books, 2002.

Boethius, Anicius Manlius Severinus. *The Consolation of Philosophy*. MobileReference, 2008.

Boorstin, Daniel J. *The Discoverers*. New York: Random House, 1983.

Bruce, F.F. *The Canon of Scripture*. Downers Grove, IL: InterVarsity Press, 1988.

Chesterton, G.K. *The Everlasting Man*. Radford, VA: Wilder Publications, LLC, 2008.

Chesterton, G.K. *Orthodoxy*. Wilder Publications, 2007.

Cherry, Shai. *Introduction to Judaism*. Chantilly, Virginia: The Teaching Company, 2008.

Cline, Eric H. *A History of Ancient Israel: From the Patriarch Through the Romans*. Prince Frederick, MD: Recorded Books, 2005.

Collins, Francis S. *The Language of God, a Scientist Presents Evidence for Belief*. New York: Free Press, 2006.

Colson, Charles and Nancy Pearcy. *How Now Shall We Live?* Wheaton, Illinois: Tyndale House Publishers, Inc., 1999.

Craig, William Lane and Paul M. Gould. *The Two Tasks of the Christian Scholar*. Wheaton, IL: Crossway Books, 2007.

Crossan, John Dominic and Jonathan L. Reed. *Excavating Jesus*. San Francisco: Harper Collins, 2001.

Dawkins, Richard. *The God Delusion*. Boston: Houghton Mifflin, 2006.

Dawkins, Richard. *The Selfish Gene*. Boston: Oxford University Press, 2006.

Descartes, René. *Discourse on Method and Meditations of First Philosophy*, translated by Elizabeth S. Haldane. Digireads.com, 2009.

Eagleton, Terry. *The Meaning of Life: A Very Short Introduction*. New York: Oxford University Press, 2007.

Eckel, Malcolm David. *Buddhism*. Chantilly, Virginia: The Teaching Company, 2007.

Ehrman, Bart D. *Lost Christianities: Christian Scriptures and the Battles of Authentication*. Chantilly, Virginia: The Teaching Company, 2008.

Ehrman, Bart D. *Misquoting Jesus*. San Francisco: Harper Collins, 2005.

Ehrman, Bart D. *New Testament.* Chantilly, Virginia: The Teaching Company, 2008.

Fernandez-Armesto, Felipe. *Ideas That Shaped Mankind.* Prince Frederick, MD: Recorded Books, 2005.

Feynman, Richard P., Ralph Leighton, Edward Hutchings, and Albert R. Hibbs. *Surely You're Joking, Mr. Feynman!* New York: W. W. Norton & Company, 1997.

Feynman, Richard P. *The Pleasure of Finding Things Out: The Best Short Works of Richard P. Feynman.* New York: Basic Books, 2005.

Frankl, Viktor. *Man's Search for Meaning.* Boston, MA: Beacon Press, 2006.

Gandhi, Mahatma. *The Bhagavad Gita According to Gandhi.* Berkeley, CA: North Atlantic Books, 2009.

Garfield, Jay L. *The Meaning of Life: Perspectives from the World's Greatest Intellectual Traditions.* Chantilly, Virginia: The Teaching Company, 2011.

Giberson, Karl W. *Saving Darwin.* New York: Harper Collins, 2008.

Grayling, A.C. *Ideas that Matter.* New York: Basic Books, 2010.

Greene, Brian. *The Elegant Universe: Superstrings, Hidden Dimensions, and the Quest for the Ultimate Theory.* New York: Vintage Books, 2000.

Hanh, Thich Nhat. *The Art of Power.* New York: HarperOne, 2007.

Hanh, Thich Nhat. *Living Buddha, Living Christ.* New York: Riverhead Trade, 1997.

Hanh, Thich Nhat. *The Miracle of Mindfulness*. New York: Beacon Press, 1999.

Hall, James. *Philosophy of Religion*. Chantilly, Virginia: The Teaching Company, 2007.

Harris, Sam. *The End of Faith*. New York: W. W. Norton and Company, 2005.

Harris, Sam. *Letter to a Christian Nation*. New York: Vintage, 2006.

Harris, Sam. *The Moral Landscape: How Science Can Determine Human Values*. New York: Free Press, 2010.

Hawking, Stephen. *A Brief History of Time*. New York: Bantam Books, 1998.

Hawking, Stephen and Leonard Mlodinow. *The Grand Design*. New York: Bantam Books, 2010.

His Holiness the Dalai Lama. *The Art of Happiness*. New York: Penguin Putnam Inc., 1993.

His Holiness the Dalai Lama. *The Dalai Lama's Book of Wisdom*. New York: Thorsons, 2000.

Hitchens, Christopher. *god is not Great*. New York: Twelve, 2007.

Holt, Jim. *Why Does the World Exist?: An Existential Detective Story*. New York, New York: Liveright Publishing Corporation, 2012.

Johnson, Luke Timothy. *Apostle Paul*. Chantilly, Virginia: The Teaching Company, 2007.

Keller, Tim. *The Reason for God: Belief in an Age of Skepticism.* Riverhead Trade, 2009.

Kimball, Charles. *Comparative Religion.* Chantilly, Virginia: The Teaching Company, 2008.

Kraus, Lawrence M. *A Universe from Nothing.* New York, New York: Free Press, 2012.

Kreeft, Peter. *Ethics: A History of Moral Thought.* Prince Frederick, MD: Recorded Books, 2006.

Kreeft, Peter. *Faith and Reason: The Philosophy of Religion.* Prince Frederick, MD: Recorded Books, 2006.

Kreeft, Peter. *Jesus-Shock.* South Bend, Indiana: St. Augustine's Press, 2008.

Kreeft, Peter and Ronald K. Tacelli. *Handbook of Christian Apologetics.* Downers Grove, IL: IntervVarsity Press, 1994.

Lederman, Leon. *The God Particle.* New York: Bantam Doubleday Dell Publishing Group, 1993.

Lewis, C.S. *The Four Loves.* Orlando, FL: Harcourt, Inc.

Lewis, C.S. *God in the Dock: Essays on Theology and Ethics.* Grand Rapids, MI: William B. Eerdmans Publishing Company.

Lewis, C.S. *Mere Christianity.* New York: HarperCollins Publishers Inc., 1980.

Lewis, C.S. *Miracles.* New York: HarperCollins Publishers Inc., 1974.

Lewis, C.S. *The Weight of Glory*. New York: HarperCollins Publishers Inc., 1980.

Littmann, Mark, Fred Espenak, and Ken Willcox. *Totality: Eclipses of the Sun, Third Edition*. New York: Oxford University Press, 2008.

Macculloch, Diarmaid. *Christianity: The First Three Thousand Years*. New York: Viking, 2009.

Madden, Thomas F. *From Jesus to Christianity: A History of the Early Church*. Prince Frederick, MD: Recorded Books, 2005.

Madden, Thomas F. *"God Wills It!: Understanding the Crusades*. Prince Frederick, MD: Recorded Books, 2005.

Madden, Thomas F. *Upon This Rock: A History of the Papacy from Peter to John Paul II*. Prince Frederick, MD: Recorded Books, 2007.

McDowell, Josh. *Evidence that Demands a Verdict: Historical Evidence for the Christian Faith*. Campus Crusade for Christ, 1972.

Meineck, Peter. *Classic Mythology: The Greeks*. Prince Frederick, MD: Recorded Books, 2005.

Meineck, Peter. *Classic Mythology: The Romans*. Prince Frederick, MD: Recorded Books, 2006.

Miller, Barbara. *The Bhagavad-Gita*. New York, New York. Bantam Classic, 1985.

Miller, Barbara. *Yoga: Discipline of Freedom: The Yoga Sutra Attributed to Patanjali*. New York, New York: Bantam Books, 1998.

Miller, James. *Examined Lives: From Socrates to Nietzsche*. New York: Farrar, Straus and Giroux, 2011.

Muesse, Mark W. *Confucius, Buddha, Jesus, and Muhammad*. Chantilly, Virginia: The Teaching Company, 2008.

Muesse, Mark W. *Great World Religions: Hinduism*. Chantilly, Virginia: The Teaching Company, 2007.

Nasr, Seyyed Hossein. *Islam and the West*. Prince Frederick, MD: Recorded Books, 2006.

Nasr, Seyyed Hossein. *Islam: Religion, History, and Civilization*. New York: HarperCollins Publishers Inc., 2003.

Pascal, Blaise. *Pascal's Pensées*. Kindle Edition by Douglas Editions, 2009.

Peters, Frank E. *Judaism, Christianity, and Islam*. Prince Frederick, MD: Recorded Books, 2007.

Plato. *The Complete Dialogues of Plato*, translated by Benjamin Jowett. MobileReference, 2008.

Plato. *The Republic*, translated by Benjamin Jowett. MobileReference, 2008.

Polkinghorne, J.C. *The Faith of a Physicist*. Princeton, NJ: Princeton University Press, 1994.

Principe, Lawrence M. *Science and Religion*. Chantilly, Virginia: The Teaching Company, 2006.

Prothero, Stephen. *Religions of the East: Paths to Enlightenment*. Prince Frederick, MD: Recorded Books, 2006.

Randall, Lisa. *Knocking on Heaven's Door*. New York: HarperCollins Publishers Inc., 2011.

Roberts, Tyler. *Skeptics and Believers: Religious Debate in the Western Intellectual Tradition*. Chantilly, Virginia: The Teaching Company, 2009.

Russell, Bertrand. *Why I Am Not a Christian and Other Essays on Religion and Related Subjects*. Barlow Press, 2008.

Sanford, David. *If God Disappears: 9 Faith Wreckers & What to Do About Them*. Carol Stream, IL: Saltriver, 2008.

Schaeffer, Francis. *How Should We Then Live? The Rise and Decline of Western Thought and Culture*. Wheaton; IL: Crossway Books, 2005.

Schiffman, Lawrence H. *The Dead Sea Scrolls: The Truth Behind the Mystique*. Prince Frederick, MD: Recorded Books, 2007.

Schmidt, James. *The Enlightenment: Reason, Tolerance, and Humanity*. Prince Frederick, MD: Recorded Books, 2005.

Shutt, Timothy B. *Dante and His Divine Comedy*. Prince Frederick, MD: Recorded Books, 2006.

The Qur'an, A new translation by M.A.S. Abdel Haleem. New York: Oxford University Press, 2005.

Tzu, Lao. *Tao Te Ching*, translated by Jonathan Star. New York: Jeremy P. Tarcher/Penguin, 2001.

The Westminster Confession of Faith. Lawrenceville, GA: Committee for Christian Education and Publications PCA Bookstore, 1990.

Yancey, Philip. *Church: Why Bother?* Grand Rapids, MI: Zondervan Publishing House, 2001.

Yancey, Philip. *The Jesus I Never Knew*. Grand Rapids, MI: Zondervan Publishing House, 1995.

Yancey, Philip. *Soul Survivor: How Thirteen Unlikely Mentors Helped My Faith Survive the Church*. Grand Rapids, MI: Zondervan Publishing House, 2003.

Yancey, Philip. *What's So Amazing About Grace?* Grand Rapids, MI: Zondervan Publishing House, 1997.

ABOUT THE AUTHOR

STEVE WHIGHAM IS A COLLEGE professor, business consultant, and a former university administrator and lay pastor. Over the past thirty years, Steve has traveled extensively through North America, Europe, and Asia as a university guest lecturer and keynote business speaker. His passion for the arts, music, philosophy, science, theology, and business keep him busy most nights, but Steve is never one to pass up an opportunity for deep conversation with anyone on various subjects concerning the Great Conversation. Steve has written one other book, the award-winning, *Throw Open the Floodgates*. Steve is deliriously happy being married to his high school sweetheart, Beth. Together, they have four adult children.

For more information about
Steve Whigham
&

Eclipse of Faith
please visit:

www.stevewhigham.com
email: stevewhigham@me.com

....

For more information about
AMBASSADOR INTERNATIONAL
please visit:

www.ambassador-international.com
@AmbassadorIntl
www.facebook.com/AmbassadorIntl